Praise for *Planting t...*

Robert McCoy's writing is straightforward and unambiguous. One begins to feel at his side as he encounters those struggling to survive in the face of the stark realities of the aftermath of war. Relief workers on the scene were hard put to find words of understanding and reassurance. War's wounds to the mind and spirit do not heal. Occasionally a survivor would say in despair, "War is not the answer," or "Why must we always have war?"

That was sixty years ago. Since then we have had Korea and Vietnam and now Iraq. Why are we so prone to violence? As you close *Planting the Good Seed,* think about that—again and again and again. If war is not the answer, surely there is a reliable answer. Can we find it?

-Louis Schneider
AFSC Executive Secretary from 1974 to 1980
AFSC European Commissioner from 1948 to 1950

Imagine a young Quaker from Ohio in the late 1930's watching the war in Europe and wondering what his future held. Imagine also the dramatic shift in perspective as he traveled overseas in his early adult years and intersected a crucial time and place in human history—post-World War II Europe. The years pass and the memories of these days fade until Bob McCoy finds the letters he dutifully sent home to his parents so many years ago. *Planting the Good Seed* reprints the letters and other insights into postwar Europe and the activities of our young author as he helped to rebuild Europe, dealt with miles of red tape, gained insight into the ravages of war, witnessed the beginning of the Cold War, and met a special young woman. *Planting the Good Seed* will deposit you into another era and leave you better for having been there.

-James A. Boland, EdD
Director, Peace Resource Center and Professor of Education
Wilmington College

Bob McCoy's letters from Europe after World War II are priceless. They offer insight into the devastation of war, the resilience of the human spirit, the looming tensions of a new cold war, and the powerful witness offered by a small group dedicated to restorative action.

Even more, these letters allow the reader to enter the world of a young man raised in rural America, with strong Quaker ideals, coming of age in an increasingly complicated world. Bob more than embraces that complexity, he jumps in with an enthusiasm and dedication that renews and refashions his vision of a better world with each new experience. In the end, he teaches us that we all possess the power within to plant good seeds for a better tomorrow.

-Mary Ellen Batiuk, PhD
Professor of Social and Political Studies
Wilmington College

Planting the Good Seed

Letters from a
Quaker Relief Worker

Robert McCoy

Wilmington College Peace Resource Center
Wilmington, Ohio

Written by
Robert McCoy

Editing and book design by
Mary Ann Mayers

Published by
Wilmington College Peace Resource Center
1870 Quaker Way
Pyle Center Box 1183
Wilmington, OH 45177

Library of Congress Control Number: 2007931217

ISBN-13:   978-0-9658866-1-1
ISBN-10:   0-9658866-1-1

Acknowledgements

The writer and editor appreciate support provided by Daniel DiBiasio, president of Wilmington College. We are also grateful to Charlotte Pack, administrative assistant, and Jim Boland, director, Peace Resource Center, and Neil Snarr, professor of social and political studies, for their advice and assistance.

*To my wife Helga, for helping
me bridge the best of two worlds*

CONTENTS

FORWARD

There is immediacy and spontaneity in these letters written during Bob McCoy's Quaker relief work in France and Austria, right after World War II had left most of Europe on its knees amid rubble. Meant for his parents in Ohio, they are practically a diary, recounting daily events. After initial accounts of culture clashes, they would probably have settled into the monotony and insignificance of most such letters and diary entries, had it not been for the reality of daily life in Europe at that time and Quaker relief attempts to adjust to it. Everything keeps changing for Bob—new work assignments, new locations, new projects, new regulations from the ever-changing authorities, new co-workers. Even free time and vacations are used to change his scenery, and Bob travels all over Austria but also much farther afield, in all directions from Paris to Prague, from Naples to Stockholm, with interesting adventures and comments along the way.

Starting as a truck driver and furniture mover in France, Bob soon becomes a mechanic and negotiator in Vienna, where locating and securing the coal, gasoline, spare parts and housing for staff is virtually impossible but absolutely fundamental for carrying out any kind of relief work. Bob's resourcefulness will keep readers smiling and gasping. At first happy when he can just exchange a few words in German, a few months later he finds himself putting on whole evening programs for young apprentices in German.

The much-decried complications of current bureaucracy pale in comparison with the almost unimaginable catch-22's of the American Army and of the other three occupying powers, as well as of the Austrian and AFSC authorities. Admirably, Bob McCoy had resourcefulness and a sense of mission strong enough to see him and his programs successfully through countless seemingly impossible red tape tangles. But Bob has other qualities that make these letters interesting today. He is capable of pulling back to put the whole AFSC program under critical examination. He is touched by a criticism that only a naïve and well-fed American with the force of the occupying American Army behind him would ever undertake volunteer relief work in such a hopeless place as Austria in 1947. In a sense his wheedling and wrangling and scrounging and waiting were a kind of game which he could leave off whenever he wanted to return to Ohio. In contrast, the Austrian population had to engage fully in these struggles just to survive. There are some horrible occasions when there is nothing to do but admit helplessness, as during a visit to a desperate family in Budapest waiting for the secret police to take them off to prison, in part because of their contacts with foreigners like Bob.

These darker moments lend contour but do not determine the overall tone of a story and experience that are basically positive and optimistic. Bob's unpretentiousness, his readiness to laugh at himself, his capacity for empathy with everyone around him, and his ability to express his feelings and thoughts clearly lift these letters far above a recounting of daily events. There is even a love interest, and like a Hollywood film or a Shakespeare comedy, the letters end with a marriage that could take place only after the lovers had overcome numerous obstacles. The book will leave readers feeling they have lived intensively in another time and place and wondering whether they wouldn't themselves like to engage in trying to make some corner of the world a better place.

-James Cool, Ph.D
Ars Linguarum, Czech Republic

PROLOGUE

In 2002, I stumbled upon a box of letters that had been carefully saved by my mother, unbeknownst to me, for over fifty years. These letters, written from me to my parents, shared details of my daily life, hopes and disappointments, unending struggles with bureaucracy, and the great friends and adversaries I encountered while engaged in European relief work after World War II.

The letters were not written with any intention other than connecting with my family during our separation. However, upon reading them some fifty years later, I found myself submerged in the joys and frustrations of that period, courtesy of the highly detailed account of day-to-day life I had shared with my parents. At the urging of friends and family, I offer this collection of letters as a window on the convergence of three forces —the rebuilding of Europe following World War II, the actions taken by the Quaker community to assist in that endeavor, and my own simple desire to make some tangible difference in the world.

The letters are presented as I originally wrote them, including my idiosyncratic expressions and writing style. I do not have the letters my parents wrote in reply, so by definition, this is a one-sided story (a handful of exceptions are noted in the text).

A brief sketch of my background may help the reader understand the setting and my perceptions of what was happening in the world at that time. I was raised on a farm in southwestern Ohio and was a member of Fairview Friends Meeting of Wilmington Yearly Meeting, part of the Five Years Meeting (now Friends United Meeting) of Quakers.

I spent the first 10 years of my schooling in the public school at New Vienna, Ohio. My high school junior and senior years were at Westtown School, a Quaker boarding school near Philadelphia, Pennsylvania. My first year in college was at Swarthmore, also near Philadelphia, and my subsequent three years of college were at Earlham College in Richmond, Indiana.

College aroused my interest in history, which ultimately became my field of study. I became actively involved with the Peace Volunteers and spent many hours debating Quaker beliefs and practices as we saw the world teetering on the brink of war.

As I neared graduation in 1942, I began to wrestle with the typical college student question—what next? Should it be the farm or graduate school? I wanted to get a higher degree in history but feared difficulty in finding a job afterwards. On the other hand, the farm beckoned me with a relatively secure, yet unexciting future.

However, the debate was moot. As soon as I graduated in 1942, I was drafted. The decision shifted to the choice between joining the Army and registering as a conscientious objector (CO). All my life I had been led by my family and the Quaker church to think in terms of becoming a CO. College experiences further strengthened this belief, as did the influence of our Quaker minister, Wendell Farr. Ultimately, the choice was clear in my mind and I chose the CO position and went to a Civilian Public Service (CPS) Camp instead of the Army. I simply could not allow myself to be put in the position of killing someone.

The American Friends Service Committee (AFSC), founded by Quakers in 1917, was created in part to provide opportunities for conscientious objectors to help rebuild war-torn Europe after the *first* World War. The program was largely financed by a government grant made possible by Herbert Hoover. Subsequent work of the AFSC was financed by charitable contributions from Quakers and others. After World War I relief work was brought to a close, the AFSC developed other programs to aid the downtrodden and to address evils that lead to war. During World War II, the AFSC, along with the Church of the Brethren and Mennonites, administered the CPS camps for conscientious objectors, who in lieu of Army service, were assigned by their local draft boards to do work of national importance.

I was assigned to Civilian Public Service Camp #46 at Big Flats, New York where I was involved mostly in forestry work. After a year, I moved to CPS Camp #104 at Ames, Iowa where I worked for three years at Iowa State College (now Iowa State University) in agricultural research.

While all CPS camps were set up to do "work of national importance," many of us called it "work of national impotence;" the work just didn't seem relevant to the crises facing the world. We felt we were not doing enough to help set the world aright. Our soldier friends were sacrificing their lives while we were living safely in middle America. Many of us had wanted to go to war-torn Europe and Asia to bind up the wounds of war, but the government would not allow us to do so for fear it would indicate a lack of American unity.

As the war drew to a close and my release from CPS was imminent, I volunteered to go with the AFSC to Europe to help with relief work, rather than return to our farm or continue my education. Farm or graduate school just had to take a back seat to this more immediate challenge.

After two months of training and orientation at Pendle Hill, near Wallingford, Pennsylvania, I left for Europe, brimming with both excitement and questions. *What will I find? What could I, a simple farm boy, contribute? Do I have what it takes to make a difference?*

This is where my letters begin.

Planting the
Good Seed

France

May to September, 1946

May 24—Crossing

Dear Mother and Dad,

Would you believe it, I have crossed the Atlantic! As you know, I was on the SS *Uruguay*, a United States Army Transport (USAT) ship. The crossing was so smooth that none of the 560 passengers got sick. We were, however, very crowded. There were six of us in a cabin no bigger than the bathroom at home! One room even had 20 in it. It has been a restful trip with no entertainment but plenty of good food. There were two shifts for meals—good old threshing type that always included first and second tables. We were assigned tables and seats and ate in the same place with the same group each and every meal. Although I was the only American Friends Service Committee (AFSC) worker on board, my Quaker uniform helped start conversation with many. Our uniforms are plain gray with a military-style short jacket. The Quaker insignia is sown into both an upper arm sleeve and cap.

Today at noon, we docked at Southampton after a nine-day crossing. Half the passengers are getting off here and tonight we leave for le Havre. My first contact with a European happened just this afternoon. I was standing on deck watching a crane on shore unload cargo. The operator of the crane was less than 20 feet away from me. I had an orange with me, which I was gently tossing in the air. Precisely at four o'clock, a whistle blew and all dock work came to a halt. A pot of tea was attached to a rope and the crane operator lifted it to his cabin. While drinking his tea, he shouted across the 20 feet asking me what I had in my hand. He said he just was not sure it was an orange since he had not seen one since before the war. Of course, I tossed mine over to a grateful Brit. My relief work had begun!

May 25—Landing in France

Although we stopped yesterday in Southampton, really the first sign that there had been a war appeared to me as we pulled into the harbor at le Havre. There were a number of ships that had been sunk during the war with only their gaunt masts sticking out of the water. By far, the most appalling thing to me was the first glimpse of a city torn asunder by the folly of man's wrath. As yet, there are no docks where a ship could tie up except floating ones built as a temporary measure.

Needless to say, I felt quite impressed to set foot on this land, Europe, which had seen so much destruction during the last few years. As I walked down that long floating dock, I walked by US soldiers, French soldiers, British soldiers, a few threadbare civilians, a number of German

Prisoners of War (PWs), and even a few Swiss soldiers. Customs was rather a farce as all they did was to ask if we had cigarettes. I guess my uniform looked official enough for they did not ask me to open any of my luggage. With no more checking, I was in France.

June 10—Off to Work

The restful days on the ship have given way to a great adventure of work and adjustment to a foreign country. I took a train down from le Havre and was picked up at a Paris station by one of the Quakers. He took me to 2 rue de Civry to our living quarters in a large garage that also houses our trucks.

The first week I was kept busy getting documented in order to live in France. I had to establish a legal right to remain here, get food ration books, get an official document to carry at all times, have a physical exam, and get a French driver's license, as well as an international one. The French license was relatively simple but I was told beforehand that for the oral test I should first memorize the words red, green and yellow in French. I stumbled through the test and passed. And so far, those are the only words I know in French. In the course of that week I also found out how to get around alone in Paris over the complicated subway system, how to do a little talking, precious little, in another language, and do a little sightseeing or should I say gawking. The people seemed to be about like any crowd in a US city except thinner and wearing shabbier clothes.

One difference I found was in restaurant food, partly cultural but also brought on by the war. One meal I had in a restaurant included, as a first course, HOT radishes, followed by the second course which consisted of a bowl of lettuce, topped off by the final course—a small fish that had no taste whatsoever—head, eyes, and all. If we had given up coupons, we could have had some bread, too. Generally we eat in the garage as a group and fare right well. However, for two weeks instead of bread we had a 10-gallon can of crackers that had been salvaged from a sunken German submarine!

I spent the next two weeks, after I finished getting documented, mostly in the garage. Each new man picks out a GMC 2½-ton truck from the five or six still available—they had previously been procured from an Army dump—and services that truck and then runs that truck and no other. For a few days I was knee deep in wheel bearing grease and the like.

That work was a bit monotonous but I had two good breaks from it. The first was two trips to Rheims to get some surplus supplies from Army dumps. The items (one truck of buttons!) had been captured by the American Army from the Germans and were now being given to the AFSC for distribution. When we got there, the Army sent around about 20

German PWs to load this German stuff. They seemed rather disgruntled until we explained to them that we were taking the supplies to Toulouse where they were to be distributed in a PW camp.

Army dump in Vincennes, France from which AFSC purchased vehicles

I was interested to see the country, as it is broken up into a patchwork of small farms and nearly all the work seems to be done by hand labor and plenty of it. People were at work in the morning at 6:00 and were still in the fields at 8:00 at night as we drove back from Rheims. One thing that struck me as singularly odd is that you can drive for several miles through this farmland and not see a single house. It seems that all the people live in villages. Every few miles you come abruptly upon a village, a crowded village with narrow and crooked streets, and then for a few more miles nothing in the way of homes. It is most weird at night to drive through these towns, since we often don't see a single light. However, the headlights of the truck pick out many people standing in front of their homes staring wordlessly as you drive by. It gave me a rather creepy feeling but that has largely dissipated now that I have gotten to know a few of the people a bit.

I had a slight scare on my second trip. Before I got back to Paris, the clutch linkage broke on my truck. I then carefully, very carefully, drove through the center of Paris to our garage with no clutch control, being sure that I could hit lights without ever having to stop.

My second break from the garage was the chance to attend Quaker French Yearly Meeting. Most of it was closed to foreigners because they didn't want to be influenced by outsiders. The part that was open to us was the session where they read the epistles. And about the only thing drier than listening to epistles in an American Yearly Meeting is sitting through two hours of them in French.

Last Sunday Jack Mote, a fellow teammate who had arrived in Paris a few days before I did, and I had an interesting experience. Genevieve, a French girl who works with the Red Cross, invited us to St. Germain for lunch with her grandmother. She met us at the station and took us through many winding streets to her grandmother's home. Grandma was a most charming woman of 80 or so who spoke good English. She was so happy to find someone to talk with about the US for she had been there 50 years ago for two or three years. She told us that Germans had killed her father in the Franco-Prussian war, Germans in the First World War had killed her husband and two sons, and Germans in the Second World War had killed her only two grandsons. Now all she has left is this one granddaughter.

Nevertheless, she said, "I don't hate the Germans. They were not the enemy—the enemy was war."

Jack Mote   Genevieve and her grandmother

The dinner she served us lasted from 1:30 to 4:30, and consisted of eight courses, one after the other. It probably took a month's rations. However, they were so glad to do it for Americans. They were particularly interested in hearing about Quakers and CPS.

June 14—My French Assignment

On Monday, two opportunities opened up. The first was a three-week trip to southern France. However, the powers that be decided I wasn't up to it since I know no French. The second one seemed to suit me better. I am going, along with Jack, for a month to St. Nazaire, on the west coast of France to join the Quaker European Transport Unit (ETU) team of five

fellows doing "demenagement" work. This consists of driving trucks daily
to homes 40 or 50 miles out of St. Nazaire to load up household goods of
people who are ready to move back to St. Nazaire. The Germans had been
making good use of a huge submarine base and many unloading docks there
during the war. They anticipated that allied bombing would be coming so
they had ordered many residents, and helped many, to move to the country
to grandma's house or a friend's house. The Germans were right. The bombing soon came from British and American bombers. Instead of hitting the
submarine base, they destroyed the town. So now, the French government
has rebuilt some housing and the displaced people are ready to go back either to this new housing or to what remains of their old homes—usually
only the cellar is left. The catch is that as yet, there is practically no way for
them to move. That is where we come in. The team has been working for
two months already so the program is well established.

New home constructed by government in St. Nazaire

Tuesday and Wednesday, I worked feverishly to get my truck finally ready. Thursday morning I mounted some good tires, finished packing
and by 2:00 was ready to leave for the gas station to tank up. Before getting
there, I ran out of gas. By various and devious means I contrived to get some
gas but I ran the battery down trying to get the gas pumped into the carburetor. I had to call the garage to get one of the fellows to come give me a push
to get started. When he arrived, he pointed out the fact that on all these
trucks the fuel pump has a hand primer that you use in such cases instead of
running your battery down. I guess I am learning. By 4:00 I was actually on
my way alone, as Jack had pulled out two hours before. I started west out of
Paris passing first through Versailles. I wanted to stop but as I was so late, I
kept moving. I passed through Chartres and le Mans before reaching Durtal
just at dark. The arrangement had been for me to be there sometime after

9:00 that morning to pick up the sister of one of the two French fellows on our team in St. Nazaire. She was to take me to a place there and get a load of furniture. Following my instructions, I finally found her, a most attractive girl of 21, who spoke some English. However, she was in a rather distraught frame of mind as I was 12 hours later than she had expected. Anyway, she took me to the family where the furniture was stored. There were six of them, none of whom spoke English. We sat around a table and talked (!) until midnight after which I went to sleep in my truck.

The next morning we loaded the truck and headed off toward St. Nazaire. As we neared the coast, I noticed the area was more densely populated than the area toward Rheims and the land more intensely farmed. I even saw some corn for the first time. Then into St. Nazaire. It was absolutely the most badly bombed town I have yet seen. Every building is now uninhabitable in the center of town. Some whole blocks were leveled. A large cathedral is in ruins except for the untouched sanctuary.

War destruction in St. Nazaire

The city railroad station is in ruins; the streets are barely passable, rocks and debris lie everywhere.

On we drove to the small town of le Baule where I unloaded the furniture and met the girl's brother who came to take me to the ETU team's home, called Ker Berny, in le Pouliguen, a town some 10 miles west of St. Nazaire. Ker Berny is a large house inside a walled courtyard, right next to a smooth sandy beach looking out on the Atlantic.

I was given a warm welcome by the team. Let me say something about them. Roger Craven, maybe 35, is the

War destruction in St. Nazaire

leader and is the only American here who speaks fluent French. He looks like an Iowa farmer but is really an easterner. He gives you a feeling of welcome and of belonging. Next is Leigh Morrell, just out of George School, young, active, but most likeable and helpful and a skilled mechanic to boot. John Robbins is from Centerville, Indiana and seems to be a solid person.

Roger Craven   *Leigh Morrell*

Then there are two French lads, Chris de Guitaud and Rene Delbes. Rene is 28, an MD, but did not intern because of the war, most of which he spent in a German concentration camp. Chris is 18 and a French veteran of the American Army!

Rene Delbes   *My picture, taken in France*

Jack and I should fit in well with this group. It seems to be a congenial, well-knit group to my first observation, and I feel at home here already, much more than with the group in Paris. Every evening we eat at a French restaurant and every morning we cook our breakfasts here. Tomorrow, I start out on my first "demenagement."

June 15—So to Work (and Wine)

Leigh went with me today to help me get the hang of the job. First, we moved some mattresses and beds to the prewar home of the International Youth Hostel, an organization with homes in many French towns. The house had obviously been used by the Germans during the war, for on one wall a huge Nazi emblem was painted with the words in German "To our Führer." Then on the opposite wall were three caricature paintings of Churchill, Chamberlain, and John Bull. Under each was a four-line poem. I only took time to translate the one under Churchill, which went something like this: "Churchill's head resembles an egg, but one difference is that there is nothing in his head. We wonder what earthly use it is; oh, perhaps it is his hat rack." In German it was poetic—but not in English with my translation.

On to my first real demenagement. We drove through St. Nazaire and took a ferryboat across the Loire River. There was just enough room on that boat for one of these large GMCs to park crosswise and the cost was about $4.00 for a round-trip. After driving a few miles, we came to a nice little cottage with a yard simply littered with junk. The family was most friendly but appeared miserably poor. There were six children, ages 10 and younger, plus the parents. The furniture consisted of three beds, one bureau, two tables, five chairs, mattresses, four broken bicycles, one good one, mirrors, two or three hundred pounds of coal, and then just plain junk —pieces of broken furniture, old pieces of metal, and scraps of wood—all precious to them.

"Demenagement" often via the second story!

Every few minutes during the loading the father insisted, no, demanded that we have some wine with him. We said no thanks in the most polite French we knew but did not make a dent in his enthusiasm. Time passed in useless argument until finally Leigh said the only way to make them feel good and get on with the loading was to take a glass, which we did. Now the real feat—to smile and have a look of pleasure on your mug while you are swallowing some of the vilest tasting stuff invented by the ingenuity of man. Well, we got by the afternoon with only two small glasses but our host in the meantime did away with two or three bottles. We finally loaded the last item, a baby carriage. Before we could load it into the truck, they took the dirty, squalling baby out of the carriage and loaded the carriage with their most precious possession—wine. So off we went, followed by poppa who clambered up on his bicycle and pedaled off with the two oldest children, while mommy walked, carrying the baby, and followed by the rest of the children. So back across the Loire and finally to their new home in St. Nazaire, a newly built government job that reminded me of a CPS barrack with plaster. My first "demenagement" was complete.

My truck with a typical load

June 18—Beer

Today Chris went with me to finish my orientation. We drove 30 miles east to Campbon. We had a lot of stuff this time—enough for both the truck and a trailer, so it took a good while to load, especially since no one took the lead in the loading. I thought that Chris, being the old-timer here, would do it. But he, being 18, thought I, being 26, would do it. It ended up with our host doing most of it. However, we got a whale of a load on despite all the time-outs for the usual "wine-ings," only this time it was beer. I managed to ward off the onslaughts of the well-meaning host until lunch. What a lunch they served. It started with some tough, grisly meat, which I could hardly stomach, followed by a refreshing bowl of spinach. Then a greasy mess of slum-gullion, topped off by something too strongly resembling Rockford cheese. There were five of us and eight bottles of beer went down the hatch.

I learned by bitter experience that it does not pay to drink your glass quickly in order to avoid dragging out the bad taste because then your glass just gets a quick refill.

June 19—On My Own

I had a 90-mile run today to Notre Dame des Landes—really up in the country. The load consisted of large, good furniture—30 or 40 chairs, mirrors galore, and marble tabletops. The helpers were all very good to let me decide what went where, but at times the language barrier made it a bit difficult.

At lunch an old woman of 70 or so with all the wrinkles of long years of servitude written on her forehead, but with the sprightly step of 40 and flashing eyes, insisted that I have some wine with the rest of the men. No? So what would I have?

"L'eau," (water) I said.

She frowned at that. Finally, she had a bright idea. "Le lait?"

I was delighted, as I hadn't had any since I left the boat. Can you imagine what le lait is? I had a whole pitcher of milk while the rest of the group drank their wine, beer, and rum. This meal was different in every way from the one yesterday. We had fresh eggs, pancakes, creamed chicken, bacon—I was really out in the country. During the afternoon, the men would stop every half hour or so for a refresher and each time they would pour me out a quart of milk!

After dinner we sat around the table and talked (?) and they all smoked. They seemed perturbed that I did not smoke. That brought on a long discussion about my not drinking or smoking. Well, what on earth did I do for entertainment? I tried to explain that Quakers have a testimony against smoking and drinking although some Quakers do not always follow that testimony.

I was interested in one other attitude that came out. The husband of the boss lady had only one eye, no glass eye, and just a vacancy. I asked no questions nor looked too long. Soon the woman volunteered the information that in 1942, some German soldiers had removed the eye—I could not tell how or why. She added that war was the enemy of all mankind—not Germans, but war!

After we finished the loading, we headed back to St. Nazaire. The railroad crossings in this country are an odd sight. Picket fences are built up to the road from the railroad at all crossings and there are either swinging gates or heavy metal bars blocking your way. At night these crossing are all shut and in order to go through, you have to wake up the railroad crossing gatekeeper to open them. Some of the gatekeepers leave them shut in the day too. (Each railroad crossing has a gatekeeper, who lives in a house right next to the gate and the tracks.) Coming into St. Nazaire I came to one that was lowered. I asked the gatekeeper, who was standing at the gate, to raise it but no amount of arguing in a language he did not understand seemed to persuade him to raise the gate. I waited and waited but no train came. I had to laboriously back up my truck and trailer three hundred yards and take off on another road that finally took me to a more hospitable gatekeeper.

Three houses from us is a sort of hotel where for some odd reason two German PWs are living and working. They are the most likeable Germans I have yet met. In their spare time, they are making each one of us very fancy homemade mirrors just because we are so friendly with them and I can speak some German with them. My college training in German, while not making me fluent in the language, was certainly helping me out here.

This evening they were here and an interesting development occurred. Our Chris, the 18-year old French lad, had joined the American Army during the invasion of France. During our conversation, one of the PWs , Helmut Ellwart, described an important battle that took place as the German Army was being driven east. In this battle many Germans were killed but he escaped to be captured later. Some of us were translating his story into English when all of a sudden Chris became very excited. Before long, we discovered that Chris and Helmut had both been at this same battle on the same day and had both taken part in a small incident that was unique enough to be distinctive. Thus, they were certain that they had been fighting each other at the same time and place. Yet here they were eating together at our table and being the best of friends. The hatreds of war seem to lessening at least in one quarter.

June 21—40 Cows

Today I went to Guemene, another of those picturesque hamlets, to move the town postmaster back to St. Nazaire to work as the government had ordered. He and his wife were what some call the typical type of people from Brittany. He looked like the salt of the earth, about 60 I would say.

Before I got there, I was driving along a gravel road when I came upon two women driving some 40 cows down the road. When I had slowly worked my way into the middle of the herd, my horn let loose with a shrill blast and would not be quieted no matter how I played with the button. I hunted down a screwdriver, opened the hood and disconnected the wires from the horn, an operation that took two or three minutes. By the time that was done, those poor cows had gone every which way. The two women looked rather scornfully at me as if to say, "These Americans can't even operate cars properly—so why are they bothering us?"

This evening four of us went to a "night club." It was just a nice little place where drinks were served and there was an orchestra. One nonalcoholic drink was available, a sort of peppermint drink which I find is pretty good stuff. The dancing is a lot different from any you would see at home. I can hardly describe it—almost jitterbug but not that either. I guess you would describe it by saying it was more sexy but not slinky. Rene had dug up two French girls for us to bring. They were not bad looking but they seemed too starved for affection. I found out later that they both have children and husbands in Paris but they come here every week or so. You would not know they had any ties!

June 25—French Attitudes

Today I drove 45 miles east to a little town called le Gavre. Again, I was out in the country, and in fact, had to drive the last three miles over a dirt road. I packed the French lady's things in the truck and thought I was done. But she pointed out a big woodpile that I had overlooked. Then she saw that I had some extra space so went next door and got some more tables and other stuff. With that loaded, I thought we were finished. But no, more and more things were found until we were really super loaded! As usual, I couldn't talk to the people but somehow I felt more at ease with them than I had before. It seemed almost as if there was some common bond of understanding between us that did not require formal words for expression. We had loaded everything with complete understanding, the lady, her mother, her one-legged father and me. We finished loading by 2:30 p.m. and then had a good meal of ham and eggs. The inevitable cider, beer, wine, and cognac went the rounds too. Then we had coffee to suit the taste of the American guest.

Before we left I noticed that one tire was low. At the first town we stopped at a garage to get some air, but I was charged five francs for it. I guess air in France is not free!

Now that I have been here a few days, you might expect me to have all the answers about French attitudes toward the Germans! Well, they are quite diverse. Some saw the Germans as just people caught up in a war machine, but many seemed to have a pent-up hatred of German soldiers. However, I could never get them to be specific as to why. What I have been able to understand goes something like this: "The German soldiers were brutes—but none ever hurt me. In fact, they warned us to leave St. Nazaire and even provided transportation for us to leave before the American bombing began. During their occupation, the looters and thieves were not Germans but our own French. The Germans shot a number of French for stealing from other French. We were able to get food under the Germans and were able to move about as we pleased within certain limits." In other words, it seems they saw the Germans, individually, as good fellows. Their hatred of them stems from the fact that they were under German control; being under someone else's control hurts any subjugated people.

June 27—Egg Day

Rene found out I was going to Campbon. He had been there before and had gotten some eggs from the housekeeper of the Presbytery of the town church. So he gave me detailed instructions how to find the place and a note to give to the lady asking if I couldn't buy a few eggs. I found the place all right but the lady did not seem to know what it was all about and would not read the note. She shunted me out into the garden and pointed to the far end where I saw someone working. I walked over to him and found that he spoke no English either. I gave the note but he could not understand it. I gave up in disgust and went to load my demenagement.

After getting loaded, we ate a late lunch in the local café. This time when I turned down the beer, they got me some pop. All this time I felt I had not done too well on the egg deal so I went back to the Presbytery to find the same woman and man eating lunch in the kitchen. She read my note this time but still did not seem to get it. In trying to talk to me, she pointed at the man and indicated he was a PW. I tried German on him and you should have seen his face light up. Here we had tried to talk in the morning in English and French, never suspecting the other spoke German. In due course, we cleared up the egg deal and I got 16 eggs for 6 francs per egg.

Today I moved some x-ray equipment to a public health center in Nantes. The police there brought out two PWs to do the actual work of unloading and added a guard with a machine gun to watch over the operation. He was rather careless with it since it wasn't really needed. From the lack of the necessity of using it, he even condescended to help with the unloading. The PWs looked as if they were leading a rather miserable life but they certainly perked up when I let out a few words of German.

During the later demenagement of the day I discovered that one of my tires on an inside duel was flat. I took time off to change it, figuring the people would go on with the truck loading. Instead, they just stood around and watched until I had changed the tire.

June 29—My Busiest Day

Yesterday was my biggest day to date. To start out I overslept and was late to my first rendezvous. I was supposed to pick up a few pieces of furniture for a man in la Baule and take them to Malville on the way to Chateaubriant. It turned out to be more of a complete demenagement. The French seem to have a way of luring you to their homes on the grounds that there isn't much to get and then it turns out they have a whole house full. Nothing was ready so it took until 11:00 to get loaded.

That made me two hours late to the next rendezvous in St. Nazaire where I picked up a young man, his wife, and his uncle. This chap could speak a little English so he took over the role of interpreter for the day. We drove to Malville and unloaded the first load at a house beside the remains of a medieval castle. A widow had lived in the castle with seven children prior to and during part of the war. When the Germans came, they used the castle for an officer's headquarters. When the American Army was approaching the Germans set fire to the castle so the Americans could not use it. They forced the widow and her children to stand and watch as it went up in flames.

When we finished the load, the man said something in French, and the English-speaking chap translated saying, "We are so grateful and thankful to have this chance to get our furniture moved but we are also grateful to see a foreigner that acts like you do. The Germans who lived in that castle, they were always strutting around, forceful, defiant, cruel looking. When the American soldiers came, we hoped for better men, but they were nearly always a little drunk. Both groups were sad down inside in their hearts. We came to feel that all foreigners were a sorry lot. You seem different—a foreigner, but not drunk, not cruel, but helpful, doing a job with a smile. That is what helps us most."

This certainly gave me a lift. I explained in a few words something of the Quaker ideals and they listened most attentively. Oh, how much difference it makes to have some means of actually communicating with people.

And so on to Chateaubriant. We passed a large gravel pit where the Germans had shot 25 French boys between the ages of 15 and 20 because they were suspected of being spies. You certainly can see why the French have no love for the Germans. I brought up the point to this English-speaking chap that just as the drunken American soldiers were not representative of all of Americans, so likewise the Germans they had seen might not be representative of all Germans. However, the logic of that statement seemed to escape him.

Chateaubriant proved to be 75 miles from le Pouliguen so it took a bit of time to get there and we did not start loading until about 3:00. The first part of the load was at a town some six kilometers beyond Chateaubriant. That took until about 5:00. Around 4:00, I noticed that we had quite an audience of about 25 eight- to fifteen-year-old youngsters. They stared in awe, wonder, and envy when I turned the truck around and hitched up the trailer. At this point, I broke the plunger on the trailer that unlocks the floating wheel, thus making it impossible to raise the wheel to support the trailer when it is not fastened to the truck. I just took the wheel off with those 25 pairs of eyes watching every move. As we pulled out I said "au revoir" and they chorused back with "good bye."

I returned to the original house to get the truck loaded by 9:00, then into the house for supper. They had found out from me earlier in the day that I prefer milk to wine and love eggs. For supper we had milk and eggs, but the eggs didn't taste right. When we cook eggs at home they are good, but when the French cook them, there is something mixed in that ruins the flavor. The milk tasted like the cows were just on new pasture and as I drank it I remembered the Army health book that says drink no water or milk in rural areas!

There were five of us who were to return to St. Nazaire with this load, but as there was no room on the load, they all rode with me in the cab. We started out for St. Nazaire after midnight. I find night driving odd. We drove 75 miles and I think we met a total of three cars, but at least 999 bicycles. When we got to the home, I found a long lane of overhanging trees. I thought I could push the branches aside with the truck, but no, the first branch caught the furniture, broke two chairs and a rear rib support on the truck. We unloaded the trailer on the spot.

As we were about finished with the trailer, an irate woman and a pugnacious man came charging out from the nearest house and a tirade of French conversation followed between my English-speaking friend and these people. It turned out that this man had a bad temper and did not like being awakened in the middle of the night by a demenagement. I managed to get the truck up to the house to unload it. There was so much and it was so tightly packed that it took us until 2:30 in the morning to finish. It was a picturesque and perhaps a grotesque sight to see me climbing over that load of furniture with a flashlight in my mouth. I even got a bit peeved at the English-speaking chap for every time I handed down a bit of furniture he would say, "sank you." When I left he was almost sickly sweet with his protestations of appreciation. I think he meant well—I was just tired of his choice of English words.

Back home to bed at 3:00 a.m. as the first signs of light began to show in the eastern sky.

Today, because of my late night yesterday I slept until 2:30 p.m! Then I actually went swimming in the ocean. At low tide I found I could walk on sand over half a mile out.

Word came down from Paris today that we will wind up this program in St. Nazaire after two more weeks, as more pressing assignments are calling us elsewhere. We will return to Paris and then split up; two men go to Austria, two go to Hungary, and three go to the Alsace-Lorraine area of France. It seems that Philadelphia put the label "Austria" on Leigh and me, but those in power in Paris don't think I am good enough for that job. I will just have to wait and see.

Maybe I can take a few moments here to make a farming observation or two about western France. By American standards, farming seems very primitive. There is no real machinery and I have seen more oxen than horses pulling loads. Little of the land is under cultivation; it is mostly in grass and some in wheat. What land is plowed is all put in ridges (as we use for sweet potatoes) and is planted in the ridges with something I do not recognize. I have not seen any four-wheeled wagons. They get in all their hay and do all their hauling with two wheeled wagons and the wheels are between four and five feet in diameter. In the farm houses there are only stone floors, and most of the cooking seems to be done in the fireplace.

July 4—A French Dairy

Yesterday was a standard move on my trip to Ligne and back with nothing particularly noteworthy except that when I finished the delivery, the people gave me 16 eggs to take home.

Today I had two demenagements. I loaded first in la Baule and went northwest for the first time to Piriac. Then on through the country north and east to Herbignac where I left the trailer and two people. I then had to go further to Camoel but had some difficulty and ended up in la Roche-Bernard by mistake. However, I got a chance to see where the Germans had blown up a huge bridge that spanned the river there—the Americans had been on the other side of the river for several months trying to get across into the St. Nazaire pocket. Then on to Camoel where I found a delightful middle-aged lady called Madame Luec in a little house in the country. By various and devious means she found out I lived on a farm in America, so after lunch of six fried eggs and a huge bowl of French fried potatoes she took me to see the livestock—which meant going into the room right off the kitchen. There I found six nondescript cows placidly batting flies and standing knee deep in manure. No wonder I had fought so many flies at lunch.

The Madame had three sisters who had lost husbands in the first war and sons in this one. A son-in-law took me to a lookout in back of the house from where you could see the river. He showed me the spot where he had signaled to the Americans during the several-month siege of the St. Nazaire pocket. He proudly explained he was a member of the resistance movement. Then back to Herbignac for the trailer and to finish loading the truck. Tonight I pulled into St. Nazaire with not only a truck and trailer loaded with furniture but also carrying eight people, five dogs, three cats and three rabbits! Someone reminded me that back home today is a holiday —July 4!

July 5—St. Nazaire Pocket

Today to Pont Chateau for a leisurely loading. One man there is from Alsace-Lorraine and spoke good German so acted as a go-between. He straightened me out on this St. Nazaire pocket. The Americans landed in France on June 6, 1944 and by August were in Paris. By the last of August, nearly all of France had fallen to the Americans and that winter they began their advance into Germany. In fact, he said, the war ended in Germany on May 5, 1945. All this time, the Germans in St. Nazaire held on clear up to May 8, 1945, which was just over a year ago!

July 6—Home Guard

Today it was my turn to stand guard alone over our little isolated castle, Ker Berny. I had one eye turned toward the top of the stonewall surrounding our house and the other turned toward the 10-foot high iron gate through which all visitors and would-be trespassers must come.

So far, I've had three visitors. First was the paper man who, I guessed, wanted some money. I could not figure out how much so I gave him a large bill and let him make the change. The second was a group of children wanting to sell me a chance on a bicycle raffle that comes off in a month or so—at least that is what I gathered. I tried to explain we would not be here then. Maybe I should have bought one from them—it was only 10 francs. Finally, a woman came on some business I could not fathom, so I told her to come back later. Oh, I guard well this spot of America hidden away in the recesses of an old French village by the sea. Two hours later, Roger had come and gone; within the next five minutes another family came wanting something, I know not what. Whenever I'm alone here, the French seem to pour in!

July 9—A Beautiful Spot

I had two demenagements today. The first was an easy one, not a long trip. I finished it before lunchtime so went on to the second one in la Guorie where I found they had already eaten. So I worked the day without lunch! Just outside Savenay, I saw the most picturesque spot I have seen in France. It was a small lake crossed in the middle by a road on a causeway. Looking north from that causeway, I saw high hills rising from the lake and the whole area was covered with the luscious green of trees in full leaf. The lake itself was the deepest blue I have ever seen—really a spot to remember.

July 10—A Lighter Day

Today was a bit different, not a demenagement. I went to the office of the mayor of St. Nazaire and picked up a man who went with me to the nearest PW camp where we picked up four German PWs. We then spent the day hauling beds, mattresses, bureaus and the like for the city. The supplies had belonged to the Germans at one time. I could not talk to this man from the mayor's office but I did with the PWs, much to their delight. Two of them had been in France for four years and were most anxious to get home to wives and children. They had heard of the Quakers in Germany from the First World War and seemed to have some idea what we are all about. When we began to unload, I pitched in and worked with them. The mayor's representative soon followed suit, as did two or three other Frenchmen who had not been helping before. Only the guard who came along did nothing and chided me for working. He had been a PW in Germany for five years, but said he really had not had it so badly there. However, he wanted the PWs to do the work.

July 11—Final Demenagements

First, I loaded six tombstones near le Pouligen. This was no light job with only two of us to carry those 200 and 300-pound tombstones—well, the man's wife helped! Then into la Baule where I loaded some new furniture. Both of these small loads went to St. Nazaire, first the furniture and then the tombstones to a cemetery on a family lot. The cemetery was like none I have ever seen in the US. The markers were so much more crowded than you usually see in the States and they had such ornate types of markings. It was a lot like one I had seen in Quebec some years ago.

Then another flat tire to change. This meant that I did not get to Prinqueau until almost 2:00 p.m. to load up the biggest load I have had yet. It took us until 7:30 p.m. to get it all on. You should have seen the load piled high in the air—a crate of chickens tied to the side of the trailer, a bicycle dangling from the rear, baling wire and linoleum tied to the side of the truck and two buckets of eggs tied to the stoplights with wire. On the way home, I met Roger who said it was the largest load he had ever seen anyone haul, and still we did not get everything. The folks seemed to be so appreciative that they sent me home at 10:00 with most of the eggs from one of those buckets!

July 15—PW Camp Visit, Farewells, Future Assignments

Saturday I worked on my truck, getting it ready to roll to Paris. However, I am waiting for a union connection for my broken oil line to come from Paris tomorrow.

Yesterday turned out to be a big day. I had intended to write letters but Roger wanted to go to the PW camp where I had been on Wednesday. We took a jeep and drove over. Roger had hoped to talk with the PWs alone but the French guards stuck around like leeches. This was only a small camp with 20 men and no barbed wire restrictions. Roger was disappointed so we decided to try to visit the main camp a few miles away where many hundreds of PWs are located. This was a different story about getting in, for you just did not drive in. The gate was barred with an armed sentry guarding it. Roger went into the office and found the French soldiers to be from Morocco. They looked at his uniform and his papers and figured he was some important American so they opened the gate and we drove in. I stayed with the jeep, for the French guards are notorious pilferers. Roger went into the next office but was immediately ousted out by a French Captain, the camp commander, who had come storming in after Roger. Roger was ousted because he had no official order from Paris. After Roger calmed him down and explained who we were, the Captain took him back into his office for a chat.

In the meantime a PW strolled by the jeep and we struck up a conversation. He had been a chemist with IG Farben industries and had been in the Army only since 1943. He said that several men in the camp had died in the past year from malnutrition. He wants to go home so badly and can see no reason why not. He cited the Geneva Convention rule governing prisoners of war, which says all prisoners are to be sent home as soon as possible after the cessation of hostilities. He seemed most happy to talk with me.

By this time, Roger had the Captain in the palm of his hand and the Captain invited us both to his quarters for tea, where Roger and he talked about the war, Conscientious Objectors (COs), and the Negro situation in the US. This conversation, all in French, went on for an hour and a half and included the next-in-command, a fine looking Negro from Morocco. We were served by a PW. I imagine the Captain was a bit mortified for as we left, Roger and I shook hands with the PW! However, the Captain remained friendly. He seemed to be rather a good egg—in fact, the PW who talked with me said the Captain was OK—the trouble was with the subordinates.

Then back to Ker Berny where we had a sort of farewell open house dinner with 21 in attendance. Our two PW friends from the hotel cooked the supper. All our previous guests were here as well as six young people who were traveling around France in the youth hostel movement. We spent the evening singing, playing recorders and in general conversation that could only go so far, as only 3 of the 21 people could speak all three languages.

Today and tomorrow, we are cleaning up and packing as we leave for Paris on Wednesday. Last night Roger talked to Paris on the phone and found out that Leigh and I have both been assigned to Vienna. There are already six AFSC workers there. They are not part of the ETU but are doing other relief and rehabilitation work. Our job will be to keep the transportation of the group moving. Since Leigh speaks no German but is a good mechanic, he will be in charge of the garage and I as a speaker of German, after a fashion, will be the scrounger—whatever that means. I think it means that I am to be the contact person with the Austrian officials and the US Army in getting parts and other stuff. Our only holdup now is waiting for the US Army to grant us permission to enter Austria. When we go, we will not take our trucks since there are already trucks in Vienna. Instead, we'll drive two new English station wagons through Switzerland. However, it will be at least the middle of August before we manage to cut through all the red tape.

July 16—St. Nazaire Project Report

All packed and ready to roll. So let me say a few words about this St. Nazaire experience. Now that it is over, what can I say we have accomplished? I fear that this is one of those rather indefinable things. On the material side, the group here has made 228 demenagements, 117 of which were the complete moving of families and their possessions. If we had not done the job—well, we don't know how they would have been moved.

As to spreading our gospel of good will, the results are not so obvious. I think the story I told before of the family who were so appreciative to see a foreigner interested in their welfare, helping them and smiling about it, enjoying helping others without remuneration, is as concrete an illustration of what we hoped we were doing as I can relate. Due to the war, these people have come to regard all foreigners with suspicion, to see foreigners as strangers who are self-seeking, frustrated individuals. Perhaps the realization that there are people who are trying to live a little differently may have its effect.

One other word of caution...I have mentioned the food I have had and the eggs I have carried back to Ker Berny several times. That may seem a bit inconsistent with the story you hear back home that there is hunger in Europe. In the first place, this area is the best off of any in France. It is the only area where there is no meat rationing. Secondly, my contacts with good food have been in the rural areas. The fact that I was glad to accept butter and eggs was because they were unobtainable even in this small town of le Pouliguen. Even though there may be a fair amount of food here, it is of little variety and not a balanced ration. Our meals in the local restaurant have made that clear.

Finally a word on the French, if I may be so bold as to generalize from my relatively few contacts. They seem to be a highly individualized people. They take no orders from superiors but, even worse, they do not even cooperate among themselves. Our group here has the feeling that the glory of France is all in the past. The chief ambition of the French we have known seems to be to get a job that will provide a pension in old age. They are looking for security and they want a quiet corner in which to retire. This may be lethargy brought on by the war, but then it may not be. That is not for me to judge. They seem to be a rather nervous people, getting into endless arguments over the slightest thing. Physically they aren't up to the standards we think of at home. I attribute that to two things, first the war and secondly, the fact that nearly every French person lives on wine. Do not take these observations too seriously—perhaps just passing thoughts.

Let me quote from an analysis of our work written by Roger in an official report:

> *"The nine men who at one time or another served at St. Nazaire certainly felt throughout the entire three months that the project was significant. Former CPS men are inclined to consider that angle with particular interest. While some doubts arose in the case of a few individual hauling jobs, by and large everybody was sold on the project—an attitude based on observation of the jobs we did, and encouraged by the frequent expressions of thanks by the grateful family as they stood before their new home in the midst of all their furniture, and fostered further by the general attitude of people about town and the newspaper, toward Quaker Transport.*
>
> *Our presence gave a significant boost to the work of a good many organizations working in the public interest, and it served, we hope, as a refreshing breeze of idealism to larger numbers in*

*the community who at least heard of our work and who had for
a long time been resigned to the uninspiring monotony of life on a
materialistic plane.*

*I say this having in mind the surprise often expressed by the
French people as they learned of our motive in doing the work.
Long hours of dirt and sweat lent a note of conviction to our
simple message that enabled people to understand."*

July 17—St. Nazaire to Paris

And so off to Paris for the six of us in six trucks. Roger led off,
followed by Chris, then Rene, followed by Leigh, me, and lastly, Jack. But
not so fast. Before we could go, Jack and
I both found each of our trucks had a flat
tire and Leigh had to fix a leak in his oil
line. After making all the necessary repairs, we finally headed out. After a long
day's drive, we finally arrived at our Paris
garage at 10:15 p.m.

The ETU director, Winslow
Ames, told us to go over to the Quaker
Center for the night, as we were all moving there anyway since the garage had to
be given up by August 1. Since we had
endured such a long day, he told us we
could sleep in the next morning and take
the day off. By the way, Roger didn't get
in until 2:00 a.m.

*Winslow Ames,
Director of ETU*

July 21—House Hunting

Thursday morning, taking Winslow at his word, I slept late; you
might say I overslept. As a result, I missed the farewell for six fellows and
trucks that left for Poland. When I got to the garage, I was branded as being
a bit lazy! It turns out there will be more fellows living in Paris for a time
than the Center can accommodate. The Center is now the AFSC office and
is located downtown at 17 rue Notre Dame des Champs. The new garage is
west of Paris, half way to St. Germain, so it was decided we should look for a
house nearer the new garage. Rene and I were chosen to find one to rent that
could house up to 10 fellows. The rest of the week, that was our project.

Although Germany is divided into specific Russian, French,
English, and American zones, France maintains its own government with

only certain areas and certain responsibilities given over to the British and Americans. Since our new garage is in the area of British responsibility, and we would like a house near the garage, our first step was to find and visit the British Town Major.

The theory was that he could best suggest housing that the British were derequisitioning. There we were told to go to the offices of the Royal Air Force (RAF). Here we were shunted up three offices until we found a Captain Brown, who turned out to be a very nice British chap who wanted to know all about our Quaker work. He told us he did not have the authority to help us and that we should go to the British Town Major where we had just been. It seems we had the wrong address! So on to the proper British Major. It took a good deal of talking to get past three secretaries, but when we finally met him, he turned out to be most polite and friendly. However, he said they were not derequisitioning anything at this time. He gave us the address of the French official in charge of all housing in Paris and wished us good luck.

So on we went to the new official who was also very friendly, yet he had jurisdiction only for Paris proper and not for the suburbs. He gave us a letter of recommendation to the proper official in Versailles. On to Versailles where we at last obtained addresses and the owners' names of two houses. Here we took time out to go through the palace, saw the Hall of Mirrors and were very impressed with all the ornamental rooms. It looks to me to be a waste to use it only as a museum. It certainly could have some more practical use!

After a long search, we found the houses. The first was totally unacceptable, as it was just a tumbled down shack. The second seemed much better. It was locked and a neighbor told us we would have to proceed through the local RAF office in order to gain access to it. Here we worked our way up four different offices from Corporal, to Sergeant, to Lieutenant, to Captain. The Captain admitted that the house had just been released and gave us the key. It was isolated in a grove of trees and was in good shape with seven rooms. It looked like the right place for us, particularly since it is only two miles from our garage. We then got in touch with the owner's wife who told us that the US Army was taking over the house! So back to Paris to check with the US Army's housing division only to find that it closes early on Friday afternoon. Upon returning Saturday morning, we found that although the US Army did not want the house, some French official had decided to take it. Worse, he could not be found. Nearby was another branch of the RAF where we talked with a Major Crampton, who was most polite, but said we should go see the British Town Major. And that was where we had started! At his office, whom should we find but the French official who had wanted the house. By now, he decided not to take it and it was at last ours. Now we could talk directly to the owner who rented it to us for $40.00 a month.

That house hunting was a valuable experience for me in my next job in Vienna. And yes, it seems settled that Leigh and I will be going there as our names have gone to Vienna to begin the long approval process. We could be leaving in two weeks but with all the red tape to be cut it may be two months.

I am glad of the chance to go but do not like the reason Lois Plumb, the new ETU chief in Paris replacing Winslow, gave for my selection. I asked her why of the three applicants Leigh and I had been chosen. Leigh was chosen because he is such a good mechanic. The other applicant wanted to go to Vienna, but since Hungary needed a top man, he will go there. I am going to Vienna by default! I hope that is not the whole story.

July 28—Garage Moving

This week we spent most of our time moving everything from our old garage in Paris at 2 rue de Civry to our new garage in Louvecienne, on the bank of the Seine. Our new house is in la Jonchere, just south of Bougival. The old garage in Paris had cost us 40,000 francs a month. Since the rent went up to 75,000 the decision was made to find a cheaper one. This garage in Louvecienne costs 5000 a month (119 francs to the dollar)!

Our garage in Louvecienne

The first three days we tried three different restaurants in Bougival for lunch, two of which were terrible at over 100 francs. The third one turned out to be very good at 75 francs.

Yesterday Leigh and I started getting a 1½-ton Chevrolet truck in shape for our trip to Vienna. We won't be taking those station wagons after all. I have been cleaning and greasing wheel bearings, removing old oil seals with wheel pullers, installing new ones, installing new king pins and bushings, rebuilding drag links, etc. Leigh has put in a new clutch and rebuilt the transmission from parts from two others. After a couple of days, the truck should be ready except for a paint job. Then we have to collect parts for the five jeeps and two trucks that are now in Vienna.

This week we spent several evenings at the Army "Sugar Bowl" where we could get ice cream and sodas, but were limited to two each. We cannot go anymore; as of yesterday all PX privileges for civilians are suspended. That means no more candy, no more film, no more cigarettes, no more ice cream, and no more razor blades from Army sources. All I will miss will be the candy and ice cream. During the last four or five years I had seldom bought a candy bar but here, I crave them as much as I did when I was 10. I still have four wholesale boxes of candy in my trunk that I have not yet opened. When I got them in Philadelphia, I was supposed to give them away. I always wondered if I would have the strength of mind to give them away. But I did today. I went out to St. Germain and paid a visit to Genevieve and her grandmother where Jack and I had lunch before we went to St. Nazaire and gave them some candy. Grandmother was overjoyed at it, almost to tears, for she had not seen any candy since the war began. Also, while we were in St. Germain we visited the birthplace of Claude Debussy.

August 4—Official Run Around

We had thought we would be leaving for Vienna by August 12. Forget that! On July 15, the Paris AFSC sent our names to AFSC Vienna and we thought that as soon as they got the Army's permission in Vienna we would be on our way. Little did we know. Let me try to explain how the process is proceeding and, hopefully, will proceed. It has to start with the US Army in the area where we currently are. Paris AFSC asked the Paris US Army to write to the Vienna US Army to give permission for us to come, permission that Vienna US Army had already given to the AFSC Vienna orally. After waiting a week we found out that was incorrect. No US civilian can go to Austria without written permission from Washington.

First, AFSC Paris cables AFSC Philadelphia asking permission for Leigh and me to go to Vienna. AFSC Philadelphia writes an approval letter to the State Department in Washington; the State Department approves with a memo to the US Army in Washington; the Washington US Army sends written approval to the Paris US Army; but the Paris US Army also needs approval from the Vienna US Army; the Vienna US Army OKs our coming with a letter back to the Paris US Army; the Paris US Army then sends the OK to Washington US Army; the Washington US Army sends a memo to the Washington State Department with an OK; the State Department then sends approval to AFSC Philadelphia from where final approval is sent to Paris AFSC. At the rate this is moving, we may celebrate Thanksgiving in Paris!

Today, Jack and I did a bit of sightseeing. We went to the American Church that has all its service in English. I might as well have gone to any stuffy, city church at home. Then after dining out—this time the meal was better than the one I reported two months ago but higher priced—we spent the afternoon walking around and finally climbed the Eiffel tower.

August 11—Translation

Another week of no news on the Austrian front. I spent only one day in the garage. Since Monday, I have been in the office at the Center drawing up a parts list that Leigh recommends we take to Vienna. No company here makes parts for Army vehicles. The only source has been the US Army, but last week the Army turned over all its parts to the French Army. That means that all parts requests to the French Army must be in French. I tried to get someone else to translate all these parts we need into French, but to no avail. So all week I have been doing the translation. Imagine that! It is nearly done now, with the help of a dictionary and Rene at odd moments. Again, I question the value of having someone like me in country for relief work who does not know the language. I really shouldn't complain too much as all AFSC workers are first funneled through France and are then sent on to the proper country.

Yet I do question relief work sometimes when you run up against the stonewall of government bureaucracy. One new example may suffice to highlight this. In June, one of our fellows flew to Rome, bought many spare parts from the Army and a truck from the United Nations Relief and Rehabilitation Administration (UNRRA) that he drove back to Paris. Then last week he took an empty truck from here to bring the rest of the parts back from Rome, but he could not get through the Italian border. He was told that no vehicles could cross unless he belonged to an automobile club. Paris got and sent him a membership card. Still his crossing was stopped because the government would allow no trucks to cross. Then later they said he could go by making a $4000 deposit, which in all likelihood he would never have gotten back. So he returned to Paris to fly to Rome to scrounge a truck in which to bring the parts back. I guess you can drive into France but not out of France into Italy!

Yesterday, Genevieve from St. Germain called to ask if I could take a food package to Austria. Some friends of hers have hungry friends in Austria. Again, I went to St. Germain to get the package.

August 17—Army Red Tape

This week I put in the time inventorying, assembling, and cleaning US Army tools we will take to Austria. They are in the original crates as packed some four years ago by the Army and in many cases are covered by rust. I am washing them all with gas and coating them with grease.

We seem to be spending most of our time waiting for the State Department and US Army permissions. Four fellows here have been waiting to go to Germany longer than we have been waiting to go to Austria. Over a month ago, a survey from Germany indicated immediate need for trucks to go to the farms to haul wheat directly from the threshing machines to the cities. Wheat harvest in Europe is in July and August and now it is in full swing in Germany. Yet the State Department has not even acknowledged the requests yet and it is doubtful if the fellows will get into Germany until the middle of September after the wheat is all harvested and stored on the farms from where it will be more difficult to move. Harvest time was the proper time and the ETU was ready.

Winslow had an experience last week that shows how absurd the Army regulations are. He took my old truck and drove to Metz to pick up a load of food for Germany as he was promised the entry permit in Metz. After getting loaded, he discovered it would be another month before the permit would be issued. He and a new team member went ahead anyway and were able to bluff their way across the border and on to Koblenz. They did hurry to get unloaded and back to France before trouble might have developed. This new member told me something of their drive in Germany. They saw much bomb damage, hundreds of transients on the roads, and the wheat harvest in full swing. He said so much of the wheat is being harvested by hand. Not being a farmer, he didn't know just how they were doing it, but after questioning him, I got the picture of the wheat being harvested with cradles—he saw no combines at all.

They kept picking up hitchhikers on the way back as they were empty. Many of the hitchhikers were shy and hesitated to get on a US Army truck. In time, he got the truck full of people. He thinks the greatest service we could do if we could just get into Germany would be to use our trucks to haul people, there are just so many going in all directions. They had not quite reached Koblenz when they noticed something dragging from the truck. On stopping, they found that a small boy had jumped onto the truck while they were moving slowly and had methodically been throwing off cartons of powdered milk. Five were missing from the truck and they had immediately disappeared from the road. At least hungry Germans got them, though not in the proper way!

August 18—This and That

Last evening I was at home alone with our French housekeeper and cook. We were able to have a nice conversation since she speaks some German. She has one phobia that has become somewhat of a nuisance to us. It seems to be rather indicative of the insecurity of the French. Every night before she goes to bed, she locks all the windows and doors after she has locked the metal shutters on the outside of the windows and doors. These shutters are iron affairs that would test the ingenuity of any burglar. She will not sleep with her windows open despite the need for air. This was all amus-

Our French housekeeper

ing at first to us but a couple of nights ago coming back late we found it impossible to get in without waking her to let us in. I would feel just as safe here with unlocked shutters as I would at home. I suppose, in her case, that the past five years of nightly fear is not easily erased.

Friday night, 15 of us went into Paris to the *Folies Bergeres*. I certainly never saw anything like it before. There were three and a half hours of continuous performances with set after set being changed, gorgeous costumes following one another across the stage in rapid procession. It was Radio City Music Hall, grand opera, Gilbert and Sullivan and burlesque all rolled into one. (*I left out a mention of the nudity because I was writing to my parents!*)

This afternoon we had our formal open house for our home here, Maison Rose. Some 60 people crowded in as it rained all day. It looks like Rene and I did all right in renting this place.

August 25—Progress?

Word has come that our permission to go to Austria is proceeding. At least Vienna has received it. It only now needs to go back to Washington and then to Paris for final clearance. It looks like we might be leaving here by September 8. Maybe! In the meantime, we helped others in the garage. And I have been both the garage and Maison Rose guard when everyone else had to be elsewhere. Wednesday night I called a square dance for the fellows of the unit plus the secretarial help at the Center. One of the girls is a good pianist so she provided the music. We had a little difficulty getting it organized, as she speaks no English. However, it worked out well.

August 31—Report from Germany

Thursday night I went into Paris to hear a report by Hertha Kraus who had just returned from a two-week visit to the French zone of Germany. The picture there, according to her, is very bleak. The French Army is living off the land. They requisition food from everyone. On the farms, they take 10% of the potatoes, every third cow, and many other items of produce entirely. In order to ensure that the peasants hold nothing back they have soldiers stationed in every little village. Not only do the soldiers have to feed themselves but also many of them have families who have to be fed. The average German diet consists of 1) breakfast—potatoes and ersatz coffee (substitute coffee made from wheat), 2) lunch—potatoes, and 3) supper—potatoes.

There are almost no young men to do the work. About five million men in the most active age of life are still prisoners of war in Russia, France, Belgium, and elsewhere. Thus, the work is being done by children, women, and old people. The de-Nazification program is cutting into the economy horribly. Every German is required to fill out papers about his or her past record. No person who ever held any office with the faintest Nazi taint is allowed to work other than as ditch diggers. Not telling the truth about your past is a prison offense. Nearly 80% of former business people are excluded from working.

The zonal division is awful. One family she knew had lived in what became the American zone. During the war, they had moved temporarily to relatives in what became the French zone. They had been in the retail dry goods business and had brought their goods with them. Since the war ended, they finally got permission to go back home but were forbidden to take any of their goods with them, yet they can't do business in the French zone because their home is the American zone. All they can now do is live off relatives. She added that there is urgent need for transport assistance but the red tape makes it prohibitive.

September 1—Opera

Friday night a group of us went to the opera in Paris and saw *Othello*. It certainly is a fancy opera house but the seating was bad. Six of us were in a box but the back two had to stand to see anything. The staging was the best I have ever seen. There was a large, well-conducted orchestra. I counted six bass viols and seven cellos—I could not see the other instruments. Admission was one dollar. I was amused by one item. All around the walls and in the lobby were no smoking signs, but the back of every other seat held an ashtray!

September 10—Permits at Last

We actually have all our permissions to leave for Vienna, but they didn't make it easy for us. Several last minute roadblocks had to be cleared away. Thursday the US embassy in Paris called the AFSC to say that our approval had arrived. On Friday, Leigh and I went to the embassy to get our passports validated for Austria. After getting them, we were told to go to the military permit office to get permits to enter the US occupied territory of Austria. When we got there, we found it was closed on Friday. Back on Saturday, we found we could not get permits until the embassy stamped in our passports that were going through Germany to get to Austria. Monday we got the notations at the embassy and finally our military permits. Then we were told to apply on the spot for military travel orders so that we could use Army facilities on our way to Vienna. This we promptly did and we were actually able to pick them up yesterday. Permits all set!

September 11—Paris Food

Before leaving Paris, I want to make a final comment on food. As far as I can tell, there is no longer a food crisis in France. Of course, you don't get dainties, little milk, chocolate, or cakes. But you do eat. Sunday I ate in restaurant and paid a fairly high price of 175 francs for the lunch. I started with a fried egg, followed with French fries, tender steak, lettuce and a very good melon. A story in the August 28 issue of TIME magazine stated that you could not get any meal in Paris better than at a subsistence level without paying 1000 francs ($8.25). This is absolutely false. We still have been eating well in Bougival for 75 francs. Yesterday I noticed along the streets at nearly every corner a butcher setting up shop with all kinds of meat hanging up for sale. Peaches are abundant at 15 cents a pound. Food may get tighter next winter but it is available now.

And yes, one other comment about Parisians before we leave France. I have been asked what I think of French girls! A few of them are attractive enough to catch my eye in a fleeting sort of way. I find most of those with possibilities cover themselves up with too much artificial paint. And too, those with dark hair take pride in bleaching their hair. Black hair must be a no-no. Tomorrow—off to Vienna. Hurrah!

September 12—The False Start

After getting last minute items loaded, pictures taken, farewells said, and a bouquet of flowers fastened to the right windshield wiper, we left Maison Rose for the Paris AFSC office. After more farewells, we were off for Vienna by 10:30 a.m. I started driving our tortuous route out of Paris.

We left Paris proper and drove on to the eastern highway that wound through innumerable narrow-street villages for a dozen miles or so. At about 11:15 we came to another small town, Meaux, where I had to pull a bit left to pass a parked car. Coming toward us was an old truck loaded with lime. Although it was a narrow street, I thought I had room. Furthermore, I was first. I nosed the front end of our truck by the parked car and headed for the right curb. But the rear didn't make it. A dull thud came to my ears and the truck quickly stopped with sort of a sigh as if mortally wounded.

Truck that I hit

My damaged truck sitting in the narrow street

We found that this was true. A rod coming from the radiator of this old charcoal burning truck had caught the rim of our left rear tire and had simply pulled the whole rear axle with it. The left rear spring was broken, the right U-bolts were sadly bent, the two left tires were in shreds, and the drive shaft had dropped to the street. At a glance, it was obvious we would go no further that day.

An Army truck heading for Paris happened by and Leigh caught a ride to go for help.

For the first 10 minutes there wasn't much for me to do. A crowd had gathered and stood idly by, gawking at it all. The lime truck had ended up on my left-hand curb with its radiator bolts broken and water pouring out in every direction. I found a sympathetic onlooker who told me the other driver was on the phone some place, as I waited. When he came out, we exchanged names, addresses and the like in a most friendly manner. Although the accident was primarily my fault, he was most courteous and polite and took it all as a matter of course. After a few more minutes, the police arrived, drew maps of the area, measured the street, and got the story from the other driver and onlookers. The police and, in fact, everyone was more polite than I would have expected at home. No one spoke English but we seemed to be able to communicate anyway. After a time the other truck managed to hobble away, and since it was such a narrow street, a cop arrived to direct the one-way traffic around my truck. A nearby storekeeper came out presently with a sandwich for me. Everyone was so friendly.

At 2:30 p.m., team members Del Eberhardt, Lois Plumb and Owen Newlin arrived with a big truck. After unloading all our Vienna parts onto their truck to lighten our truck, we lifted its rear onto the front bumper of their truck. For the 20 miles or so of our trip back through Paris, Del pushed me as I guided the truck back to our garage, where we arrived by 6:00 p.m. Then back to Maison Rose for supper and early to bed to be ready to work on the truck in the morning. I had not seen Leigh since he left me to get help. Others told me he was a bit upset about it. Why wouldn't he be? Everyone else has been swell about the accident. I do appreciate that.

September 13—This Time It Is True

After breakfast we headed to the garage, my mind all set for two or three day's work. On going into the garage, we saw the truck, axle all straight, springs and U-bolts in place, good tires mounted; in short, we were ready to go. Upon looking into the office, we spied the sleeping form of Leigh. He soon came awake with his story. He had come to the garage last night to see how bad the damage was and had just started working on it. He got more interested as he went along, particularly on finding that the axle was not damaged and that all he had to do was to put on a new spring, drive shaft, and tires! I wreck the trucks and he fixes them! We spent the rest of the morning reloading the truck. The last thing we did was to remove the flowers that were still on the windshield wiper. Yesterday on the way back, we had seen three funeral processions with similar wreaths (quite common in Europe).

Starting at four o'clock, I drove until 7:30 when we stopped for the night in a wheat stubble field (a recently harvested field of wheat). We ate

K rations (US Army emergency field rations) for supper and went to sleep with Leigh under the truck and me on the boxes of spare parts in the truck. At last, we were really on our way.

September 14—The First Lap

We were up by 7:00 for another K ration meal and then headed east. By midafternoon we reached Metz. We had heard it was in pretty bad shape but were surprised to find it not as bad as we had expected, not nearly as bad as St. Nazaire had been. We left the main road and headed in the direction of Bitche. The last 50 miles were quite hilly, a bit more rugged than eastern Ohio. At various hilltops, we began to see pillboxes sticking out of the ground and often we saw barbed wire entanglements. Each valley was surrounded with these hilltop pillboxes. Later we learned that this was the Maginot line. It was not in a line as I had expected, but was spread all over the hills. We also were told that there were tunnels connecting all these pillboxes (small, low structures of reinforced concrete, enclosing machine guns). The Maginot Line was build in the thirties by the French in the mistaken belief it would protect them from a future German invasion

At about 6:00 p.m., we came down a high hill into a tiny valley just large enough to contain the town of Bitche. We found we had been within 10 miles of the German border for the last 25 miles. We had just been parallel to it. When we located the Quaker group, we found they were all English except for one American, Irwin Graeber, whom I had known in Pendle Hill. They were doing work similar to ours in St. Nazaire. We spent the night with them in their barracks. Irwin and I took a late night walk through the town. The full moon was just behind the church steeple, from which came the strokes of the richest and most sonorous sounding bell I had ever heard. Just to think that this town is in the heart of a piece of land that has been disputed and fought over as much as any land in the world—the French/German border.

Glimpse of Germany

September 1946

September 15—Deutschland at Last

After another K ration breakfast (the team at Bitche eats with a French family who could not take visitors), we took off on a lonely, narrow road and headed east again. The hills had grown by now and reminded me of parts of Vermont. We knew we were only a mile or two from the border but suddenly we were blocked by a border pole and French policemen. The border didn't look quite right so after giving up our papers Leigh asked if we really were entering Germany. No, Leigh was told, we were entering France from Germany! For the last two miles, we had been in Germany illegally and hadn't even known it. We told the policeman we had come from Paris and he apologized for thinking we had been deep in Germany somewhere.

The next 10 miles to the border town of Wissembourg were dotted with little French villages. Every house seemed to be part barn. In front of the door step of each "barn" was a neat pile of manure, even in the center of the towns. Every time a horse would leave some manure on the street, two or three housewives armed with brooms and dustpans would vie with each other to pick up the precious stuff because it makes such good fertilizer.

Every little town had its ruined buildings and bridges. The people seemed to be going on about their business as usual as if they little knew or cared that this land was the prized plaything of Germany and France. And so on to the French border through which we passed with no difficulty. After two miles we came to another border, manned this time with French soldiers, as it was the border to French-occupied Germany. Shortly after going through this border, we crossed through the Siegfried line, the German counterpoint for the Maginot line. It was just as I had always imagined it to

I am standing at the Siegfried Line on the German border

be, one continuous line. Every few hundred yards were pillboxes sticking out of the ground and all along the way between them was this line of tank blocks some four feet or so high, two feet apart and eight blocks deep. It certainly seemed to be more capable of stopping tanks than the Maginot Line. Germany, too, had feared invasion and had prepared for it. Now we knew we were really in Germany.

The country soon flattened out and we were driving through good farmland. The towns looked different and in much better shape than those in France. At first I couldn't figure out why, as the towns had destruction on a par with French towns. Then I realized the difference. There were no walls around the houses and the streets often were as wide as in an American town. There was no manure in front of the houses and many of the houses had flowers in the windows. I was fascinated trying to read the signs on the stores and actually understanding what was for sale there.

One other distinction is worthy of note—the people. In France, I had been used to seeing people going about their usual business, which on Sunday means market day. In these German villages, the people seemed to be going or coming from church and mostly appeared well groomed. Their clothes were old and worn but clean and colorful, though a bit faded. More than once, I saw the typical German girl's costume that we all have associated with Little Red Riding Hood.

We soon arrived at the Rhine, which was about the size of the Ohio River in Cincinnati, and passed through the French control before crossing the river on a pontoon bridge, a temporary floating bridge, the only bridge between Mannheim to the north and Strasbourg to the south.

Next came the American control, which put us into the American zone of Germany. Soon we passed through the city of Karlsruhe and started out on the autobahn, the German equivalent of the Pennsylvania turnpike. Hitler had built this super highway all the way from Frankfurt to Salzburg. He knew such a road was not only good propaganda but also made the movement of military troops easier. It was thus possible for us to make better time now, not having to pass through villages. However, we were slowed almost as much by the many bridges that had been destroyed, causing difficult detours.

Crossing into the U.S. zone of Germany

By the middle of the afternoon, we came close to Stuttgart and decided to go into the city in search of Army gas. Shortly, we descended into a great valley which seemed to be entirely filled with a city, that is, if you can call it a city now. Nowhere did we see the complete destruction that characterized St. Nazaire, but the area of Stuttgart that is damaged is many times larger than the area of St. Nazaire. Here we saw the whole heart of the city torn apart—buildings with one side ripped away, many floors caved in, just one wall standing, or all walls standing with the inside just blown up. The streets were littered with rubble making it very difficult to drive through. It was the largest scale destruction I have ever seen.

We found the Army HQ, talked them out of 25 gallons of gas (we had no coupons), and headed out of town for the autobahn. Again, I had to ask directions and a German policeman answered me in beautiful German after giving me a smart military salute, which I was not quite able to bring myself to return.

One other little incident of the day must not go unnoticed. Leigh was driving on the autobahn and making good time—going down a hill we were rolling at a good 45 mph. Around the corner an American MP stopped us and told us we had been caught speeding in a speed trap and would have to report to his senior officer a few hundred yards back. The officer was nonplussed to have a civilian truck and two civilians fall into his snare. Finally, he said he would report it as a misdemeanor and send the report to our Paris office for the proper disciplinary action. We are expecting dire things from the Paris AFSC office any day!

Night found us some 40 miles beyond Stuttgart so we pulled off the road into the edge of a pine forest to spend the night in the same fashion we have done the two previous nights in France. Speaking of pine forests, we had driven past forest after forest of beautiful conifers standing high and limbless half way to the tops. I don't think I have ever seen so much good timber in one day.

September 16—Farewell Germany

After we had eaten our K ration breakfast, I noticed that in a nearby field a farmer had brought a team and wagon to a compost pile and was beginning to fork the contents of the pile onto his wagon. Since I wasn't going to have much chance for personal contact with people in Germany on this trip, I thought I would try him now. At my greeting he looked up and grunted after glancing at my uniform. It was an inauspicious beginning.

I just stood around and rubbed the horses' necks while he went on working. "Good farming weather, isn't it?" I said.

He stopped working and grudging replied about the weather. By then curiosity had gotten the better of his animosity. "Is your truck broken down?" he asked.

"No, we slept here last night and haven't gotten back on the road just yet."

With surprise across his face, he replied, "It's odd for an American officer to sleep on the ground in an enemy country, all alone."

That was my opening so I explained, "We are not soldiers—we are here to help rebuild."

With that, he really warmed up. "I have not seen an American civilian in years. What do you do in America?" He was surprised when I told him I was from a farm. We talked on for a time about red clover, the value of manure, horses vs. tractors, etc.

Then as if something we had said earlier came back to him, he said, "Soldiers are all bad. War is all bad. Why can't we live without war and without soldiers?" His words stayed with me for some time as we drove on.

In the middle of the morning, we turned off the autobahn to go to a little village in order to mail some letters we had brought from Paris. No mail can yet go from France to Germany. I found the post office to be in a private residence. The postmistress quietly, but with a bit of hostility, made my transactions. Again, curiosity helped. She asked just what kind of an American soldier I was. She said she had not seen this kind of a uniform before. As soon as I told a little about myself, she became very friendly. Her husband had been killed on the Russian front and she and her daughter were carrying on with the small farm and the post office, which, incidentally looked spick-and-span.

One sentence in our conversation stood out when she said, "Why must we always have war?" She said food was scarce but they, at least, had potatoes and milk. I gave her some candy and left thinking of the question she had asked.

We drove on eastward seeing lots of productive land that was given over mostly to potatoes and pasture. The rest of the land either was in forest or freshly plowed in preparation for sowing wheat. I saw almost no tractors, only horses, or a horse teamed with a cow or a bull, and sometimes two cows alone.

I cannot report much on our drive through Munich as I was driving and was hard put to keep on the right street. I did see evidence of destruction but not the complete desolation of Stuttgart.

In the afternoon we came in sight of mountains some 40 miles away, a similar experience to the time we drove from Kansas to Colorado Springs, when I was 10 years old. All afternoon and into early evening we were approaching these mountains—high forbidding piles of earth, some covered with forests, others were rough and barren with rocky protuberances, and again others covered with beautiful seedings of grass. It was a brilliantly sunny afternoon, with contrasts of light and shadow on the tops of the mountains, the lower hills, and on the houses, trees, and meadows. It gave the whole vista a Shangri-la glow. We kept guessing which of the many valleys between the mountains we would eventually drive through, but alas, we never did. The autobahn veered to the left and we skirted the northern edge without ever entering them.

Suddenly we were at the Austrian border through which we passed without incident. In a few more miles, we observed the city of Salzburg nestled placidly in a wide valley to our right beyond which the Austrian Alps towered solidly. As soon as we had passed Salzburg, the autobahn played out and we took the regular road on toward Linz, the most eastern outpost in the American zone. In all of Germany, we had not seen the transients we had expected, perhaps because we had been on the autobahn. Now in Austria it was different. Many people were on the highway going in both directions and nearly all laden down with parcels of food. For the first time I saw many people barefoot. We drove on into the night in order to reach Linz where we found quarters at the Army transient station and spent the night in a crowded room, in fact on cots on the stage of a large auditorium.

Austria

September to
December, 1946

September 17—Red Country

Right after breakfast in the Army mess we went to the HQ to get a "four powered pass." This pass, in four languages, is commonly known as the "gray card" and is necessary to gain entry to the Russian zone! I spent an hour getting it, as the Colonel was hesitant for we had no written proof that Vienna AFSC had approved our coming. Finally, the AFSC travel order did the trick. Just before getting to the Russian border, we stopped to put enough gas in our tank to get us to Vienna. I handed Leigh a can the contents of which he began siphoning into the tank. The can was half empty before he discovered it was water! We thought we might be able to burn it through so started off. After a minute the truck stopped completely. We then had to drain not only the tank, but also the filter, the fuel pump, and the lines. However, this was our last mishap of the trip.

Just around the next curve, we came to the Enns River, the end of the American zone. We passed easily through the American control, on to the no-man's-land of the bridge, and onto the other side to the Russian pole and the Russian guards. I crossed this bridge with rather mixed feelings. Here we were going, in a sense, through that famous iron curtain that we have heard so much about. I was half expecting to see seven-foot Hussars, with sword in one hand, a machine gun in the other, and topped off with a huge fez hat. In a sense I was disappointed to find that these, my first Russian guards, were just about like any other soldiers in appearance. In fact, they didn't seem as belligerent as some Americans I have seen. These chaps happened to be rather short and their simple trim uniforms seemed to add to their apparent humility—humility in contrast to the vision I previously had of them.

Everything went well with my pass. The soldier spoke German but as he handed me back my pass I made a mistake and thanked him in French. He looked at me again with a bit more interest and asked if I were French. That is the first and last time I have been accused of being French! When I told him I was American he wanted to know if I was a soldier. My "no" startled him enough to cause another look at my pass. After careful perusal, he waved us on. We were now officially in the Russian zone. And they don't let you forget it. Atop the bridge was a large blood red flag, and below a large colorful picture of Stalin.

As we left the Russian control post, an Austrian pled with us to take him to Vienna. We had not intended to take anyone inside the truck with all our tools, parts, and food, but did not have the heart to say no. As soon as we said "yes," another man and a girl jumped out of the bushes and wanted to go too. We pushed the two men through the porthole in the rear canvas and took the girl up front with us (that was their choice, not ours!). They were all carrying food parcels, heading home to Vienna. I asked the girl how she would have gone without our ride and she said she would have hitched another ride, walked, or possibly taken the bus. The bus was too crowded, cost too much money, and took 11 hours to get to Vienna, and we made it in three. We passed many more people walking but did not feel we should take any more.

At about 3:00 p.m. in the afternoon we pulled into Vienna, took our passengers where they wanted to go, and started hunting for the AFSC office at 17 Rotenturmstrasse. We had some difficulty and started asking pedestrians where it might be. They were always glad to oblige but never quite got it right. Generally, their answers were something like "just around the second corner to the right—you can't miss it!" We did miss it.

I saw two Russian soldiers walking toward us so I thought I would see if they spoke German and if they knew where Rotenturmstrasse was. I walked up to them but something in their manner arrested my tongue and I uttered not a word. The thing that caught my attention was simply the fact that they did not recognize my physical presence with the slightest movement of limb or eye. Generally, when you walk toward someone, they at least glance in your direction. These two soldiers did not. I might as well have been air as far as they were concerned. At any rate, we soon found the office and were heartily welcomed by AFSC staff in the office. We had reached our destination.

September 20—Orientation

We have had a great three days becoming acquainted with the team, with this city, and getting temporarily settled into this nice hotel that the Army has set aside for US civilian employees. The team consists of five men and four women each of whom has a particular relief project. They meet together for a staff meeting every Monday morning. The leader, at least the man who signs the papers as leader, is George Mathues, a Catholic who was in CPS. He is probably around 35 and unmarried. He seems very capable although inclined to be overcritical at times. I have had very good relations with him.

George Mathues

The next is Ed Fredericks, a 40-ish engineer who works on an industrial rehabilitation project near Enns in the American zone. He is not often in Vienna.

The team also includes Arthur Billing, who was in Leavenworth prison in Kansas as a conscientious objector (CO). I asked him if he had known my old college history professor who had been in Leavenworth dur-

ing the First World War. He said no and then I discovered later that he had been in Leavenworth during the Second World War but because of his bald head, I had placed him at least over 50! He is also unmarried and belongs to no particular church. He can be very opinionated on some topics but is a delight. Before the war, he was in Moscow for a couple of years as a translator so he speaks fluent Russian and tells many Russian stories. Last year he attended a Child Welfare Congress in Zagreb, Yugoslavia where he met and talked

Arthur Billings

with Marshal Tito.

Arthur meeting Marshall Tito in Yugoslavia

Carlton Maybee is a rather famous CPS man for he has written a book about his CPS experience. He is 35, a Baptist, and is married. In fact, his wife had a baby last week.

Then we have Mel Luerson, a Swede from Texas, an Episcopalian, I think. He too is a CPS man and is about 30. He has been in charge of transportation and is happy to teach me the ropes so that he can spend more time with the Österreichischer Gewerkschaftsbund (ÖGB) Federation of

Mel Luerson

Austrian Trade Unions. Others of the group find him a bit difficult to get along with because of his gruff manner, but we all see he does not mean it and have a lot of fun with him. He is sometimes in opposition to George on policy matters, but nothing serious.

Now to the women. Marlis Guildemeister, about 30, has an unusual background. She is from Peru, has lived some years in the US, was one of the first women to attend Haverford College, and lived some years at her father's castle near Zell am See in what is now the American zone of Austria.

(On July 25, 2005, I met Marlis again at her old homestead, Fischhorn, after more than 55 years.)

Marlis Guildemeister

Marlis and me in 2005

Polly Campion, 29, is quite self-sufficient. She takes care of personnel services, meeting all the people who come to the office. We have a lot of fun with her although I think of her as definitely in the "old maid" class.

Then there is Comfort Cary, 28, not particularly pretty, but a wonderful buddy. She worked in UNRRA for a year before coming here in July. She is a most efficient person and is very companionable.

Polly Campion

Comfort Cary

Finally, we have Mary Forman, 27, who is far from the "old maid" type. She is a Columbus, Ohio Quaker who is here to do youth work. Everyone likes Mary. And, oh yes, everyone speaks fluent German. Leigh and I round out this group of very interesting people.

Even though I have been here only three days, I think I see a sizeable rift between two of them and I think they are wooing us as newcomers to their respective camps. So even in the AFSC you have politics and personality clashes—just like back in CPS. Remember, I have been here only three days so of course I know all the answers already!

Mary Forman

I should mention one other person. Bert Smucker, a young man my age who arrived in Vienna at the same time, is living with us in the same hotel. He is with the Mennonite Central Committee (MCC). I imagine we will often be working together even though our programs are completely separate.

This city has fabulous buildings, parks, and streets but it certainly has been scarred by the war, not nearly as badly as St. Nazaire or Stuttgart, but there are many areas with total destruction. Right across the street from our office on Rotenturmstrasse lay the remains of a former office building.

Vienna destruction as seen from the Marienbrücke

The center of the city is the international sector and the outlying sectors are divided up among the four powers, the English, French, American, and Russian. We can travel unhindered in all of these sectors but cannot go beyond them into the Russian zone that surrounds Vienna. There are only two roads out of Vienna on which we can travel, the American road west to Linz to the American zone, and the British road over the Semmering pass to the British zone.

The team felt that Leigh and I should have the last three days of this week off to get settled and get our documents in order. Mel, who has been sharing the transportation chores with Comfort, took Leigh and me around the city helping us with our documentation. He also introduced us to several Army officials with whom I will need to work, took us to the Army Ordnance Center, the PX garage, and to the gas station. We also began the search for a garage where Leigh can set up shop. However, we may have trouble finding one as the Army has already requisitioned about every one available.

September 22—First Sunday

Carlton took me to a local Baptist church. It was just like a good country Methodist church in Iowa, or so it seemed to me. I did not understand much of the sermon but all else seemed so natural. In the afternoon I delivered some items I had brought from Genevieve in Paris for a family here. They told me their supply of food was poor but I did not understand much more. The accent is not what I thought in Paris a German accent should be, probably because they are Austrian, and Austrians speak a somewhat different version of German than the Germans.

This evening I went to a home for undernourished children run by the Swiss Quakers. The occasion was a farewell party for Emma Cadbury, who had worked with the AFSC in Vienna after World War I. In good Austrian fashion, the party took the form of a concert by a good violinist. I arrived too late for worship so instead ate supper with the children. Supper was porridge covered with chocolate chips—very good but not a lot of it. To the children it was wonderful. I found it most difficult to communicate with them. I never did learn the grammar forms to use when addressing children, Du etc. and when I used the standard forms, Sie etc., the children were so surprised to be addressed as adults that they would not talk anymore.

September 29—My First Week

This has been a week of introduction for me to Vienna, the Army, the Austrians, our team, and even an opera! Some of us drove one day to the Kahlenberg, which is a high hill, almost a mountain, north of Vienna that is still in the American sector. From there we could see not only all of Vienna in the wide valley below and the brown, not blue, Danube River, but also the level plain eastward to the Hungarian border. Awe inspiring sites.

The weekly Monday morning staff meeting was most interesting. As each person on the staff has his own pet work project, the meeting is really a clearinghouse so that all know what the others are doing. The antagonisms I first thought I saw were not antagonisms. These are just strong personalities pushing their views on each other, and the barbs were mostly in fun.

Monday night I attended a sort of club meeting at the office. Carlton and Mary had organized this group of young Austrians (15–25 years old) for a social gathering. I had a great time in trying out my German. That reminds me, I am taking German lessons three times a week. The Army provides free lessons for any Americans here. The teacher is a middle-aged Austrian University professor. He too has fallen on hard times. He gets a meal a day from the Army for his three hours of teaching, and he lets his frail wife eat the meal. He is a charming individual who somehow symbol-izes the fine qualities and yet the pathetic position of Austria today. Just his manner somehow tugs at the heartstrings. A couple of Army chaps in the class seem very nice, as do many of the Army contacts I have made here in Vienna.

One other nonwork event of the week was last night. Bert, Mary, Polly, Leigh, and I went to see *Madame Butterfly*. As the Staatsoper was so badly bombed, opera is now performed in an older building, the Theater an der Wien. We all agreed it was poorly done. Maybe Paris opera spoiled us. I'm sure that the bombing of the Staatsoper just before the end of the war was a great setback to opera production in Vienna.

One day this week I took a few American women to a vacation camp for children of displaced persons (DPs). The children and their fami-lies were actually Volksdeutsch, whose "crimes" had been their German ancestry while living in Czechoslovakia, Yugoslavia, or Hungary, and their German language. An American woman here had contacted and asked American civilians living in Vienna to contribute a little money to do some-thing nice for the children. As a result of contributions, this woman's group was able to buy five gallons of ice cream from the Army and bring it to the camp. This camp had a hundred children ranging in age from eight to twelve. They were all children of DPs and have been living with their parents since the war in various camps around Vienna. The average caloric intake per day of the DPs is around 800. They only get one meal a day. These children have been getting an additional 300 calories from the Austrian government. You can imagine a child of that age living in a room with 20 other families, eating 1100 to 1200 calories a day. This camp is set up to bring in 100 children every three weeks and feed them up to 2500 calories a day in order to build them up a bit, give them each a bed entirely to themselves, and give them a bit of en-couragement toward living. Most of the extra food comes from the AFSC, although the British Quakers do the actual administration of the feeding.

The American civilians took great delight in serving this ice cream to the children who were in ecstasies of delight over having ice cream, many for the first time in their

*Displaced Persons child
enjoying ice cream*

memory. After seeing the great pleasure on those wistful faces, I would say that anything that can be sent over in the way of food is worthwhile.

We really did do some work this week. Mel, Leigh, and I spent a lot of time searching for a garage. The United Nations Relief and Rehabilitation Administration (UNRRA) had told us that there were no garages available in Vienna. We could not go to the Army in our search for they would requisition any they knew about. We went to a man who is in a high position in the Austrian government and is friendly to the Quakers. He promised to turn up one for us by next week.

I also got initiated to the frustrations of using the Army international telephone lines. Free they may be, but service is terrible. In Paris I had heard that we were to get a jeep from Rome, but I did not know any details. After a four-hour attempt, I finally reached Lois in Paris. Our conversation was short, and the connection bad, but before we were cut off, she confirmed that a jeep had been reserved for us and then gave me the name of our contact in Rome. Another four-hour phone attempt to our contact in Rome revealed that he was out for the day. However, his secretary said the jeep had been assigned to us and would be shipped in a week or so along with 10 jeeps being shipped to the Jewish Joint Distribution Committee (JDC) here.

October 6—First Big Trip

Tuesday this Austrian government friend of the Quakers gave us a list of several possible garages. Mel, Leigh, and I spent that day and part of Wednesday checking them out. We finally found a small one that is still large enough for our trucks. We even found the owner who is not able to operate his garage due to lack of parts and gas. We negotiated a deal with him and Thursday Leigh moved in. At least something is accomplished. I couldn't help Leigh as I was off on an interesting trip. Let me tell you about it.

Mel found he could get a truckload of recreational equipment from the Army in Salzburg. A recuperation home in Frankenmarkt, near Salzburg, needed a barrack, which was in sections in Vienna. Wednesday afternoon Mel and I loaded this barrack onto two trucks. Then Thursday we drove out the American highway through the Russian zone to Frankenmarkt and unloaded the barrack. He then went on to Salzburg leaving me in the recuperation home for the night.

This recuperation home is run by the ÖGB for apprentice boys aged 14 to 18. Let me explain. In Austria most noncollege-bound boys become apprentices; that is, they work for some person, business, or company to learn a trade while they are finishing school. This recuperation home can house up to 120 boys—and this group changes every month. None of these still growing boys has enough to eat. So those worst off are selected to come here for a month of better food to build up their physical condition. There are about 10 of these camps throughout Austria and it was possible to set them up based only on the promise of food being provided by the AFSC.

ÖGB recuperation home in Frankenmarkt

Mel came back that night but we stayed until this morning, Sunday, as the home director wanted to go to Vienna with us but could not leave until today. Eating with the boys, I found the diet to be very uninteresting. It consisted of the following: at breakfast there was a large bowl of oatmeal and a cup of coffee; at noon, a sort of a bean and potato hash, plenty of it, a small piece of meat, some sort of potato cakes made mostly from Ralston cereal product, and one piece of black bread; at four o'clock there was another piece of black bread and a cup of milk; at supper there was all the potato salad one could eat, again made partly from the Ralston cereal, plus one cup of milk. Many of the boys told me it was the best diet they had experienced in years and was far superior to anything they could get in Vienna.

We spent Friday and Saturday getting acquainted with the boys. They almost fell all over themselves treating us like visiting celebrities. They knew where the food was coming from! We ate with them, played "fussball" (soccer) with them, hiked, and chatted with them as best we could. I hope we were able to let them know that "enemy" Americans can be regular fellows too. They seemed really interested in the concept of democracy. They were too young to have been in the German Army but were in school during that time. They felt they were sold down the river by the Nazi line and deplored their own thoughts and actions then. They detested any display of militarism. The town had a celebration a few days ago and sent out its band, but the boys jeered and hooted because the band suggested the military to them. They are ripe for good leadership along the lines of rights of the individual and freedom of thought. At home you often hear that these are the youth who have been completely indoctrinated with Nazism. I don't believe that at all after this week. I don't think you could have found a more earnest, upright group of young fellows anywhere.

On our way back to Vienna we stopped at an Army gas station for gas. The Army chap who gave us gas wanted to know who we were. Then he said we must have been getting high salaries to be willing to stay over here and work with these "krauts." When we said we working for nothing you should have seen his look of astonishment.

He said, "You can do it if you want to but let me tell you, they would have to pay me well and conscript me too to keep me over here with these damn krauts."

If that is the attitude that young Austrians see in Americans, they certainly would lose respect for Americans and for America. Those Austrian chaps are ready for a new attitude for life and are getting it, I think, from the ÖGB leadership and from their contact with AFSC representatives. Mel, for one, has been very active in visiting and taking food to the homes and hopes to do more now that Leigh and I are here to handle the transportation.

Saturday I took a dozen fellows with me into the town of Frankenmarkt where we picked up a load of apples to take to Vienna. Then this morning Mel, with his truck of recreational equipment, and I, with my load of apples, started back to Vienna. The home director, who came with us, posed a question that was a real dilemma. One of his office staff from Vienna who was with him in Frankenmarkt had lost his identity card. He wanted to go home to Vienna but could not pass into the Russian zone without his card. Could we smuggle him in with us? Ouch! After considerable deliberation, we decided to try since we knew he was a legitimate citizen of Vienna. A mile or so before we got to the Russian zone border we stopped and buried this man in my load of apples. At the border the Russian guard inspected our truck, in the cab, under the hood, under the truck, and even took an apple to eat. We were through and I had become a lawbreaker! Even tonight, I half expect a knock on the door from a Russian officer!

October 13—A Very Full Week

This week I really got a lesson in Army procedure. Before we had our garage, we took one of our jeeps to the PX Army garage for repair. They discovered it needed a new clutch, a flywheel, and a pressure plate. This garage only does service in a minor way, as they have no access to parts. However, as a special consideration to us (Mel had done some favors for them), they agreed to do the work if we could find the parts. We then arranged with the Ordnance division of the Army whereby they agreed to give us any needed parts if we would turn in our damaged parts. The PX garage agreed to remove the damaged parts from our jeep. I picked up the damaged parts from them and went to Ordnance for new replacements.

I had a letter of introduction from Mel who had made the original agreement, but the officer to whom it was addressed was not in. I was shunted to a Lieutenant who said that a new order had just come down that they could no longer deal with individual agencies but only with UNRRA, which was supposedly coordinating all private agencies. All I would have to do was to get an order signed by UNRRA and that should be easy, he said, because he saw that AFSC was on the top of UNRRA's list. Before leaving to go to UNRRA, I pointed out what parts I would need. He checked to see if they were in stock and found they were available; he said we could not have them under any circumstances as they were third echelon repair parts. The UNRRA order would only qualify us for second echelon ones. Third echelon parts are considered by the Army to be major parts—just the ones I needed. Second echelon repair parts are such things as spark plugs, fuel pumps and the like. I had a rather lengthy discussion with the Lieutenant about how we could possibly get these parts. Finally, he relented a bit, agreed that if I would take the jeep to the UNRRA garage, and get a written statement from them that the jeep needed third echelon repair parts and have UNRRA bring the jeep to Ordnance, that Ordnance would repair the jeep. Then I explained that we now had our own garage and could install the parts ourselves. All we needed was the parts.

To that he replied, "Brother, I can see you haven't been in the Army! Orders are that no third echelon parts go out of here. So no parts are going out. Just bring your jeep here through UNRRA."

Off I went to UNRRA. I finally found the right man at the UNRRA garage and felt that he was an OK guy. After chewing the fat with him a few minutes, I got down to the jeep business. Yes, he knew of this new Army directive and he would be glad to do all he could to help us. But there was a problem. (I'm finding out there is ALWAYS a problem when you deal with the Army.) There was no point in his taking our jeep to Ordnance with the damaged parts the PX garage had removed and I now had with me, as they would not accept a jeep for repair that had been torn down. So back I went to the PX garage where they agreed to reinstall the damaged parts in the jeep. They promised to have it done by next morning. I then arranged with the UNRRA man to come to the PX garage at 10:00 the next morning to pull our "defective parts repaired jeep" to Ordnance.

The next morning, being a little suspicious, I went to the PX garage to see if the jeep was ready. Of course, it was not! They guaranteed it would be ready by 2:00. I went to UNRRA, got the UNRRA signed authorization for Ordnance, and at 2:00 p.m. went with an UNRRA driver to the PX garage where we picked up the famous jeep and delivered it to Ordnance. Ordnance promised it would be ready in two weeks! We have our own garage where Leigh could have done this in one day—if we only could have gotten the parts!

Even though I had spent all this time at Ordnance, I went back there twice more this week on other matters. First, I needed to get a set of rings for Leigh to install in another jeep. Lieutenant McCauffrey first said it was impossible. After a good Ohio farm boy chat with him, he said if I would get an UNRRA order he would wink at the requirement and get them for me. After I got the UNRRA order and presented it to him, he apologized that he had forgotten to tell me I also needed an UNRRA order authorizing me as the person to pick them up. So back to UNRRA I went. He certainly seems to be a nice person and goes out on a limb to be helpful. Then the next day I went back again to discuss the problem we have of getting tops for these open jeeps. He indicated it is possible that they could get canvas ones for us in Linz. In another week he will know for sure.

I should report one other item of work. I went to the JDC to inquire as to the status of the jeeps coming from Rome. He said he expected them any day now at the Swiss border, but maybe I should call Rome to find out. I did so and no one in the office in Rome knew anything about the jeeps. The proper official was out for the day. Seems he's always out when I call.

The Monday morning staff meeting was long and argumentative. For some time now, we had been taking food to a few towns outside of Vienna in the Russian zone (the Russians had given us permission to do so). Now the Russians refuse to let us come into their zone. They have told us to keep sending the food and they will distribute it. Can we trust them to do this properly? Or should we cease sending the food? Everything we hear leads us to believe that without our personal supervision the food will all disappear into the Russian soldiers' use. After a lengthy discussion no decision was reached.

One final note for this week—Saturday's activities. Leigh and I went with Mary to work on her café. This project focuses on fixing up and converting an old café into a Community Center for young people. It was filthy so we, along with three or four Austrian fellows, scrubbed the floors and washed the furniture. Last night Comfort and I ended the week by going to see the *Tales of Hoffman.* The music was wonderful but the action seemed a little involved—maybe it was just that I didn't get the language too well!

October 16—My Initial Impression of Austria

Let me share with you some of my three-week-old views of Austria and the food situation. Austria is in a peculiarly unfortunate position. The Allied governments think of Austria as a conquered enemy country but do not have the concern for her that they have for Germany. Germany is the political football between the US and Russia while Austria is just a small country to be forgotten. Austria feels she has no friends. The people think Germany sold them down the river and now the rest of the world looks badly at Austria.

I have only been here three weeks but already I have forgotten I am in an enemy country. The people are genuinely looking toward America for a helping hand, at first for food, and later in many other ways.

Vienna is a city of nearly two million while the whole country is only six million. The treaty of Versailles took away most of the food producing part of this country and she had to import food to live. Now the occupying armies are taking what little food there is for themselves, particularly the Russians.

Some people in the US have said that the Austrians eat as well as the Army. I emphatically deny that statement. Yet it is easy to see how a soldier might think so. It is even hard for me not to think so at times. For here I am eating nearly 4000 calories a day at an Army mess (we eat at the Eiles Café, set aside by the Army for civilian American employees), and it's always good food. When I am well fed, it is hard to realize that the average Austrian gets only 1200 calories a day. You should see the way people line up to get any kind of scarce food article that is for sale. Children are always begging for candy or food of any kind. One of the programs of the AFSC this winter will be the supplementary feeding in the schools.

The only people who really get along pretty well are those who have relatives living in the country and the time to go there for fruit, vegetables, bread, or other staples. Driving into Vienna, we passed so many people walking with their arms loaded with basic staples. They walk as far as fifty miles out and back to get food. The old people of Vienna aren't able to do this, so beginning next week, the AFSC will give supplemental feeding to everyone in Vienna over 70 who is on the register. That means feeding 25,000 people a day! Many people here need basic nutrition. In the US, we used to hear about people starving in the streets in Europe. We just don't see that. People generally get enough to stay alive; it is just that it isn't enough to stay alive and thrive. You get susceptible to diseases when you are so undernourished.

October 19—Work and Housing

Instead of detailing my work activities of the week, let me list many of the projects on which I am working, some of which I have already written about.

- Bugging the Army for spare parts for jeeps and trucks.

- Major overhaul of vehicles at Army Ordnance? Army PX Garage? UNRRA? Leigh?

- Procurement of gas, oil, grease, antifreeze, brake fluid. Each requires a different approach.

- Trying to keep up on the location of the jeep supposedly coming from Rome.

- Planning our aid to the Hungarian unit due to arrive from Paris any day.

- Informing Paris if and how we can help the new team arriving in Innsbruck in December.

- Buy, build, beg, borrow, or requisition winter tops for our jeeps.

- Coordinate the use of vehicles for the staff.

- Vehicle registration with the Army, with the Austrians, with ETU in Paris.

- Finding casters for a movable workbench for Leigh. I went to five stores to find them.

Since we arrived in Vienna, Leigh, Bert, and I have been living in this Army-requisitioned hotel for American civilians. Originally this was at no cost but last month the Army began charging $35 a month per person. We had originally put our names on a list for private housing. This week Bert and I went back to the Army housing office for the third time to see if our names were any nearer to the top of the list. The Lieutenant said we still had a long way to go. After a nice, long friendly chat with him, he came up with an apartment that turns out to be only a block from our garage. It is a nice three-room apartment, with a bedroom, a living room and a kitchen. The only trouble is that there is not a scrap of furniture in the place. That was why the Lieutenant was able to offer it to us when are names were still so far down on his list. Finally, he said he could possibly get some of the bare essentials.

Now we have an apartment, at least on paper. If we can find some more furniture, we can move in next week. And we get it for $15 a month per person, including light, heat and cleaning service. The other men of our group are already living in private quarters. The Army will not let any American women live in Austrian homes or private apartments. They must stay in Army requisitioned hotels and pay the $35 a month per person. You may ask why that requirement. The answer I always got was, "Why we must protect American womanhood, of course!"

Speaking of Bert reminds me of a little language incident we had a few days ago. Bert is also taking this German class with me. In addition to studying grammar, we learn some phrases and expressions that may or may not be of any use. Anyway, that day I was riding with Bert in his jeep when an Austrian policeman stopped him for speeding. Without proper thought, Bert came up with one of those sentences we had learned in German class.

To the policeman he said "Kümmern Sie sich um Ihre eigenen Angelegenheiten," which means, "Mind your own business!"

The policeman did not take offense. He merely said, "Excuse me; I didn't realize you were an American!"

October 20—Weekend Trip

Thursday, impulsive Mary came up with the idea that it would make for a nice weekend for a group of us to take a little trip. So Army travel orders had to be "cut" (Army term) for Leigh, Bert, Mary, and me to travel out through the Russian Zone. You can never leave Vienna without such an order. We got the orders Friday afternoon. By 5:30 (it gets dark by then), after Leigh and I had dressed warmly, packed a few things, gathered up some food to add to the K rations that Mary had spent most of the afternoon sweet-talking out of the Army, we left the hotel. At the last minute, Bert decided not to go.

After picking up Mary we headed southwest out of Vienna. I drove that night through the Russian Zone—something that is not looked on with much favor by the group, as there have been a number of incidents in said Zone at night. We had intended to leave much earlier but just did not. We were on the British road south through the Russian Zone. It is about 50 miles while the American road west through the Russian Zone is nearer 100 miles. We drove through Wiener Neustadt and even in the dark, I could see it was the most war damaged city I had seen since St. Nazaire. We were stopped a couple of times by routine Russian checks but all went well. Then after getting into the British Zone we were stopped by three different British checks, again only routine. As you can imagine I was most chilled, as the temperature was around 40 degrees and here we were speeding through the night in an open jeep.

When we reached Bruck we put up for the night in a British Officers Transient Hotel and each of us had a very large and comfortable room. The next morning we ate breakfast with the British officers and were served what I would imagine is a typical British breakfast with plenty of tea, and more silverware than I knew what to do with. We were given tickets for lunch, tea, and dinner along with the night's lodging and breakfast for two Austrian schillings ($0.02).

After bundling up well, as it was a cloudy, gray, cool morning, we headed south through some beautiful country and by 11:00 had reached Austria's second largest city, Graz. It too had some war damage but not on the scale of many I have seen. We walked through a small market that was similar to what I had seen in France, only there were not nearly so many things to sell. Apples seemed to be rather plentiful, eggs were available, and there even was a little meat, but at very high price between $2 and $3 a pound. Remember that a skilled worker here earns $0.18 an hour. Although there were some things available there really wasn't much considering it was all rationed, cost a fabulous price, and further the fact that we were down in the farming country where food should have been more available.

We headed west toward Klagenfurt and it proved to be the most beautiful scenery of the whole trip. We crossed two series of mountain ranges. They were not like the Rocky Mountains, just very large hills. I suppose it was something like the roughest country in Pennsylvania only the mountains here were higher. The sun came out and we found many a picturesque valley, peasant home, stream, etc. to gape at in wonder.

When we got to Klagenfurt, we decided to try to get some gas as it looked as if we would be driving further than our gas supply would take us. Up to a British Army "Petrol point" we went. Our US and Russian travel orders didn't seem to impress the "bloke" at all until I pulled out an UNRRA travel order for our jeep which I had made out and signed myself. With that we could have gotten all the gas we wanted and at no cost! As evening fell, we drove on west along the north side of Wörther See. In prewar times this was the "Riviera" of Austria. On we went around the west end of the lake and back east on the southern side to the resort town of Maria Wörth. The hotel here, where we spent the night, was also requisitioned for British officers. We arrived after dark but were still in time for Tea. The evening was most chilly so we appreciated the one warm room, the dining room with its beautiful pine paneled walls and its very warm Austrian Kackelofen (a glazed tile stove). After tea we went up to a 12th century church and had its high points explained to us by the janitor. Then at 8:00 p.m. back to the dining room for a delicious dinner over which we lingered two hours. One other sensation that wasn't very real but still tingles a bit was the realization that we were only about 12 miles from the Yugoslavian border. In fact, during the afternoon the towering mountains to our left had been Yugoslavia.

After another good British breakfast, we headed back into Klagenfurt and directly north on a shorter road to Bruck for a British lunch (we hadn't needed those K rations after all) at the same hotel we had stayed at on Friday. After another hour's drive, we stopped a bit in Kapfenberg to visit with three British Quakers working there. Finally, we headed back toward the Russian Zone with the hope of making Vienna before dark, but we were delightfully delayed for a time. Coming into another of the picturesque villages, I think it was Niklasdorf, we found the only street through it was completely blocked off by a huge crowd of people.

Upon closer investigation, we found that it was a celebration of some kind. It turned out to be the annual (at least before the war) fall harvest festival. It consisted of some 15 or 20 floats, but not floats like any we had ever seen at home. Each float was a farm wagon of one kind or another and drawn by every combination of four-footed animal you can think of. Each wagon was decorated with extravagant colors of crepe paper and on each wagon was an exhibit of some phase of the life they led to earn their living. One wagon had a sample of grain on it, another had a crude machine for hackling (combing) flax, another had a wood carver lathe, another a wagon makers shop, another a harness makers outfit, another a crude threshing machine, another had only manure on it to show the staff of life for good crops, another had a German band, and another had a group doing folk

Parade in Niklasdorf

dancing. On each wagon were the proper people for that exhibit. They were dressed in beautifully colored clothes and each machine was in operation.

Both sides of the street were jammed with people who smiled broadly at Mary and me as we walked down the street, half in the parade, and half in the crowd. It was the most happy, carefree, spontaneous group I have seen in Europe. They seemed to take Mary and me in as part of the group even though we were obviously American. Leigh soon managed to get our jeep into the middle of the parade, as otherwise, he would have had to wait too long on the edge of the town. Through the length of that little town, the size of New Vienna, Ohio, went the parade with our jeep in the middle of it. Leigh was able to pick up eight lads to ride with him in the jeep. It was great to see some happy people again. What a contrast between the Austrians here in the country to the dour life of the Viennese.

Then on to Vienna, without incident. Looking at our speedometer, we were surprised to find we had covered 500 miles in those 48 hours and had spent a total of $0.90 each for the whole trip, mostly thanks to British taxpayers. There was only one objection to the trip as we did it. We had planned to hike up in the mountains somewhere. Instead, we had just kept driving until we ended up in Klagenfurt and had to spend all the time driving to get back. Next time maybe we will just go to Bruck and spend more time on foot. Still, it was a delightful weekend break.

October 27—Continuing Problems

Usable transportation requires gasoline, oil and grease, and antifreeze. Until recently we had been getting our gasoline from UNRRA. Part of that gasoline we actually got through a US Army station by means of coupons acquired from UNRRA. Two weeks ago, the Army exchange station abolished all rationing and any US civilian can buy all the gas he needs for his car at the rate of $0.11 per gallon. It is very difficult to get any grease or oil except as you use it up in your car or when the car is serviced. I had hoped to get a bulk supply of oil and grease so that we could do our own servicing in the garage. So far we have not been able to do so. However, I still have hopes of finding it and thus saving the cost of the servicing by the Army.

Antifreeze is almost unavailable. At first we counted on getting a part of the shipment from Philadelphia but I understand that the order has not yet arrived in Paris. UNRRA said they would not be able to get any this winter, and the Army was, as usual, very vague about it all. However, UNRRA stirred itself enough this week to get a little from the Army and we were allotted enough for three jeeps. There is also a promise of antifreeze through the PX garage "sometime in the future." For the rest of the antifreeze requirement we are counting on two promises of "sometime in the future," the Army and the AFSC shipment from Philadelphia. I might mention that I have found one necessary item available in limited supplies on the Austrian market and that is brake fluid. We may be able to get a liter every month or two, but at least we have gotten the first liter without difficulty.

Jeep tops are also a headache. I'm not sure just how critical this item appears to be to a person on your side of the Atlantic but to us it is very important. Rumor has it that winters in Austria are not noted for their mildness and we feel that it would be practically impossible for us to drive an open jeep through zero weather and snow. On our weekend trip to Klagenfurt, we found it well nigh impossible to keep warm even though the temperature was yet well above freezing. At any rate I have been spending a good deal of time on this project of getting tops built on our jeeps, tops that would at least keep part of the wind out. Before I arrived in Vienna, Mel had arranged with the ÖGB whereby they were to build wooden tops on all our jeeps. They have finished one and are working on the second now (it took them three weeks to do the first one!). However, they have only enough wood for this second one. I have found any number of wood working shops that will agree to build a top if we will bring the wood. The ÖGB will build them free, if only we could find the wood. Alas, it is not to be found. I thought I had arranged with the Army for us to buy some of their cozy metal tops but at the last minute, an order came down saying jeep tops were in critical supply and were not to be sold to any civilians. We thought we were going to get six canvas tops in Linz but that also fell through. No one seems to have any material for jeep tops except the Army and they will not release it. However, we are hoping that Paris will be able to furnish us with two or three canvas tops.

Insurance has also been a problem. Since we insured all our vehicles with an Austrian company, we cancelled the insurance we had on them in Paris. Last week the Provost Marshal's Office, through which we must register all our vehicles in order to get gasoline, said that a directive would soon be handed down from Frankfurt which would invalidate all insurance not paid in dollars. The point seems to be that they want to protect any American here whom we might injure, in dollar currency, not shillings. Thus, it looks as if we would have to insure with a company in the States. This, of course, would mean losing the value of the $400 we have paid out here for insurance. However, this ruling has not yet become official and we are hoping there has been an error in that announcement. In the meantime, I heard from Paris AFSC that ETU vehicles in Europe were insured on a fleet policy in Philadelphia. I will have to check to see if our vehicles are included even though here in Vienna we are not part of the ETU.

Leigh and I arrived in Vienna to find that in order to stabilize the transportation for the team we had to "hospitalize" most of the jeeps. So temporarily, instead of improving the situation, our arrival made it worse! Simultaneously two jeeps are having tops built on them, a third is in Ordnance getting a new motor, a fourth is waiting for Leigh to install new rings, and the fifth is running more or less spasmodically. We do hope that by December we will have all these items taken care of. With the two additions from Paris, including the one going there from Rome by mistake (it never arrived at the Swiss border with the JDC jeeps), we should be able to keep five jeeps on the road—we hope.

Now the Russians again. The skis and apples we brought to Vienna a couple of weeks ago are stored in an ÖGB building just outside of Vienna, ¾ mile inside the Russian Zone. Last Sunday the Russians were looking around a bit and found both the skis and the apples. They seemed delighted at the find and told the ÖGB people living there that they would be back to get them as soon as they could find a truck. The ÖGB people protested that these were American property but that seemed to just whet the Russian appetite more! We found out about it this Monday morning but our two trucks, which we needed to pick up the skis and apples, were gone for the day. Tuesday I got one of our Austrian drivers on the job to go and check it out. I could not dare go for the place is now under Russian scrutiny and besides, I couldn't go there legally anyway. He scooted out with one of our trucks, found the skis still there, loaded all 300 pairs and they are now safely reposing here in Vienna. The apples do not belong to us but to the ÖGB and the ÖGB decided to take a chance on leaving them there rather than bruise them more by moving them.

Our troubles are not only with the Russians. Yesterday, Leigh told me that one section of the American Army had found our garage and were most interested in the fact that a big truck could go through the garage doors. Now it seems the American Army is going to requisition our garage away from us. It is only in rumor stage so far and I have already gotten Dr. Heiser, our friendly US Army contact, working up a counterattack for us. By the way, I think Dr. Heiser has worked it out for us to get grease and oil now from the Army. Hurrah! Friday I went to the Austrian telephone office to request telephones for our garage and apartment. Guess what they did? They sent me to the US Army. However, I did get some satisfaction there. And so it goes every day it seems, more dealing with the Army for this and that and the other.

It looks like I won't ever have much contact with the relief end of our program. I'm just the cog that keeps the wheels rolling, or tries too. Still, it is worth it just to live here for a time. In the relief end of it, we have gotten started with feeding all people in Vienna who have TB who are not open cases (the open cases are cared for by the city). All people in the city over age 70, who are on relief rolls, get our supplemental rations. By the way, we are looking forward to one more relief worker joining us from the States, Jean Fairfax.

November 3—Possible Changes

I think I may have mentioned before that the AFSC is sending five or six fellows from Paris to start a program in Budapest. They could be arriving here in two or three weeks. I hear that AFSC is starting an ETU program in Innsbruck. It is my guess that we will be expected to service both groups. To complicate the matter, our team wants me to consider taking over our warehousing job. That could only happen if I could be replaced from my present assignment. So it looks as if we will try to get Howard Suits, who is in Paris (I had known him there) to replace me. All these shifts take time. The Innsbruck team will not arrive until next year. But maybe I won't change jobs after all. Two or three days ago, Dr. Heiser called George into his office and informed him that AFSC has too many people here already and he could not allow anymore to come. Our nice little pipe dream about Howard seems to be stymied. So here we are with a warehousing job, which no one seems to have time or the inclination to do. Mel will continue handling it for the moment.

November 5—Paris Phone Call

I talked a long time tonight with Lois in Paris. These calls are on Army lines and cost us nothing. We decided that it would be necessary for two or three of us to make a trip to Paris. We need to return our Chevrolet truck and bring back a larger GMC one. Then there are two jeeps to bring plus a "cannibal jeep" for parts plus an assortment of tools and parts. We would like to make this trip before winter if possible. Meantime, I gave a list of items to Lois to send with the Hungarian team who will soon be coming our way. You might be interested in the list I gave Lois, items that according to Leigh are urgent:

- Screws—assortment
- Cotter pins—assortment
- Bolts—assortment
- Files—4 metal, 1 rat tail (a small round file)
- Copper tubing—assorted sizes

- Brake fluid

- 6-volt bulbs—5 or 6

I also asked her to send other items or at least get them ready for us to bring when we go to Paris:

- Air compressor—must be large enough to give steady pressure

- Electric grinder—ordered on the French market before we left

- Shock absorbers for jeeps—6

- One jeep windshield—safety glass

- Jeep tarps—3 or 4

- Tap and die sets

- Jeep wheel bearings

November 7—Prediction

This looks like it will be the worst winter yet for the Austrians. Food and shelter have not improved since last winter—and last winter they had the hope of UNRRA and allied aid to look forward to, which now they realize doesn't make enough difference to help. They no longer have hope that things will get better. There is no coal for heating and many homes are without glass. They have a diet of 1200 calories a day unless they can afford the black market.

Electricity is getting to be an item now. It gets dark about 4:30 in the afternoon and there is no electricity during the day until 5:00 p.m. In the evening the current often goes off, leaving streetcars stranded all over and the city in total blackness. In fact, all over Austria all trains except military ones have been stopped because there is no coal to make electricity. Only in Army billets do you find heated rooms. Anyone who says things are fine here just does not know. Yet if you live as we do in Army comfort you just don't realize the dire need of the Austrians.

November 10—A Brief Trip

Guess what I did all day Thursday? I hauled coal. We finally got a requisition from the Army for three tons of coal, but we could only get it if we hauled it ourselves. Carlton and I did the dirty job of shoveling the coal onto our truck and unloading it at the office, at the garage, and at the community center. Guess I'm just the general handy man!

Friday was a bit different. A so-called professional photographer was sent here a few days ago by AFSC to take pictures of our work. Once she had finished in Vienna, she then needed to go to Enns to get pictures of Ed's dam project and particularly pictures of the dedication of the dam and power plant, which was to be Saturday.

Dam building project near Enns

Mel and I picked her up and headed west over the now famous Russian road. We traveled over it without incident and arrived at the location of the dam only to discover that the dedication had been canceled. General Clark, the US Army headman in Austria, had been scheduled to officiate at the dedication. When it was discovered that the dedication, scheduled for the power plant side of the river, was in the Russian Zone, it was postponed. General Clark could only go on that side after another week of red tape. After she took a few pictures of the dam, we headed further west to the ÖGB recuperation home at Frankenmarkt, where I had been a month ago. We figured some pictures there would add to the pictorial record of our work.

She is supposed to be a professional, but she didn't seem to be any better than an average amateur. In fact, her camera seemed to have something wrong with it nearly every time she tried to use it. What was worse was that she had on an Army uniform, although she is not in the Army. (All press representatives are permitted to wear an Army uniform.) Further, she didn't seem to know much about the AFSC, although they were paying her $500 for her work here. I know several fellows in CPS who would have jumped at the chance to come here to do this job and could have done it better. Guess the head office can make mistakes too.

November 11—A Visit

Armistice Day! It is a holiday with the Allied Forces all over Europe. I'm not just sure why. At one time, I suppose, it was a day of rejoicing, a commemoration of the end of that war, which was to free all mankind. Yet since then—another war—and today, what are people here looking forward to? A democratic, abundant, happy life? Obviously, people are not that optimistic. This whole train of thinking takes me back to an evening I spent a few days ago. It was an evening that did not give me encouragement about the future but I think it gave me a little insight into the thoughts and feelings of Austria, perhaps of Europe. It made me ask that old question with which we dealt in CPS, "What makes a man sell his birthright for a mess of pottage?"

Let me tell you about this particular evening, and I will begin by telling about some very mundane matters, but matters that had a bearing on the state of mind I encountered. On this evening, I spent about three hours in the home of a university professor and his wife. I had some acquaintance with him since I had arrived in Vienna and had found him to be a most friendly, gentle, intelligent, and yet an eternally sad individual. He had seemed old before his time, almost hopeless, and yet relatively cheerful in the daily round of living. As such, he seemed to embody the spirit of Austria. He is about 40 and his charming wife is about 35.

This particular evening was one of those October previews of dire things to come. The temperature was hovering around the freezing point and the wind was cheerfully chilling me as I walked the streets to a three-room apartment where Dr. Kober and his wife lived. I found little physical warmth in that apartment. We sat and talked for those three hours in a room that was not a degree over 40. I began to realize what a dreary view one must take of the coming winter when one has to live in an unheated house.

We started talking casually about fuel. He told me that civilians cannot get any coal yet for another month or so, and then very little. Last winter they had practically no coal; with a grimace, he said that after a time you sort of get used to being continually frozen—but that seemed to me to be whistling in the dark. From fuel, we drifted to the subject of food. I mentioned that I had heard from the States that soldiers who had been in Vienna were saying that the people here were getting plenty to eat, at least enough to keep going well. Dr. Kober was almost bitter in answering that this might easily be said by Americans who eat too well and care little how others fare. Then Mrs. Kober got out a list of that week's rations for me to see. This ration is the basic ration that an Austrian gets. It was what Mrs.

Kober gets. Her husband gets a little more because he is a worker. Let me give you the complete list of that week's rations:

- Black pudding—6 oz.
- Fat—2½ oz
- Cracked corn for cereal—6 oz
- Bouillon cubes—1½ cubes
- Coffee—¼ oz
- Malt—7 oz
- Flour—6½ oz
- Bread—4 lb
- Vinegar—½ pint
- Potatoes—3 lb. 2 oz
- Beans—3 ½ oz

That is all, for one whole week. Worse, they cannot always get even this much. In order to get it, the housewife has to stand her turn in line nearly every morning in the week and often when it is her turn the supply is gone. Now remember this ration is only the basic one. A worker gets a bit more and a heavy worker gets a little more. Yet the wife, in this case, does more physical work in getting food than her husband, who gets the worker's share. Those figures are hard to understand in terms of actual food, but there they are—just under 1200 calories per day.

Mrs. Kober admitted that the ration wasn't enough for anyone to live on and maintain health. She admitted she patronized the black market. "Everyone does, for he has to."

The black market is not in stores but is with individuals. She knows a man who has connections in the country and can slip her some food on the side, although the prices are very high, the source uncertain, and the quality often bad.

The entire basic ration listed above costs about $1.50 for the week. Last week she got one serving of fish on the black market for $3.00, most of which turned out to be spoiled.

Then she said, "Let me tell you about the wage scale so you can get an idea of what that means. A professional worker, i.e., a teacher, gets about $10.00 a week."

(In the AFSC here in Vienna, we are allowed to pay our chauffeurs and our mechanics about $7.50 a week). How does a professional worker with a family of five use his $10.00? $7.50 of it goes for the basic food ration. Some more goes for his extra ration as a worker. Then clothes, rent, light, gas for cooking, medical expenses, etc. come from the remaining $2.50. You can well see how much he has left to spend on the black market. Yet, in order to eat most people sell everything they own to buy on the black market. After a time it became clear that Mrs. Kober wished to be the hospitable hostess, but what could she offer? She made some tea, saved from a ration received long ago, and brought in two cups, one for her guest and one for herself. They could not afford to have tea for all three, just one for the guest and one for one of them to be hospitable.

From the subject of food we wandered to other things, for as Dr. Kober said, "Food is only the temporary, immediate problem."

What of the future of Austria? In his opinion, there is none since he believes that in a few years, Austria and Germany will be the battleground of the war, which may actually end all wars. During the recent war, he had held hope that American democratic ideals might prove a solution to oppressed peoples. Those hopes have all evaporated in his mind. And Russia? Before the war he used to think that Communism was the answer—for theoretically it gives a rosy view. As it is practiced in Russia, it means the end of freedom, intellectual integrity, and is practically a return to savagery. Americans think of Austria as an enemy and still act accordingly. While the Americans are here, their real job is to maintain a front to Russia, not to help or reform the Austrians. Russia looks on Austria as legitimate spoils of war to be plundered at will. In fact, the presence of either country's soldiers here is a great detriment to Austria.

He went further than Austria...what hope is there for the world? He felt that the ideal way of life was that of democracy. He would like to see the world come to it, but it will not come from America. America is so naïve. She thinks she has the answer to all the world's problems. America says, "We can live a life of fullness, ease, and peace—you, the rest of the world, just do as we do and everyone will reap the same reward." Americans do not seem to realize that America has been able to live as she has not because of any superior philosophy, but because of two factors—her unique geographic position and her lack of overpopulation. Europe has been plagued for centuries by overpopulation. Europe has therefore fought for centuries and starved for centuries.

There is only one solution to the world's problem, one way to make the rest of the world a place of peace and plenty. That way is simply to limit the number of children born. Since men will not do that, there is only one thing to do. We must kill a certain percentage of children at birth! Naturally I raised a hue and cry at this point. He calmly said he would expect any American to react in that way. Only an American could live in the dream world where he could not see the problem or agree to do anything about it. There is only so much good earth available, and when populations get crowded, people starve. Starvation brings unrest, the willingness of people to give up freedom for a piece of bread and thus the acceptance of dictators. Then comes war and children whom you spared in your naïve innocence when they were born are sent forth to suffer and kill when they have reached manhood. Now which is the more humane method?

Of course, I couldn't go along with him at all but he seemed to be at least thinking logically. I questioned him a good bit on it but he always had an answer to back up his theory. For example, I contested his point that the earth would not support more people. He admitted that theoretically it could, if some power controlled the earth to enhance production. However, that again means giving unlimited power to one group.

"Any group in complete control tends to become ruthless, and the individual becomes only a cog in a machine."

Here was a man who had opposed the Nazis machine, in his quiet way, a man who held dear all the things in life most of us cherish, a man who believed that men should be free, and yet here was a man who was willing to stoop to the doctrine of state domination, of mass killing of children because he felt it was the only way of survival even though he detested it. He was falling into the snare of what has been called Nazis ideology and yet he deplores the thought of such a step. Why? Partly because he can see no alternative ahead. And partly because of the conditions of life at the moment.

Actually, the most telling arguments are the things that affect you personally and daily. And these conditions—our sitting there talking in a freezing room, he and his wife spending most of their time in talking, scheming, fighting for a pittance of food in order to exist, the lack of faith in anything really constructive coming from any government. I fear he had fallen into the trap of believing that the end is justified by any means.

Mrs. Kober seemed interested in what I had to tell of life in America. She has a sister there and both she and Dr. Kober lived three years in England between the wars. She longs for a life without starvation, without freezing, and without fear. Would it not be possible for her husband to get a job teaching in an American college? He didn't seem particularly interested. What good would it do to go to all the effort to get to America when America would soon be in the same situation as the rest of the world?

I asked him if he saw no hope in any of the political leaders in government. His answer was simply that public office corrupts. I suggested that not all people in high places were corrupt and cited Henry Wallace, the former US Vice President, as an example of a relatively honest man in government. Dr. Kober replied that he didn't know about his honesty but that he did know that world peace had been damaged by his recent famous speech. I asked how and why and was surprised by his answer. He did not necessarily oppose Wallace's policy of friendship with Russia, but he said that he should never have been allowed to say what he did—that the present administration is preparing for war. I pointed out that this was not what he had said but that his statement was something to the effect that the present policy might lead to war.

"No difference," was his answer. The world and particularly the Russians interpreted Wallace's words to say that the present government is preparing for war. They are convinced of the truth of those words because he was fired from the government for saying so. "He should never have been allowed to say what he did!"

I asked, "What do you think is the best course for Austria?"

He answered, "There is no best course. There is no course. We have no friends. There is one chance of survival, as much as I detest it. If we would embrace Communism, the Russians would really be our friends. Those in power there recognize and respect us intellectually but they will despise and persecute us unless we take to Communism. If we were to do so, we would have bread and a measure of security. A year ago, our people would have done so willingly, but the Russian leaders could not control the hordes of soldiers who have committed all kinds of vile deeds here. These acts have alienated our people. They wish they could look to America for guidance and leadership but they know that America offers no security. In time, maybe in a year or two, we Austrians will forget the Russian atrocities for we will see that Russia offers bread. We will give up our measure of freedom and join the satellites of people in the Russian orbit. It means the end of all we hold dear, but it means we can stay alive. I can see no hope of the good life with Russia, but I can see no hope of life without Russia."

I asked him why he thought we Quakers were here in Austria. He seemed to know fairly well for he said, "Yes, I understand you came to demonstrate to us that a faith in God can surmount all difficulties, that the power of love is the only real power. You are trying to do so through the medium of bringing relief of a physical nature to us. Your relief is greatly appreciated and we are glad to know that there are still people who believe that by simply doing good you can reform the world. But I think you will fail. You come with that faith because you are from America where you can afford to indulge in such beliefs, where such a faith seems to have a chance of really doing something. If the world were in either of two conditions, we could look forward to the future. First, if the world were made up largely of people like you, Quakers, there would be much hope. Secondly, if the world were physically as well off as America there might be a period of relative peace and prosperity for several centuries. Neither is the case. All the good works you will do and all the good will you spread will not materially affect the course of the world. People will not change. The nature of man is not to profit from the experiences of someone else and any good you do now will be lost on the next generation. You might as well pack up and go home, except for the food you bring. You have a wonderful, high-sounding message, but its effect will be but a drop in the bucket, so small that the world will not be changed enough to avert catastrophe."

As I came home that night I wondered just how long a person could live in a freezing home, eat a starvation diet, and feel insecure before he might yield to the domination of the State. When it seems that such well-intentioned people as Quakers (!) are but beating their heads against a wall and when you see that many of the trials of life could be lessened by yielding to Communism, how long would you hold out? Many Austrians fell for Nazism at a similar point some years ago. Most of them regret it bitterly today. If life continues as it is, they may come, not to Nazism of course, but to Communism.

The worst part is that now they have little hope. A year ago they hoped for real help from UNRRA, from the Allies, from America, even from Russia. Now they are no better off then they were then. Dr. Kober believed that a free, democratic existence is the ideal but even now, he is unwillingly turning to a philosophy that gives the State all power. He has the intellectual background and ability to withstand such a tendency, much better than many people do. How much truth is there in Dr. Kober's accusation that we can indulge in our faith simply because we are from America where war and famine have hardly scratched the surface? I fear there is more truth to it than I want to admit.

Still, there is more to our faith than the fact that we are the children of luxury. It seems to me that Dr. Kober has lost faith in anything but tangibles. He would say that the good or bad of an action could only be judged by its obvious results. In other words, it seems to me that Dr. Kober, and probably many in Austria, have come to the point where it is impossible for them to take a long range view of things, impossible for them to have faith in the ultimate power of love, in the groping of mankind for something above and beyond. It seems to me that it is just this loss of faith that we as relief workers must try to restore. I cannot say how, for I certainly did not do any of that with Dr. Kober. Yet we must keep trying. That is why we are here.

This whole discussion made me realize a little better that there is a strong possibility that all our work and efforts may not produce tangible results on a world scale. The world very probably will go down into the abyss of a third world war despite anything we may do. If our faith is such that we must see a change on the world scene as the result of our work, it is not of great value. We must be deeply enough grounded to be able to withstand the trials that may come, and that may include the destruction of all that we hold dear. We must carry on with the faith that even though our way of life may not triumph in our time, it is the right way and must be followed regardless. Then maybe, just maybe, peace in our time will come. Either way, we must keep trying.

November 19—The Hungarian Team

Friday evening the team scheduled for Hungary arrived from Paris. It consists of seven people, most of whom have just arrived from the States. Their leader is Del Eberhardt, whom I had known in Paris. All day Saturday we were busy unloading our parts, which they brought from Paris, and placing them in our garage. We got their vehicles inspected at the PX garage so the Army could license them in order to qualify for parts. We then got them loaded with other parts and all gassed up for the trip on to Budapest. That evening we had a sort of party in our community center for them and all our team. Yesterday after our biggest staff meeting ever, we loaded two more of their trucks with shoes and clothing from our warehouse, items they will distribute in Budapest. I even taught one of their members, Joan, how to drive a truck. I hope she makes it to Budapest! Finally, this morning after checking at our garage for oil and air they departed for Budapest. I hope they are not counting on us too much for help. Although Budapest is only 150 miles from Vienna, it might as well be a thousand considering all the red tape required to go there.

November 20—Average Work Day

Yesterday, after the Hungarian team left, I helped Hans George, one of our Austrian drivers, change a flat tire so he could get started on a long trip to haul bricks for the ÖGB. I then went to the PX garage, got a set of gaskets for the jeep, and asked for a new piston. Of course, they didn't have one! In the afternoon, I went to the wood shop to get the jeep that was to have had its top installed. It was actually ready but wouldn't start because of a dead battery. I called Comfort at the office for help but there were no jeeps there. She promised to call back when one showed up. I waited until 4:30 when I remembered that the electricity goes off at the office at 4:00. I took the subway to the office to find there were still no jeeps there. A wasted afternoon!

This morning Leigh and I went directly to the wood shop and got the jeep going by pushing it. He took it back to the garage to get a charged battery and I went to the Community Center to give one of the Austrian boys the key to our garage so he can get some duplicates made. (I had previously tried other places, to no avail.) So on to Ordnance in search of a piston, and of course, they didn't have one the right size. Here we are with a broken piston and none to be had in Vienna. Well, that is not quite true. At that moment, I ran into the UNRRA garage manager who told me he thought he had an old jeep engine lying around and maybe I could use one of the pistons from it. At that moment, Leigh picked me up to take me to get the jeep with the new top from the garage and take it to a metal working shop located in the Russian sector of Vienna. This shop was to fasten the top to the body of the jeep. Then he dropped me off and I rode the subway and walked to the UNRRA garage to check on that piston. It looked as if it might do and they promised to take it out for me.

At lunch I found that one of our two running jeeps had stalled, so I went in search of Bert to borrow his jeep to push it. When I returned, Comfort had it running. I hurried over to the office to dictate two letters, one was our coal order for December and the other was for gasoline for the Innsbruck team for January. Then I went to the Provost Marshall's office for further information on registering the Hungarian vehicles. Then back to the office to sign and pick up the letters. Comfort and I tried the jeep that had stalled at noon and it started fine, but two blocks later it left us stranded at a busy intersection. I called Leigh and he came down in a truck to pull it to the garage. Since I had to have those orders for coal and gas in today, I left on foot and Comfort stayed with the jeep that was to be pulled to the garage. She told me later that after being pulled two blocks the jeep started fine! I went back to UNRRA with the gas order and picked up our new PX cards. Then a long hard struggle on the streetcar to the coal office to drop off the coal order only to find they had changed the basis of figuring coal requirements. Up to now they had figured each person's allotment based on the square feet of space to be heated. Now they are figuring it based on cubic feet, so I had to take the order back to the office and do it all over again.

I then hurried to Dr Heiser's office to report the jeep number of the Army unit that is trying to take over our garage. After picking up my laundry at the United States Forces Austria (USFA) office, I went back to UNRRA where I was able to get the piston. Next came German class, after which I went to the Eiles Café to find Mary to get the garage key duplicates that the Austrian boy was to give to her. It had been a normal busy day.

November 21—That Jeep Again

The first thing this morning Leigh drained all the water out of the gasoline in that troublesome jeep, put in new spark plugs, and announced the jeep was ready to go. I headed off to the office with it but had to return for something I had forgotten. When I got ready to start again, the jeep refused to start. Leigh worked on it a few minutes and was able to get it started. I took off for the ÖGB but en route the jeep stopped twice. I managed to coast to the ÖGB where it died again. I called the office for help but there were no jeeps there. I called the garage but there were no jeeps there either. I called UNRRA for help, again in vain. Finally I called poor Bert, who came to my rescue. He pushed me to the UNRRA garage where they decided the jeep needed a new coil, which of course, they didn't have.

Meanwhile, they discovered that by temporarily attaching the wire to the old coil in a certain way, the jeep would run. So off I went to the PX garage to find that they had no coils either. However, I figured that since all one had to do, when the jeep stopped, was to push the wire in certain way, I could get along. Off I headed for the office.

The jeep decided to stop right in the middle of the busiest intersection of Vienna, and no amount of pushing the wire in the right way did any good! The policeman directing traffic got disturbed and he finally got a car to push me. The jeep started and then stopped again. This time I coasted into the middle of a large circular street and stopped in a taxi parking stand. By this time the helpful driver had disappeared so I was stuck. I walked to the office for help but there was no jeep there. Off I walked to the UNRRA garage, but again in vain. So back to the office I walked, arriving in time to walk with them across town to lunch, hoping we would find a jeep there. One had just left!

Off I went to get Bert out of his German class to borrow his jeep. By the time I drove back to the restaurant everyone had gone. Here I was with a jeep to push and no person to help me do it! I waited until five minutes until two (I had promised Bert his jeep back by 2:00) and Comfort showed up. We pushed the jeep to UNRRA and I hurriedly left to return Bert's jeep. Then I walked back to UNRRA and learned they had found an old coil in the wrecked jeep—and our jeep was running again.

With the happily running jeep, I was off to the Austrian permit office to get ration tickets to purchase wood if you can find it. I had been looking for plywood for weeks to no avail but now had a lead that a certain shop might have some if one brought in ration tickets. We shall see tomorrow.

November 22—Plywood or Something

Off this morning I went, with my happily running jeep, to the Austrian permit office in search of ration tickets for the purchase of plywood. The office was dark and dingy and I had to inquire a number of times as to the right room. There I found a man who was very cordial and who listened patiently to my plea for plywood for the rest of our jeeps. He said he had been in a number of PW camps in America but he spoke no English. He told me my tip about finding plywood was false but he thought he knew where I could get some wallboard and wondered if that would help. I readily agreed and asked for 60 square meters. I had gone before to the wood working shop where our jeeps are done to find out how much we needed. He had his secretary fill out a bunch of papers. She then sent me to another office where I paid $0.12 for more ration tickets. I noticed that the tickets called for 0.24 of a cubic meter of wallboard. I could not tell if that equaled my request of 60 square meters so had to trust that it did. Later a secretary back at our office verified that it did. I then went to the warehouse in search of the wallboard to find that it was actually available, but I could not get it until next week.

To round out the day we had an evening of folk dancing at the Community Center lead by an Austrian woman who knows it well—genuine Austrian folk dancing. About 20 university students participated—most in quaint Tyrolean costumes!

November 23—Hans George's Accidents

This morning I talked for an hour with our insurance man about Hans George's accident on his most recent trip. He is one of our Austrian drivers. He is turning out to be not as good a driver as we had thought. He side swiped a telephone and electrical pole and as a result, had broken all the wires and left a small town in darkness for a couple of days. A rumored bill of $200 in damages may be coming to us. Fortunately, there was no damage to the truck, but this was not his only accident. On his trip to St. Pölten, he asked directions and ended up in a Russian compound. At the gate on one side was a huge picture of Stalin and on the other, a huge picture of Lenin. The Russians had not placed these pictures with an eye to the width of an American truck. When Hans, now inside the compound, climbed down from his truck, he found that Stalin and Lenin were no longer standing imposingly at the entrance! The Russians were rather perturbed but agreed to let him go on payment of $5.90 on the spot. As this is not covered by our insurance, it will appear in our accounting to Philadelphia as an interesting charge "For repair of Stalin and Lenin—$5.90."

November 26—Another Russian Incident

Erika, one of our Austrian secretaries, and I were driving near the southern edge of Vienna looking for the Steyr automobile plant but somehow we got lost. We came shortly to the usual Russian barrier between the Russian Sector and Russian Zone where we were, of course, barred from going further. At first we saw only an Austrian policeman and I inquired of him as to the direction we should go. At this point a Russian guard came out of the hut and demanded to see my papers. I showed him my identification card but it didn't seem to mean anything to him. He wanted the usual gray four-powered pass we get in order to go into the Russian Zone. I explained we didn't want to go into the Russian Zone and I started to turn around to return to Vienna proper. The Russian let me know in no uncertain terms that I was not to return.

"You can't go into the Russian Zone without papers and you can't go back without papers!" or something like that.

He pointed his machine gun at Erika and said "Frau raus" (Woman get out).

He then clambered into the rear of the jeep, ordered Erika back into the passenger seat, pushed the point of his gun in my back, and ordered me to drive into the Russian Zone. Wishing to cooperate and show that traditional Quaker spirit, I amiably complied, although inwardly I had a doubt or two about the whole affair!

After driving about three miles, we arrived at the headquarters where I was ushered into the office to see the Commandant. I had little success in making my German understandable to him and soon he pounded his fist on the table and yelled "Stille" which from his tone of voice obviously meant "Shut up." After a lengthy conversation in Russian with another officer, he told me to take the guard back to his post and get back into Vienna "schnell" (quickly). I did so without further adieu. It may sound rather drab on paper but it really was a rather harrowing experience while it lasted!

November 27—AFSC Vienna Programs

I don't think I have written much as to the nature of the team's work here other than my own transportation problems. Let me try to outline them. Our major emphasis is in providing supplemental feeding. When the AFSC came to Vienna last spring they looked for groups of people who were not able to supplement their meager diet of less than 1200 calories by going out on the black market or to friends in the country, and were not being helped by any other relief organization. Our feeding program has developed in three ways:

1) We give a supplemental ration of 500 calories per day to every one in Vienna who is over 70 and is on relief. This amounts to about 25,000 people.

2) We give the same ration to everyone in Vienna under 25 who has TB but is not in a hospital.

3) We provide major and supplemental food to the apprentice program of the ÖGB. All have had exams and have been classified according to their physical condition. The very worst, about 1500, are sent to some 10 recuperation homes throughout Austria for a month at a time for a high diet of 3000 calories to get them back on their feet. The AFSC provides the major amount of this food. Then the next 9000 worst cases who don't qualify to go to the recuperation homes get a glass of milk and a bit of chocolate every working day here in Vienna.

Ned Weaver presenting the
1,000,000th food parcel

AFSC clothing distribution

However, we are also carrying on nonfood programs to meet other needs in the area:

4) Clothing distribution. Anyone in Vienna who has been below a certain standard of living and who gets a card from his or her local relief agency is eligible to receive an article of clothing.

5) Individual service. Polly's assignment is to provide individual service to all who come to our office for help. This amounts to a steady stream of people. She channels them to people or agencies that can really help them.

6) Community Center. A few weeks ago, I mentioned the arrival of another team member, Jean. She came to assist Mary in our Community Center. This is an interesting project, one I wish I had more time with which to work. We rented an old café in the twelfth district, one of the worst bombed areas of the city. (I think I mentioned a few weeks ago that we had scrubbed it out and cleaned it up.) Every night of the week a different group of young

AFSC Community House in Meidling, Vienna's 12th District

people meet there. One is purely recreational, one is an English-speaking group, one is a discussion group, and one is a university folk dancing group. (No, I don't lead them, I follow them—I'm charmed by Austrian folk dancing.) In the mornings, the Café is always open as a warming and reading room for old people. In the afternoon, it is open to all young people who wish to play games or study. This center is really a good way to get close to the people of the community.

I don't have much to do with most of the relief work, as I along with Leigh, must keep transportation rolling.

December 1—Quaker Bureaucracy

Some weeks ago, I reported to Philadelphia about our relations with the British Quakers in Vienna. Let me quote here from that report. "The British Quakers here in Vienna seem to be in a rather bad way along transportation lines. They have no garage nor do they have any person assigned to handle transportation problems. At any rate, when they realized that the AFSC had two men here for transportation support and also had a garage, they came wondering if perhaps we could service their vehicles along with our own. At that time, Leigh didn't have much work lined up ahead and it seemed that there would be some time for that. Since then we have hit several snags with our own vehicles and are not doing anything about the British at the moment.

One of the problems is the fact that the British Friends are working with the British Red Cross who would want us to service all their vehicles too. In regard to repairing their vehicles, we told them that it would be impossible because of the parts situation—their vehicles being entirely different from ours. We did agree that as soon as we get more of our vehicles on the road we would take on servicing their three strictly Quaker cars. That means merely grease, oil, and minor repairs. We told them that at some indefinite future date we might see our way clear to servicing all 10 vehicles, but only after ours were completed. We must be careful not to follow Dr. Heiser's suggestion that we become the garaging facilities for all the private relief agencies in Vienna. We have had enough headaches just dealing with one "Danish" jeep. The question of servicing British vehicles will further depend on how much of our time will be taken up by the Hungarian relief team and by the Innsbruck ETU unit."

Now let me explain the story of this "Danish" jeep. The Danish Quakers in Vienna first approached AFSC Austria last summer with a request for a loan of a jeep for a month. George let them have it for the month. During that time, the Danes were to contact the AFSC Commissioners in Paris to find out if the Commissioners would sell them a jeep. The fact that the Austrian AFSC had loaned them a jeep possibly was a talking point for them. At any rate, between the Commissioners and the Austrian AFSC, the Danes got a promise of a jeep in a month or so from a large purchase the Commissioners were making in Italy. During the wait, they used this jeep of ours. As you know, that month grew longer—in fact, it isn't even over yet. During those many weeks there were many interpretations about that Danish jeep. In fact, in my letters I have mentioned "the Danish Jeep" referring to the one that we had loaned them for a month. I had not understood too well that it was loaned only until this replacement for them arrived from

Paris (I think the word "loaned" has been confusing. In one sense, it meant the jeep we let them have for a month. In another sense, it refers to the type of financial transaction with regard to the jeep they were to get from Paris—loaned or sold.)

The Danes tell me that they have always considered the jeep we loaned them to be strictly a temporary loan. Mel also thought so as he licensed it with the US Army, which would not have been necessary if it was to have been their permanent jeep. One of the two jeeps Paris is sending to us will go to the Danes and we will get back our loaned one. A further complication is the fact that over two months ago, this jeep developed a bad clutch and the Danes returned it to us for repair. I have already written at length about that problem. For the past two months the Danes have actually had no jeep at all, as their loaned jeep was back with us for repair. Willis Weatherford, one of the Commissioners, who is visiting us for a few days, wondered why the Danes actually need a jeep since they had not had one for the past two months. He suggested that I talk with them and sound them out on the matter of their need.

I visited the Danes feeling that I was more an agent of the Commissioners office than of Austria AFSC. The question really boiled down to the relative needs of the Danish Quakers here vs. some project of AFSC other than Vienna. I was not in a position to make that decision. As the leader of the Danish Quakers, Elise Thompsen, was in Copenhagen for the moment, it seemed best for her to contact Paris AFSC directly.

Let me say a word about the Danish need of a jeep based on my conversation with them. It seems there are four Danish Quakers in Vienna. One of the four works full time in one place, the Swiss Kinderheim, and thus requires no transportation. A second is ill right now. The third, the leader, is now in Copenhagen. Just one needs transportation at this time. They have no cars of any kind. Sometimes they are able to borrow from the Danish Red Cross but they cannot rely on that. They are hoping to get permission to work in the Russian Zone, in which case they would desperately need a jeep. I asked them if they could buy a car in Denmark or in Sweden, but they are not allowed to export any vehicles from Denmark or for that matter export the money to buy one here! (That seems to be the reason that this jeep they were to get from us on a permanent basis was to be a "loaned" jeep.)

If this group were an AFSC group I would say that they need one jeep for their work in Vienna and possibly another for use in the Russian Zone. However, there is another consideration than that of need. This is in regard to their identity. In the first place, they are not an American group. There may be some precedent for providing vehicles to other than American Quakers in the fact that the Commissioners are turning over one or both of their Canadian Chevrolets to the British Quakers. The second consideration is that Quakers in Denmark are members of London Yearly Meeting. Wouldn't it be proper procedure for them to get their vehicle through the British Quakers? Lastly, the four Danes here are not even representing Danish Quakers in a strict sense. They also represent some other Danish group such as the Peace Volunteers. My conclusion—they should have a jeep subject to AFSC needs elsewhere. That is a decision the Commissioners will have to make.

December 5—Appreciation

This week a copy of a letter that Arthur had written home last spring surfaced in the office. At that time we still had Russian permission to do relief work in the Russian Zone. Let me give you Arthur's letter.

"Sunday, April 28, 1946

Some of those who have done a great deal to give the Friends the good name which they have today the world over, might be interested in a little incident which occurred this afternoon. Carleton, Mary, Michael, and I took some Austrian students out for a picnic excursion in a town in the Russian Zone some twenty-odd miles outside Vienna. (The British Friends supplied the gasoline and we the truck, both groups contributing to the food supply.)

Along the way we stopped to pick up pedestrians (both Russians and Austrians) until the truck was so full it could hold no more. One of those whom we picked up was a white-haired old gentleman who was trudging wearily up a long and steep incline when we came upon him. He didn't try to flag us down, but was obviously very grateful when we stopped and asked him if he wouldn't like to ride. He clambered in and we drove him to the town for which he was headed.

There he got out and came around to me (I happened to be driving) and asked, 'Wie viel bin ich Ihnen schuldig?' (What do I owe you?).

'Nichts' (Nothing), I replied, 'Wir sind froh, das wir Ihnen helfen konnten' (We are happy we could help).

He looked at me puzzled a moment and then his eye happened to fall upon the insignia upon my cap, his face broke into a warm smile and he exclaimed with great feeling, 'Ach, Quäker...das sagt Alles' (Oh, Quaker, that says it all).

He took my hand in both of his and shook it but I was
so moved that I couldn't say anything more to him. Incidents
like this, and it is not the first one of its kind, remind one what
a great privilege it is to be representing the Service Committee
here."

This letter gave us all a much-needed lift.

December 8—Gasoline

A month ago, Marlis and Willis had been in Innsbruck setting up plans for the arrival of our ETU team from Paris. The only remaining problem was where and how to get gasoline. Major Graham, a US Army liaison officer with the French in Innsbruck, had come up with a sort of solution. We would have to register all the Innsbruck vehicles with the Provost Marshall here in Vienna. Then we would be authorized to buy 105 gallon coupon books for each designated vehicle and the gas would be available at the French Army station in Innsbruck.

The only catch was that we could not get more than one book at a time for each vehicle and had to turn in the empty book in order to get the next one. This was just too impractical for us to do here so far away from Innsbruck. I made alternative arrangements with UNRRA for them to supply the gas. I had even filled out a requisition for the first month's supply. Then we discovered that UNRRA is closing down its Innsbruck operation on January 1. So what to do? A bright idea that paid off finally hit me. I had almost milked UNRRA dry by now. I had worked on the Army Exchange Service (AES) only to get the run around with completely vague answers. Still, I had not gone to the Army proper. AES is for civilians, but we do have a working agreement with Army Ordnance for parts. Why not try them for gas? I talked for half an hour with a Lieutenant Colonel in the supply division of Ordnance, supply division for all Army points in Austria. He saw no reason why we couldn't buy all the books we needed at one time but the matter of gas supply was the problem. We would need about 2000 gallons a month and he said Major Graham in Innsbruck was only getting 1000 for all his needs. Therefore, he wrote me a note to take to the Quartermaster division with the suggestion that we buy our gasoline in Garmisch in Germany, which is 40 miles north of Innsbruck, and truck it over to Innsbruck.

At Quartermaster I found a Major who was also most cooperative, agreeing that it would be entirely possible, but he could not handle it. Only the third Army in Garmisch could authorize the deal and there is no third Army representative in Vienna. Someone from AFSC would have to go to Garmisch to close the deal.

By this time it was Wednesday night. I had talked to Paris Tuesday and found that the Innsbruck team was almost ready to leave, pending a sure source of gas in Innsbruck. It looked as if I should go to Garmisch to order the gas. George did not think I should take the time to go, as Innsbruck is not our responsibility. I called Frankfurt AFSC to see if someone from there could go to Garmisch, but no one could go. Paris urged me to go despite George's opposition, as no one else seemed to be available. First I thought of going Saturday night, thus arriving Sunday, doing the job on Monday and returning here Monday night. Then I decided I might as well go Friday night and have Sunday to either climb the highest mountain in Germany or go over to Oberammergau.

First, I had to get Army permission to enter Germany. Next, I needed travel orders to use Army facilities in Garmisch. Finally, I had to get a train and Pullman reservation to Munich. Pullman reservations are usually very difficult to get. However, when the AFSC first came to Vienna, George had managed to get us an Army travel category of CAF 12, which I think, put us in the rank of a Colonel! At any rate, I got all my papers ready. At this point, I decided to call Major Graham in Innsbruck to see if this was the proper course for us. I found that he was due in Vienna Thursday afternoon. Thursday evening Major Graham called me (I had left word for that) and he made an appointment to see me Friday morning.

I found him to be a most affable man. He couldn't see why he could not get us all the gas we needed right in Innsbruck. He promised to spend all day Friday trying to arrange it for us. If he succeeded I would not need to go to Garmisch. If he failed, I was prepared to go. The train left Friday night at 8:00. At 5:30 he called me at the office and said it was all cleared. He could furnish us the gas directly in Innsbruck. I'll have to go to Garmisch and climb the Zugspitze some other day.

In order for this gas deal with Major Graham to work, I had to purchase the coupons here in Vienna. So yesterday, Saturday morning, I went to the Quartermaster to buy 2000-gallon coupons for the Innsbruck January supply. The Quartermaster Officer decided they would rather sell us 5000-gallon coupons at a time. That suited me very well, as that would save us going through the process every month. However, he wanted cash on the line and next week the price was going up from $0.09 a gallon to $0.11 a gallon.

At 10:30, I hurried back to the office to try to scare up $500. The financier was not to be found. I finally dug up one of the team who had traveler's checks, and got other members to contribute about all their cash. I made it back to the Quartermaster at 11:50 (They were to close at noon). Everything was cleared but as he gave me the coupon book, he saw that it was for 5500 gallons plus 300 quarts of oil, and the bill was $739.20. Still, with the down payment of $500 he was willing to consider the deal closed. While I was there, the head officer from Salzburg came in and agreed to ship a tank load of gas tomorrow to Innsbruck. I then called Lois in Paris to give her the green light for the Innsbruck team to get under way. You can find cooperation in the Army more often than you might expect.

This last man with whom I dealt was a George Harvey. If you read the December 2 issue of Time Magazine, you will see a story about a plane crash in the Swiss Alps that occurred a month or less ago. It told about the hero of the crash, a George Harvey—the same. He had arrived in Vienna from Frankfurt about an hour before I bought the gas from him!

December 9—Extracurricular Activities

A week ago Friday evening I went to the Red Cross Club to a folk dancing group where I knew the leader slightly. She got me to call one square dance, which seemed to go over very well. There were some 30 people there, mostly US soldiers and WACS with a few French soldiers too. Then the next evening was the official opening of our Community Center. Over 150 people crowded in to hear a few speeches given to dedicate the Center.

Last Wednesday we all went to a farewell party put on for one of the British Quakers who is leaving Vienna. The odd part was that she both sent out the invitations and ran the party herself. Then sometime last week, Arthur, Jean, Comfort, and I went to a Russian movie. It was a delightful fairy tale fantasy, so different from the lavish Hollywood productions. It was in Russian but had German subtitles, which were easy to follow.

The biggest event of the week occurred Sunday morning. This was the holiday celebration of the ÖGB in one of the theaters in Vienna. Some 3,000 young people attended, some of the leading politicians in Austria spoke, skits were put on, and slides of the recuperation homes were shown. A skit on the Quaker food program in which Mel and George took part was presented. They really played up the Quaker part in the work of the ÖGB. Oh, I almost forgot something else. Sunday night Jean and I went to a choral offering of a group of Viennese young people. It was something like a city production of the Messiah at home and was very well done.

December 10—Job Shift?

I spent some time during the last few days working on warehousing problems. George wants me to work slowly into that job. The theory is that after Christmas, the transportation job won't be so heavy and I should have some time to take over the warehousing position. Now I am getting acquainted with the job. The problem at the moment is to get the seven carloads of goods we received from Antwerp recently shipped off to Budapest. It is so difficult to find freight cars for the shipment, as no one wants to send cars into Hungary for fear the Russians will take them. Still, I think we will get them off next week.

December 12—Inconsistency

For some time several of us have been talking among ourselves about the inconsistencies of our position here in Austria. We came here to show a friendly way of life, show that spirit of the Brotherhood of Man and all that. Yet we still accept all the special privileges of the Army and thus identify ourselves with the "Conquerors." The other evening at the Community Center, I was with some of the Austrian young people in the kitchen. I saw they were stirring up cocoa, which we usually have. In an offhand manner I laughed that I was good and hungry for it. One of the young people turned to me with a scathing eye and said, "You, with your 4000 calorie diet, are hungry? You know we only get 1200!"

I don't intend to reduce to 1200. It just emphasizes the fact that you cannot try to make them feel you are one of them; you can't identify yourself with the Austrians when you are so far apart from them in a material way. It comes down to this—why we are here? Is it just to distribute relief goods like UNRRA and a dozen other agencies? Or is it to bring a message of friendship and hope to these people? It seems to many of us that it is more the latter.

At any rate, yesterday noon Leigh, Mary, Bert, Jean and I ate together and hashed over the whole matter. The upshot is that we are thinking strongly of pulling out of the Army mess, at least as a first step in the right direction. We are not ready to reduce our daily intake to 1500 calories, but we will try to set up a central kitchen for those in our group who are interested in using it. We will have the AFSC send us packages from which we can cook—not the elaborate trimmings we get at the Army mess—but just plain, simple food at about a 3500 calorie a day level.

If possible, we intend to try to live in a house together if one can be found. In our Army billets we are not allowed to entertain Austrian guests. We are so tied up with the Army that it will be difficult to remove ourselves from it. I pointed out that our transportation would become well nigh impossible without Army assistance. Yet some felt we should at least take one step in the right direction, no matter how feeble. After all, we lived in Paris without the Army.

Here they just have us wrapped around their fingers. We appear to the Austrians to be their masters due only to circumstances. We are really in a quandary. Logically we should eat 1500 calories a day, but could we keep doing our work efficiently on that? We really came to no conclusions on these ideas. We will just have to think more about it after Christmas.

December 15—Christmas and Later Plans

Most of the group are going skiing Christmas week near Zell am See at Marlis' castle. However, Mel and I have accepted an invitation from the ÖGB to go to their recuperation home at Moosham near Tamsweg with the leaders of that organization for a holiday of skiing. Mel leaves Thursday to do some business in Salzburg and will drive to Moosham on Saturday. Saturday I will go with the ÖGB group to Moosham in a bus. On December 25, I will take Mel's jeep (he will stay with the ÖGB group) and drive over the Alps to Zell am See to join the rest of our team at Marlis' castle, Fischhorn. That drive should only be about 75 miles if the pass is still open. I may, however, have to drive 150 miles around that alpine range.

On December 29 most of the team returns to Vienna. Marlis and I plan to go on to Innsbruck by train. She will finish her negotiations there for food and lodging for the Innsbruck team and I will make the final negotiations for gasoline, garaging, etc. Then if things work out in Paris, the Innsbruck team of six men and four trucks will arrive in Innsbruck on January 2.

On January 4, Marlis and I will bring two jeeps, which the Innsbruck team will have brought for us, back to Vienna. Then two of our team will take our old Chevrolet truck, drive back to Innsbruck, trade it for the GMC truck they are bringing from Paris, pick up one of their other jeeps and take them back to Vienna. Two of these jeeps are scheduled for the Hungarian team and the other is our long awaited jeep from Rome.

In the meantime, about January 6, Leigh will take a train to Paris, pick up tools and parts, and meet up with Percy Andrews, one of the British Quakers who operates in Vienna. Percy left Vienna yesterday for Christmas leave in London from where he will go to Paris to drive back a vehicle which ETU is turning over to the British. Leigh will come back to Vienna with him. Is that complicated enough? I'm willing to wager that this tight schedule will never work out. At least you have to set up a plan before you can break it. And too, you have to plan in order to get the proper travel orders.

For my trip I had to get a pass to travel through the Russian Zone, another to go through the British Zone, another to enter the American Zone, and finally another one to go into Innsbruck, in the French Zone. Approval for each Zone has to be cleared by that particular occupying power. Life is so complicated here, but it is interesting. All Christmas week I am supposed to be skiing (I have never been skiing in my life) and talking only German with the ÖGB. Always a challenge.

December 16—Last Minute Details

Before we all leave for Christmas I have a number of items to take care of. One I successfully handled last week. After visiting Ordnance for the umpteenth time, I actually drove away from there with five jeep tires, three GMC tires, three GMC tubes, and two Personnel Carrier tubes. We needed all these items badly but had little hope of getting them. Hurrah!

But this week I have to get the jeep with the broken transmission (hopefully repaired) back from Ordnance, get the doors repaired on our other closed jeep, take care of finishing the tops on two other jeeps, get our gasoline request in for January, find out the new system for getting it, get our coal request in for January, try to find out why the December allotment has never been delivered, go to a meeting tomorrow night in honor of all relief agencies in Vienna at which medals are supposed to be liberally handed out, attend an international Quaker party Thursday night, go to the folk dance group Friday night, finish the licensing of the Hungarian vehicles, get the licenses off to them this week, try to get a battery for Hungary from Ordnance, get my skis ready, get packed, and Saturday off with the ÖGB for Tamsweg.

I've needed a haircut for two weeks. On the other hand, with long hair I look more Austrian! I hope to find time to read some of the home mail I hope comes this week. By the way, I was amused at a comment in a letter from James Terrell from Ohio last week.

He wrote, "I keep thinking I'll write you and then to be honest I don't, just for fear of starting up a correspondence which, however enjoyable, would be a burden (I hate writing letters)!" Then he writes a long letter!

December 20—Updated Last Minute Details

Wednesday evening just at dusk, before the city lights came on, the Army arrived with our December coal delivery. However, the owners of the building didn't want the coal put where we wanted it. We had a terrible time in German, English, and unprintables before we got it solved. Thursday evening I was so bushed I decided not to go to the Quaker party and told Leigh to go on alone. At 8:15 he called to say he was out of gas. I went over to the garage to find that all the gas was locked in the basement and he had the key. He called later and told me where to find the key, but I hunted in vain for it. I took another jeep to find him, and I found a can of gas in that jeep. I got back home at 9:00 and found that dear Bert had drawn a tub of hot water for me, as he knew that the gas went off at 9:00. So a hot bath and to bed. But not for long. At 11:00 p.m., Carlton rang the bell to tell me the personnel carrier had stopped on him. I got dressed, got a jeep, and went to the stalled carrier. I wasn't able to do anything with it! At that point, Leigh showed up, got into the carrier, and started it right away! We drove it to the garage for Leigh to work on the next morning. Some restful night!

This afternoon, Friday, I had to run more errands than usual as Leigh was not available. He had to spend two hours in a dentist chair after which he was playing Santa Claus to some party or other. After supper Bert and I took a truck to a hospital near here where we picked up most of the Friday night folk dancing group. They had been Christmas caroling for the patients. We took them to the Community Center for a Christmas party for all our Austrian groups. It was a most happy time—the expectancy of Christmas upon us all—singing and listening to the Christmas story in German. Before the party ended, I left and went to the Red Cross where I had agreed to lead some square dancing. It was all soldiers and I didn't get along so well. They weren't particularly interested in square dancing; they just wanted a leader of some quaint thing or other.

Christmas Break

December 1946

December 21—Trip to Tamsweg

The ÖGB bus was scheduled to leave their office at 7:00 a.m. I set my alarm for 6:00 a.m., but Leigh, Bert, and I were so tired we slept right through it and didn't wake up until 7:10. You should have seen us get dressed. By 7:30 Leigh had me at the ÖGB office some four miles away! The bus had already left, but the doorman told me it had gone to the AFSC office looking for me and that it would return in a few minutes, which it did. They all took it in good humor but I was really embarrassed about it.

Seventeen of us took off by 8:00 for our trip on another cold Austrian day. The temperature was around zero. I had become acquainted with about half of the Austrians in the bus, but before long, I was to know all of them. However, I only talked with two or three of them on the trip, as it was just too cold to talk on that unheated bus. Some 30 or 40 miles out of Vienna we drove into the first snow of the winter for me. At the Russian/British border, our leader purposely stated that we were all Austrian. He did this to avoid the time consuming stop that the Russian inspection of one American passenger would have taken. It was risky but it worked. Then on through the British Zone and finally into the American where Tamsweg is located. Tamsweg is famous as the coldest place in Austria and it was. It was 20 below this morning and the cold part of the winter hasn't even come yet. There was real snow on the ground and you should have seen the view. It looked as if we were in a long valley completely surrounded by mountains. We are staying in the barracks of one of the newer recuperation homes at a place called Moosham. There are 20 of us, heads of recuperation homes, the leaders from Vienna and a couple of young leaders my age.

December 22—Our Group

Let me introduce you to some of the ÖGB group. First, there is Frau Mela Zvacek, the director of the recuperation home program, and her husband, Fritz. They won't be here for a day or two yet and will be arriving with Mel. The second in command is Herr Rohm and his wife. The eternal clown is Herr Novotny, affectionately called Noverl. He had been with me on that first trip I took to Frankenmarkt. The two youth leaders are Herbert and Fritzel. Then the head secretary in the Vienna office is Frau Billi. She lost her husband at the Russian front. Then we have the Uncle Leo of the group, Herr Meisel. I have met two other couples, Herr and Frau Idawitz and Herr and Frau Snyder. I'm sure I will get acquainted with the others in the next few days.

December 22 to 25—Christmastime at Moosham

Bright and early Sunday morning, we started skiing, my first attempt. Herr Novotny and the pro skiing teacher took me in hand and taught me the rudiments of it, at least enough so I shouldn't get hurt. We were out all morning and again all afternoon, and I really did make some progress.

We had six meals throughout the day. Of course, there was breakfast. In mid-morning it was "Gabelfrühstuck" (fork breakfast, which means essentially, eggs), then lunch, afternoon tea, supper, and finally, a late night snack. All this time I heard not a word of English. I could talk reasonably well with most of the people on a one-to-one basis, but when they talked to each other, I was really lost!

Monday we took a long hike up one of the mountains on skis. It was a beautifully clear, sunny day with deep snow all around and clear, cold mountain air. It was wonderful.

Tuesday I did some more skiing and found that if I went down the mountain with my eyes almost closed I could do better than when I

Herr Karl Novotny (Noverl)

was looking intently at the slope! I visited a combination Gasthaus and farm where the barns are always part of the houses. It seemed good to be in a barn again with cows, sheep, hay, and animal warmth.

The rest of the day was given over to Christmas Eve. In Austria, the evening of the 24th is more really Christmas than the 25th. The Home Director has two small children for whom we decorated a tree with real candles. All the people at the camp assembled for the occasion, even Frau Billi who had broken her ankle skiing. The children were ushered into the room last after the candles had been lit, and did they scream with joy. They received a number of very simple presents and we tackled the imposing pile of packages. There really wasn't much but everyone got something. Mela Zvacek gave me a book about Adelbert Stifter.

The rest of the evening was spent in singing to a guitar and an accordion, songs I did not know, but they were beautiful. About 11:00, the party began to get hilarious for some of the more playful began playing tricks on each other. The tricks were mostly on the newcomers and I think I got more than my share of them. The keg of beer they had was well along the way to being drained! Then someone with a flute and another with a guitar accompanied the group in singing until 3:00 in the morning!

Today I was up at 8:00 in order to be in on the fun planned for Mel and the Zvaceks. The day before some of us had elaborately fixed up a hose system through the ceiling over the beds of those three, Mel in my room and the Zvaceks in the next room. One of us was to pour water down those hoses at 8:45 into the faces of the three sleeping people. The whole camp was in on it and had great fun in planning it all. However, Mel got up too early and the Zvaceks were aware that something was afoot so they moved their beds to another part of the room. The water went harmlessly onto the floor. This was just to give you an idea of the spirit of Christmas at Moosham.

December 25—The Rest of Christmas Day—Jeep Trouble

By 10:30 I was packed and starting off in Mel's jeep across the mountains to Zell am See. It was another beautiful, clear day and it turned out to be one of the most scenic drives I have ever made. I kept climbing higher and higher through this mountain pass, the snow getting deeper and deeper on each side of me, although the road had long since been plowed clean. I stopped frequently just to absorb the beauty of it all. At last I came above the timberline and was in a surrounding of only snow and high, rocky mountains. As I passed a little farmhouse, a cloaked figure with a long umbrella rushed out, waving his umbrella frantically. I stopped and picked up a hitchhiker who proved to be a Catholic Priest who had been paying a few Christmas morning visits on foot to some of his flock. He turned out to be a most interesting companion, explaining the countryside, Catholicism, the world problems, etc. and, of course, all in German. He even had heard of Quakers. His knowledge of them consisted of knowing they are a small religious group in America who never drink alcohol!

After dropping him in the next town I proceeded further and further down toward the valley, getting stuck twice in snow drifts as the road was really too narrow to meet anyone. I met two trucks on that whole trip and both times, I preferred being stuck in a snowdrift to hitting the trucks. The first time I had hardly gotten out of the jeep before a neighbor turned up with a shovel and had my path cleared before I could say a word. Everyone seemed to be so friendly around that area. By now the sun had disappeared and the day grew dreary. I hastened on toward Zell am See, passing through the picturesque town of Radstadt and thinking I would be with our team within the hour.

At 2:15, everything was going nicely when all of a sudden the jeep rolled to a stop, the motor still running but the wheels not going round. I thought at first it was transmission trouble but upon a little investigation, I realized it was the clutch. Something had gone radically wrong there and it was impossible to move the jeep an inch. Christmas afternoon, no traffic, 40 miles from Zell am See, what was I to do? I went to the nearest farmhouse where I found a friendly family sitting in the kitchen. They told me there was a little telephone house out back by the railroad tracks. They gave me the key to the house and out I went to give it a try. The railroad operator told me there was no connection today between the railroad line and the public line, so there was nothing left to do but to walk to the next town, Bishopshofen, a little town about two miles away. There I was able to find a phone and after an hour, managed to get a call through to the team at Zell am See. They promised to send their last jeep on its way as soon as possible. I walked back to my jeep.

I guess I made quite a figure walking through that town with my coveralls and farmer's hat. Still, just about everyone I met spoke to me as if they knew me. It certainly was friendly there, so different from Vienna. Leigh arrived around 4:30 with a jeep and by 6:00, he pulled me in my sick jeep to Fischhorn where we were heartily greeted by the rest of the Quaker delegation. It was relaxing to be back with a group of English speaking people again, to be there safe and sound. It had been a long Christmas Day.

Just a word here about Fischhorn. That is the name of this castle in which we are staying and it is also the name of the estate. It is located near the little town of Bruck an der Glocknerstrasse, not far from the larger town of Zell am See. In 1920 or so, Marlis' father bought the estate and remodeled the castle. As castles go, it is small but it still is a castle. I was taken to my room—yes, private rooms for each of us—with 15-foot high ceilings. After supper I got completely lost in the place and couldn't find my room. Supper was served in the dining room, a room about twice as big as our living room and library combined. A maid served us very nicely and I felt a bit out of place with my overalls, which had been just the thing at Moosham.

December 29—Final Vacation Days at Fischhorn

Thursday morning after breakfast, which was served whenever you wanted it, I went skiing with Carlton and Polly. They too were beginners and we just went up on a small hill back of the castle. All went well until noon when I started down a hill on the way back to the castle. The path led through sort of a tree nursery. When I arrived at the last small tree I did what I had done many times before, I fell down. Only this time the tree had something to say about it. As a result I pulled a ligament in my left knee and hobbled back to the castle—my skiing for the week a thing of the past. It gave me a lot of trouble that night, but Leigh worked on it and by the next evening, the swelling and the pain had gone down. That afternoon I contented myself with a chess game with Arthur, snapping a few pictures of the castle, and taking a short walk around the castle. Leigh and George had gone hunting up in the mountains and George came back having bagged a gams (chamois).

Fischhorn, Marlis' family castle

Friday the group decided to climb the Schmittenhöhe Mountain to go skiing again and I went along to see it all even though I didn't dare try skiing with my knee. We all crowded into a cable car, which lifted us up to the top of the mountain, some 7000 feet high. It was a gorgeous view with mountain peaks in every direction and the lake of Zeller See far below. The good skiers took off immediately and made two round trips. Carlton and Jean tried to go down the mountain by skiing but it got too tough for them so they just walked the rest of the way down with difficulty. I had gone back down on the cable car and met them at the bottom.

Oh, I forgot. In the morning Leigh and I took the broken-down jeep to UNRRA. Fortunately, Zell am See is the headquarters for UNRRA car repair in Austria. They had not been very cooperative with George, and would not give him any gas,

Jean's attempt at skiing

but I managed to get them to promise to look into that jeep. After I got down from the mountain I went back there to find that they had taken the motor out, had found that the clutch was torn to ribbons, had replaced it and had the jeep nearly ready to go. Saturday morning I went back and picked it up. We still had no gas, at least not enough to get us to the nearest Army station. I finally talked them out of five gallons and that was enough to do us. I spent the rest of the morning at an Army switchboard, trying to get through to Paris. When I finally reached Lois, I found out that the Innsbruck team was not leaving Paris until Monday. Thus, there was not much point in Marlis and me going to Innsbruck now, so we decided to go back to Vienna with the rest of the group.

Yesterday afternoon Marlis took us on a tour of the estate, but mostly the castle and the barns. This castle was taken over by the Nazis some time in 1943 and it later became the home of Goering. In fact, the Americans captured him in this very place. We were shown his room. A small amount of Nazi furniture is left as well as a number of books. The Nazis kept the place in good shape and didn't take anything away.

Then the Americans moved in. During 1945 they lived there and simply wrecked the place. Marlis' household servants remained all the time and were able to tell what happened. The Americans had the keys to everything in the castle. Instead of hunting up the right key, they just broke into everything by force, ruining many a valuable old cupboard, chest, or whatnot. Instead of washing dishes, they would often just throw the exquisite but dirty china out the window. By appealing to General Tate, Marlis at last got the Army out of the castle and found that very little of the furnishings were left. Then last spring she took a tour and found many an old table, chair, painting, etc adorning American Army quarters in Austria and Germany. She was able to get some of this returned but much has been forever lost.

Marlis then took us out to the barns to see the cows, all 110 of them. They are Pinzgauers, sort of a cross between Shorthorns and Holsteins. Their complete ration is very immature silage and thin looking hay. Corn never ripens in this climate. There are 59 working men on the farm, all hired hands who work by the hour. They get a little house, milk, a garden, and the prevailing wage. They seem to live pretty well compared to the Viennese, but to me the whole thing was just a picture of the old feudal system, the lord and his peasants. All the milking is done by hand and much of the work is done with horses. However, I did see four diesel tractors. It is a most interesting set up and I had a delightful time seeing this feudal farm and castle.

One other story might be of interest. Saturday, George went hunting again. Four of the 59 men on the farm are hunters. That is their full time job. One of them was telling George how last year he had saved up a lot of money, around $300, with which he bought a pair of binoculars, something essential for a hunter. One day some American soldiers came along and asked if they could look through them. After he let them do it, one of the soldiers took a fancy to the binoculars and told the Austrian to get moving. He started to protest but another soldier pulled a gun and told him to leave without his binoculars. The Austrian went to the US Commander of the region to report the trouble. The Commander told him to get out and not bother him with such details. The hunter says he is not so sure America is the land of idealism that it is supposed to be!

This morning everyone but Comfort, George, and I took the six o'clock train to Salzburg in order to go with a couple of Austrians who could not drive with us as our route would take us through a corner of Germany. By 8:00 a.m. we three were off with the two jeeps and the loaded trailer to drive through more beautiful mountains through the jutting corner of Germany and into Salzburg where we picked up gasoline and our other passengers. We got a noon meal at the Army mess in Wels and arrived "home" in Vienna by 6:00 this evening. It was quite a Christmas vacation.

Winter Problems

January to February, 1947

January 1, 1947—New Challenges

At our last Monday morning staff meeting, our discussion centered on two problems. First Philadelphia wanted our opinion on the wisdom of setting up one or two work camps this summer here in Austria. Secondly, Philadelphia informed us of an impending serious budget cut and requested our recommendation on how to handle it in Austria. After considerable discussion we decided to postpone decisions on these items for a couple of days and settle them at a special meeting this morning, January 1. We agreed to work today as we had a bit of an extended Christmas vacation.

After more discussion, we recommended against having the work camps. We felt that the need here is not people to do the work but materials to work with. There is plenty of unskilled labor here. Although the main purpose of a work camp is the fellowship of the group rather than the actual work accomplished, it was felt that foreigners should not be brought in yet to eat up food, take up much needed housing, and not really accomplish much material gain. Austrians would look upon it too much as a sort of good vacation for rich Americans and not realize the mutual sharing experience it would be. We recommended that the same amount of money be used to send some Austrians to American work camps.

The budget crunch was a tougher matter to settle. Our monthly budget of $50,000 for Vienna must be cut immediately or we must stop all feeding in June and wait for the next budget year to begin again in October. We finally decided to keep on with our present programs even though that would mean ending them June 1. Our programs are now in full swing and the critical period is now until June rather than between June and October. I forgot to mention earlier that in a December staff meeting we decided to send no more food to the Russian Zone unless the Russians would relent and let us monitor it. So far they have not.

Monday afternoon I got word that the Army was ceasing all repair and maintenance operations for UNRRA and UNRRA-sponsored agencies as of December 31. Yesterday, I hurried to Ordnance and was able to buy five batteries just as they were closing their books for the year. I don't know what we are going to do for major repairs and parts in the future. I spent the rest of the day getting all our vehicles gassed at UNRRA and I filled up every spare can in our garage with gas, for as of today we go back to Army coupons and cannot get any gas in cans. Yesterday was New Year's Eve. We did no celebrating. In fact, I was in bed and asleep by 11:00. Rumor has it that there were some Americans in Vienna who did otherwise.

Staff Meeting decided that since the Innsbruck team was delayed in leaving Paris I should go directly to Paris right away, collect all the parts, tools and supplies we needed, and come back with them to Innsbruck. I was to go in place of Leigh for I needed to help the team get established in Innsbruck. If I can get ready, I will be off to Paris on Friday.

January 5—Trip to Paris

Thursday and Friday, I spent too much time in getting a French visa, travel orders, and a rail ticket. I also discovered that progress on building our last two jeep tops was halted as Viennese workers were laid off for the week due to the lack of electricity. At 9:50 Friday night, I was on the Orient Express pulling out of Vienna. This was my first experience on a Pullman in Europe. It was doubly enjoyable because it did not cost the AFSC a penny; it was all on the Army. Pullmans are not as they are in the States. The car is made up entirely of compartments and I shared a compartment with one other person. In the beginning it was an Englishman going only to Linz. I slept in the upper and made out so well that I didn't wake up until 10:00 the next morning.

My car stayed in Salzburg until 1:30 in the afternoon to be picked up by the rest of the train, which comes from Prague to Salzburg and then on to Paris. I found time to walk around in Salzburg a bit. Judging from the shop displays it is the best off of any town I have seen in Austria.

At 2:00 that afternoon we were rolling into Germany. My new compartment mate was a US Army Captain. I am glad to say he seemed to be to be one of those individuals of whom the US could well be proud to say, "He is one of our ambassadors in uniform," a type seen all too seldom. There was no diner but the train stopped an hour in Stuttgart where the Captain and I ate at an Army mess. The next day we pulled into Paris at about noon.

January 9—Paris Revisited

Paris after four months! Any changes? On leaving the train, the inevitable porter had my bags whisked away before I could do a thing. When I claimed them at the front of the station, I handed him a half a pack of cigarettes, which would have been a handsome tip four months ago. He looked at me scornfully and asked for money! That really is a sign of a return to normalcy. As I rode out to the Center on the metro I was impressed by the magnificence of the cars, the good-looking clothes people were wearing, and general attitude of satisfaction with life. To this day, I don't know whether these observations were valid. It may have been only the contrast to Vienna. Maybe the people looked the same as they did on my first arrival in Paris but then I was contrasting them with America.

Upon arrival at the Center, I could find only one person. I took a jeep and went out to Maison Rose, the house that Rene and I had rented many months ago. I arrived in the midst of dinner to find Madame overjoyed and the fellows most cordial at my return. It was particularly good to see Jack Mote, Owen Newlin, and Howard Suits again. We spent the rest of the evening in filling in the gaps in our stories. The next morning Gordon Coffin and I took that jeep back to Paris. Half way to the Center the jeep froze up. We slowly worked our way in, stopping now and then to put in water and allowing time for it to cool off and thaw out.

At the Center, I was nabbed by Willis Weatherford, one of the Commissioners, for a three-hour debriefing on Vienna. By 4:00 I began to drag. France had gotten to me with that feeling of exhaustion I had here last summer. Until today I have not been up to par. That day I talked twice with Vienna. They had a tale of woe to report. The night before the temperature had dropped to 15 below and two of the jeeps and three batteries had frozen.

Because of the bitter weather, the rivers were frozen over and there was practically no electricity. Accordingly, there was not a light in Vienna from 6:00 in the morning until 10:00 at night. As a result, one of the orders they gave me was to buy lanterns on the French market. On Tuesday, Howard and I started a tour of French stores in search of lanterns and other items that Vienna needed. I was astonished at the number of things available on the Paris market. It seems that now if you have money you can get almost any thing you want, although prices are about double what they were last summer. Metro tickets have doubled. An afternoon movie now costs $1.00 instead of the $0.50 last August. However, this availability of goods does not extend to food. Food at Maison Rose seemed worse than it had been last summer. Then again, that may have been my reaction in contrast to Army food in Vienna.

The rest of the time, I spent in the garage collecting parts and tools to take to Vienna, finding only about half of our needs. Wednesday night Percy, the British chap from Vienna, turned up from London on his way back to Vienna. At the last minute word came in from somewhere that not only was Percy to take the Canadian Chevrolet 3-ton truck but that he was to drag the other broken down truck behind him. However, since his truck was not in good enough condition to tow the wreck, we tied the wreck behind Jack's GMC and are now ready to leave Paris tomorrow. The four days in Paris have been filled with work without time for anything else. Still, it has been good to see so many people I had known before and get some better idea of projects in other areas.

January 14—Our Eastward Trek to Innsbruck

Friday morning we started out from the garage about 9:00. Percy and I were in the Canadian Chevy loaded with my parts and a jeep. Jack and a chap we called "the Kid" were in another truck. The deadhead truck was attached to their truck and behind it was a trailer. Then came Owen and Bob Forthman in a truck with a jeep on it. They were also pulling a trailer. We made some procession! It had been raining all week but that morning it was clear—a good omen, we thought, for our trip to Austria. However, this trip eastward from Paris turned out to be as hexed as my trip last September.

We were only halfway from the garage to the Center when incident #1 occurred. The clutch linkage on Jack's truck came loose. We found that a nut had simply come off, but none of the boys had a nut that size. I climbed into the back of Percy's truck, got out my big box of stuff for Vienna, found the proper nut—and we were off again. After fond farewells at the Center, we asked who best knew the way out of Paris. I more or less did but was glad to defer to anyone who really knew. The Kid said that, sure, he knew the way and so led us out. The Kid is about 22, had six months at Harvard, and lets you know it. That was at 11:00. After winding our way all through Paris, we finally reached the last Metro stop at one, only 10 miles from the Center. At last we were out of Paris headed east, with everything in order. Or was it?

After a mile or so, Jack's truck sputtered and died. Before the rest of us could do anything, the Kid was under the hood with the word that any minute now he would have us on our way. There was only one really good mechanic in our crew, Owen, but he too let the Kid have his way. After a suitable length of time the Kid came up for air and announced that the truck must have a new coil. Of course, the Innsbruck team had packed no coils. I opened my Vienna box again and got one out. Off we went in good shape, we thought. After about 500 yards the truck stopped once more. Again the Kid; again a long wait; finally, the diagnosis—the carburetor was at fault. There was no carburetor with the Innsbruck team. Back I went to my Vienna box to take out the only one I had (I had bought it in Paris for $22). This time, we found it was a slightly different model and would not fit. We went to a telephone, called the garage, and asked for a proper carburetor and for a real mechanic to install it. Three hours later a nonmechanic worker from the Center turned up with a carburetor, which he had just purchased for us. It did not quite fit! In disgust, the Kid made it fit in a haphazard sort of way. And off we started, but after another five hundred yards, the truck stopped again. This time the Kid came up with the story that it was the condenser.

This time I did not have one so we took one off the deadhead truck. Did this fix the problem? No. Another 500 yards and we stopped again.

After a council of war we decided to send the truck back to the garage for the night, get it fixed by a good mechanic the next morning, and let it try to catch up with the rest of us the next day. We unhooked the dead head truck from Jack's truck and fastened it to Owens' truck. I turned the troublesome truck around to head back for Paris, and it started running beautifully. Without further delay, we all turned back east and let them roll. It was 7:00 p.m. as we passed the city limits of Paris. After about 25 kilometers, we stopped for the night to sleep in our trucks in the rain.

Truck procession from Paris to Innsbruck

Saturday was a gray, rainy day, but we pushed on in spite of the fact that Jack's truck at times was as bad as the day before. However, as it was not pulling the deadhead truck, it moved along at a fairly good clip, in fact as fast as our sluggish Canadian Chevrolet could lead the procession. Toward evening we stopped again to see what could be done. The Kid finally relinquished his position as head mechanic and our British friend, Percy, mildly suggested we test the wiring between the battery and the coil. In a couple of minutes we found that the ignition switch was faulty. Again my box yielded forth the necessary part. The truck ran like a charm for the rest of the trip.

We ate supper in a restaurant in Metz. You can now get restaurant meals in France without coupons. We decided to move just outside of Metz and spend the night. The Kid was in the lead truck and kept pushing on. We soon ran into a heavy fog but he still kept driving. I was driving Owen's truck with the deadhead behind and just couldn't keep up with the Kid. We drove on and on through that fog with the four us in the second and third trucks wondering when on earth the Kid would stop for the night. Later the Kid said he just felt like driving! About 11:30 my truck ran out of gas but we had a can of gas with us. So on to midnight when we came to the last town in France. I just stopped for the night, Kid or no Kid. A few minutes later, he reappeared out of the fog to join us in another sloppy, damp night.

We spent half the next morning getting gas. However, French gas station attendants seemed singularly unresponsive to our pleas early on a Sunday morning. Now we were in an area that spoke both French and German and I certainly felt more at ease. I had been completely at a loss in Paris with the language, having forgotten what few words I had learned last summer.

In due course, after finally getting gas, we crossed the French border and entered the town of Saarbrücken in Germany. By 4:30 we had reached the city of Ludwigshafen, where a unit of AFSC workers was supposed to be, but none of us knew where to find them. We patrolled the city until 8:30 that night before we finally found them. They all lived in private homes, not together. We really reveled in the luxury of a hot meal, hot water, good fellowship and a comfortable, warm bed. We talked until midnight. I was mentally comparing notes of our Vienna projects with theirs. I had known Merton Scott, a pastor from Oklahoma, and Dan Boehm in Paris.

This was a very delightful respite from a rather tiresome journey from Paris. Incidentally the city of Ludwigshafen, 100,000 or so, is about the most destroyed town I have seen. The whole city seems to be just a shell, gaunt specters of buildings, not just here and there, but everywhere, jutting into the night. The basic food ration here amounts to only 1100 calories a day.

Monday we crossed the Rhine on a US Army-built pontoon bridge into Mannheim and then on to the autobahn. I was now in vaguely familiar territory; at least I had been on the autobahn once before, in September. Twice more that day I had to open my Vienna box to get minor items for the trucks. We spent another rainy night half way between Stuttgart and Munich. This morning we decided to make a dash for Innsbruck. We got started in good time only to skid all over a steep hill when we unexpectedly came upon icy roads. Luckily, nothing serious happened.

At 4:00 we left Percy, who continued in the direction of Vienna with the Chevrolet truck, a jeep, and my parts, and the rest of us turned south at Rosenheim. At last I had the chance to enter that range of mountains Leigh and I had admired last September but had never entered. We headed right into them over a tortuous, winding road, which was covered with snow. Before we had gone far it got dark. Driving on through the night, we arrived in Innsbruck by 8:30 where the two fellows who had preceded us from Paris, Irwin Graeber and John Eliot met us. Despite our many mishaps and the Kid, we had made it.

January 20—Innsbruck to Vienna

Wednesday I spent in doing the things I had come to Innsbruck to do, namely, getting the team set up to live in Innsbruck. We unloaded trucks, met officials, got the vehicles inspected, and made a beginning on finding homes for the team. I had planned to drive a jeep back to Vienna, Thursday, but one of our Vienna drivers, Richard, had brought a truck down. On Thursday he took that jeep and headed back for Vienna while I stayed on a couple of days to see Innsbruck.

Friday I went with skiers on a cable car up the Hafelekar Mountain, north of Innsbruck. It was a beautiful day and after I had climbed from the top of the cable car to the top of the mountain I found about the best mountain view I have ever seen. It was not a long climb but I got very warm. I saw several skiers without any shirts and yet the snow was not nearly warm enough to melt. Innsbruck did look so tiny down in the valley far below. I had always thought of Innsbruck as a one street town with sharp mountains on each side. The valley is at least 10 miles wide, but from the mountaintop, it looked very narrow. From the peak I could see Germany to the north and Italy to the south!

Saturday morning I slept late, to be awakened by a phone call from Leigh from Salzburg. It seems he and Mary were taking this week off for a vacation in Innsbruck. They had taken the Friday night train from Vienna but had overslept in Salzburg and had missed the Innsbruck connection. They could get a bus as far as Kitzbühel and asked if I could pick them up there. After an early lunch I took a jeep and drove the 60 miles east to Kitzbühel where I waited a couple of hours for that bus. They finally arrived and we were back in Innsbruck by 8:00. On Sunday the three of us went back up the Hafelekar. This time it was snowing and we could see little.

As we neared the top, gliding over rocky crags in the cable car, we were suddenly thrown to the floor. For an instant, I thought the cable had broken. Soon I realized that it simply was that the electricity had gone dead and the automatic brakes had suddenly set so that the car swung crazily in midair for a time. We dangled there some 15 minutes until the electricity came on. It certainly gave us a weird feeling. Shortly after noon, we came down and I packed. At 4:00, I took the Arlberg Express for Vienna, had a good meal in the diner, a good night's sleep, and arrived in Vienna this morning just in time for Staff Meeting.

The rest of today I was deep in the swirl of piled up work here, renewing contacts, getting this and that done to the jeeps, and doing what of Leigh's work needed to be done. It was a long, hard trip, and I fear I did not do all the things done I was supposed to. Still, it was very enjoyable. I got some much-needed parts, I've seen more AFSC projects, and I've visited Innsbruck. However, it is good to be back in Vienna.

January 26—Routine Details Again

With Leigh gone on vacation, I spent most of the week in the garage with coveralls and greasy hands. I will just touch lightly on some of my other projects of the week. The two jeeps destined for Hungary had to be put in running order. They had to be Army inspected in order to get licenses, I took two jeeps to a glass shop, got a top fastened down on a third, got doors put on a fourth, took the fifth to Ordnance for a complete over-haul. At Ordnance I discovered, to my delight, that the Army has decided to extend its services to UNRRA for six more months. And so it went.

Oh, I had to visit the US Summary Court on summons to ex-plain why two of our jeeps had been parked in a wrong place sometime in December, and none of us could remember what it was all about. Today, George talked some of us into going to a movie. It was *Notorious* with Ingrid Bergman. Either it was pretty poor or else my taste is getting so that I don't like most movies. I haven't been to enough lately to really say. I did enjoy one in Paris called, *Fantasia*.

February 3—Snow, Repairs, Fun

What a winter. Before I went to Paris, there had not been a sign of snow in Vienna but since returning, it has snowed nearly every day. Each day there are crowds of workers, Nazi prisoners, women, city workers, chil-dren, shoveling snow. Along each street the snow is piled five to six feet high so that from the street you can hardly see the sidewalks. When the thaw comes, there will really be a lot of water. The authorities expect a flood in three of the twenty-one city districts.

There has been a noticeable increase in the crime rate and the expectation is for it to increase in the next few months as UNRRA supplies are cut off and private stocks are exhausted. We had two cases of milk stolen from the back of one of our trucks the other day as it was driving through the city.

Last Monday, Ordnance called to tell me the jeep I had taken to them for repair was such a complete wreck that it would take $600 to repair it. Leigh and I went there to go over the details with their mechanic. We found his estimate had been wrong. They are now putting in a new motor, new springs, a new clutch, and a number of minor items for $250. The biggest headache of the week was the matter of the compressor I had brought from Paris. We have never had one and so far have had to pump up all our tires the old-fashioned way, by hand. I found that when I got the compressor in Paris I had failed to note that it was an AC one. Our current in the garage is all DC current. That presented a problem, as you cannot buy any motors in Vienna. I went to a radio shop and asked if they knew a place where I could have an AC motor changed to DC. They sent me off to another shop that sent me to a third. They thought that perhaps they could make the change, so I left it with them. I went back every day for three days, and finally they said they couldn't do the job. They suggested that I read the papers daily until I found an ad offering a DC motor for trade with an AC one. Tedious. At this point I went to Ordnance to find they could do nothing as they handle only parts. They sent me to the Army Signal Corps. After first going to the wrong branch, I found the proper place but was told they had nothing to do with motors; they referred me to the Army VAC Engineers. They wanted to help but didn't have any motors. They gave me the name of an Austrian shop where they thought I might have some success.

They were right. The shop had DC motors but none were for sale. After a bit of dickering with them they finally agreed to trade a DC motor for our motor, but at a price. At any rate, Friday I went back there and picked up our compressor with the DC motor installed. Leigh has not yet tried it out as we have had no electricity lately, but we think it will work! We now have an Austrian mechanic to help Leigh so I won't have to spend much time in the garage.

Beginning today, I finally took over the complete job of vehicle coordination. Comfort has been doing a bit of up to now. George decided I wouldn't have time to do the warehousing. He and Comfort had to spend so much time on transportation while I was in Paris that he realized I wouldn't have time for warehousing.

During the week we had a bit of culture and fun. Mary and I went to the Vienna Philharmonic concert where we heard Wagner, Brahms and Shostakovich. The audience certainly did not like Shostakovich. They left in droves during his music and applauded hardly at all. I thought it might be because he is Russian. However, my seat neighbor told me it was just that they didn't like his music!

Saturday Del, who was in from Budapest, Leigh, Carlton, Jean and I went up on the Kahlenberg, just outside of Vienna but still in the American Zone, and went skiing. I'm still not good enough to really enjoy it but we had fun.

Yesterday it snowed all day so I stayed home writing letters and getting the apartment warm at last. We had gotten our month's supply of coal, five tons, this past week. It was so warm that George convened our weekly staff meeting this morning in our apartment. At this meeting, staff asked me to consider staying three more months beyond my year's contract that ends on May 15. I'll have to consider it.

February 10—Weekend Visitors

I spent some time this past week feeling my oats in getting into the complete coordination of the use of vehicles. At times I had to assume an almost dictatorial approach while still keeping all in good spirits. I think the transition from Comfort to me has been a success despite a bit of reluctance on her part to give up the job.

Friday morning I went to one of the railroad stations to meet two ETU men who were arriving on the same train quite by accident. Bob Bent was coming from Paris en route to Budapest and Jack was coming up from Innsbruck to spend a long weekend in Vienna to learn more about our work here. They had run into each other in the middle of the night on the train somewhere in western Austria. We spent most of the time that afternoon in getting them legalized to eat in Vienna.

That night we all went to the regular folk dance group and Jack was much impressed by the Community Center type of work and wished he could be in something like this rather than in transport work.

Saturday morning we took Bob to the train station for Budapest and had to wait for an hour. During that wait six Russian soldiers came up to us, six of the lowest ranking soldiers and started asking us questions. We spent most of that hour in friendly attempts at conversation. Only one of them could speak anything like a language resembling German; Bob didn't understand a word of German; Jack spoke just little more. Therefore, the two groups talked through this one soldier and me. We didn't get to anything important but we did establish a friendly relationship for a time. They seemed much interested to know what we were but never did seem to be able to understand. The idea of volunteers to help people just did not get across. You only do things because you are ordered to, seemed to be their only understanding. I finally tried to tell them we were a small group something like UNRRA, but none of them had ever heard of UNRRA. They were all farmers from the Ukraine but had not been home for several years. They are supposed to get 30 days a year off but none had gotten any time off for four years. They grumbled about it but did not question it.

After seeing Bob off, Jack and I went to see Rudi Böck, a Viennese Quaker who has been looking for a place where we might all live together and set up our own mess. This was for what we call the "Simple Life Group." He had not been able to find anything suitable for us. The housing situation in Vienna is just impossible. All he could offer was a whole second floor, some 50 rooms, of a sort of palace, but completely unfurnished! Saturday night the "simple life" group met—Jean, Mary, Bert, Leigh me, and our guest, Jack. After much discussion, it seemed best that we give up these plans for the present and keep eating with the Army, not because of any change of heart, but because of the impracticality of it.

We also had found out a couple of days before that it is a court martial offense for an American to spend a penny for Austrian food. When you are in an occupied country, you just have to depend on the Army whether you like it or not. Still, we have hopes that the Army will pull out of Austria by midsummer, although many will tell you that may be overly optimistic.

That afternoon Jack, Leigh, and Bert went skiing but I went to a Tea held by the British Quakers in honor of two big shots from London. It was a boring Tea and I wished I had not gone. However, I did have an interesting talk with one of the British Quakers about COs in England.

I forgot to mention a happening last Thursday evening. I attended a new International Club. It is a club started for individuals in Vienna who are on relief teams. I'm not too sure of its value yet but it might be quite worthwhile. Arthur is the main founder of this group.

Sunday afternoon George, Comfort, Jack, and I went to an English-speaking movie, *Henry V,* which we enjoyed very much. For some unknown reason they ran the film on slow speed so that the speaking was almost unintelligible. I suppose the theory was that if it was slow Austrians might understand the English better! That made it worse, but you would not have understood the English anyway unless you had been exposed to Shakespeare!

After supper Leigh, Jack, and I went to the Vienna Symphony where we enjoyed Wagner, Mozart, and Schubert. That made it really a cultural Sunday.

This morning we had a long staff meeting in our apartment at which time Jack told of all the troubles of the Innsbruck team. Then tonight I took him to catch a train back to Innsbruck. I think he had a very enjoyable long weekend with us.

February 17—US Summary Court and Other Events

Thursday I went to the Army Summary Court to appear with one of our Austrian drivers, Frederick, who had been summoned on a charge of speeding. I got there late after he had already appeared. He told me the

Judge would let him off if he would get the Quakers to give some food to his Secretary. I went in then to check it out with the American soldier, who was the Judge, and got the same story. He said he wanted to help us out if we would just cooperate. I told him that there could be no connection between the court's decision about speeding and the food he had requested. If she needed food and was in one of the categories that we feed, we would be glad to help. If not, we couldn't help her on the side. Then the judge admitted that he had no real charge against Frederick anyway, as the MP had not turned in the complaint on the right form. It didn't seem right to me for a Judge, in essence, to request a bribe for his decision. I reported the incident at staff meeting and the group decided I should write it up and turn it in to the Judge's superior! This may cause us some trouble in the future, but the feeling was that a thing of this kind should be made known.

Friday night, I took a truck to our Community Center where I picked up the Friday night group and took them to the Red Cross to join the American folk dancing group there. There is a law that no Austrian is allowed in at the Red Cross, so it took a special order to get them in. The evening turned out fairly well.

However, I made one mistake. I allowed myself to be persuaded to lead a square dance. I can usually get along fairly well with Americans who know a little of square dancing, but this time, over half the group spoke no English and I had a terrible time. In trying to call the dance in English, I forgot all the German I ever knew. Then too, most square dance calls can't be translated into any language—they don't even mean much in English!

Yesterday afternoon I visited a Dr. Keller whom Dean Buchanan's wife had referred to me. Dean Buchanan is the Dean at Iowa State College and had been in charge of our CPS camp at Ames. Dr. Keller had had a fellowship at Iowa State College in 1931. He is the director of a small agricultural school somewhere near Klagenfurt. He was most cordial and I certainly enjoyed my talk with him. He invited me to visit his school if I ever get down that way. I do hope I can.

Saturday afternoon our garage owner invited me to go with him and his family to an operetta. It was *Straussbuben*, all Strauss music with the story of the Strauss family. None of the music was familiar to me but I liked it anyway. It was written with the lesser-known Strauss music.

I haven't said anything about work this week. It continued at its usual pace. It seemed that nearly every day I had to visit Ordnance about some problem. At staff meeting this morning it was decided to send Leigh to Innsbruck for a time. Three of their four trucks are off the road and need repair. Who better than Leigh to do it! Here it is 10:30 at night and I am home alone. Leigh is out with his widow this evening. He met an Austrian girl who lives near here and speaks English. She is 27 with a five-year-old daughter. Her husband was killed in the war. Who knows if anything will come of it, particularly now that he will be in Innsbruck for a time. He did take her to one of the many pre-Lent Viennese Balls Saturday night and did not get home until after 5:00. You can't blame him for the hour. Streetcars stop at midnight and do not start again until 5:00 a.m. The Balls just keep on going until morning!

February 24—Del from Budapest, a Viennese Ball, a PW

On February 10, Del showed up here from Budapest with a jeep that needed a complete overhaul. Ordnance promised to have it ready by last Monday. Del had gone back on the train to Budapest and planned to return last Monday to get his jeep. I called Budapest to tell Del not to come, as it was not ready, but he had already left on a train for Vienna. He showed up at our office midmorning on Tuesday. It had taken 14 hours for his train to come the 150 miles from Budapest and as he had arrived in Vienna at 2:00 a.m., he had just stayed on the train until daybreak.

I checked and found his jeep should be ready by last Friday. However, since his Russian permit to travel was to expire last Thursday he couldn't wait for the jeep. He then tried to get a train and even a plane back to Budapest on Tuesday, but everything was grounded due to snow. It has snowed here everyday since I returned from Paris. Here in Vienna the snow has even gotten ahead of the maintenance crews. At last, we got the bright idea of talking with the Russian Liaison officer, an American whom I knew slightly from the Army mess. After the pulling of many strings, he was able to get the Russians to extend Del's pass by five days. And Friday his jeep was ready! On Saturday, he took off with it to work his way through the snow to Budapest.

Speaking of snow, it has blocked Leigh's trip to Innsbruck. He was packed ready to go last Thursday but found that the road to Innsbruck was blocked. Only today did word come of its opening so he took off this morning. A phone call from him a few minutes ago told me he had at least made it as far as Salzburg.

At the Red Cross dance, a couple of weeks ago, I met a fairly interesting Austrian girl. I had decided it was time to get a bit better acquainted with Austrians so I had asked her for a date. Her answer was that she would like to go out with me but that she could not because her parents did not know me. Instead, she invited me to her home Thursday evening to meet her parents. She speaks fair English but the parents spoke none. I went to their home and had an interesting evening talking to the three of them. It ended by them inviting me to go with them Saturday night to the last Viennese Ball of the season.

Saturday afternoon I slept late in anticipation of a long night. At 7:30 I arrived at their home to find them all decked out for the Ball, the daughter and the mother in masquerade costumes and the father in full dress. As usual, I was wearing my Quaker uniform that seems to be accepted everywhere. The four of us went on a streetcar to the huge building in which the ball was held. It took us until 10:00 to actually get there, get in, and get our coats checked. The evening then began to grind slowly on. I enjoyed it only as a novelty for as far as intrinsic values were concerned, I saw none. There were nearly 3000 people there. It included four dance bands in different large ballrooms and in the corridors between there was just a struggling mass of humanity. In a couple of the smaller rooms one could find a merry-go-round, a slide, hit the bottle concessions, and souvenirs for sale, etc.

I had worn my long underwear, as I do all the time in this winter weather, and since the rooms were stifling hot I was burning up! It was so crowded that it was almost impossible to dance. I had a thoroughly miserable time except that I enjoyed seeing every one else pretend to enjoy it. I think many of them did, for it was a noble attempt to have prewar gayety. There were high prices, ration free drinks, black market cigarettes, and too many people. I only saw three American soldiers and a like number of Russians. Everyone else was Austrian. I had hoped the crowd might thin out by midnight but everyone stayed on, as the streetcars do not start until 5:00. I had five more long weary hours there. I staggered home at 6:00, glad to have seen it all, but happier that I would not have to do it again. Then I slept until noon.

You may remember that during the latter part of the war several German and Austrian PWs were stationed in Wilmington, Ohio and were taken daily to work on local farms. One Austrian PW worked for some time on Harry Hamilton's farm and Harry had become friendly with him. Since the Hamiltons had sent me his name, Franz Pfliegler, and his address I went to see him yesterday. I found him to be a most likeable chap and spent over two hours in his home. Neither he nor his parents spoke any English but we got along. You should have seen his eyes light up with pleasure when I first said that I knew the Hamiltons. He had a letter from them, which he had not yet had translated, so I read it to him in German. He was pleased as punch to hear it. He was so appreciative of the things they had sent him. He asked if I would translate a letter, which he would write them, into English. It seems that few of the PWs had made much contact with their employers but what little he had with the Hamiltons made them stand out as the best family he had worked for.

He lived in a typical, small, overcrowded apartment but it was neat and clean. He is now a member of the Vienna police force. The family had supper while I was there and they simply demanded that I eat of their meager rations. They served cocoa, sent by the Hamiltons, and some delicious bread with a Viennese sour cheese heart. I think they got the greatest pleasure out of sharing that meal with me—a small token of return for what the Hamiltons had done for them.

March 4—Work Camp Planning, Steve's Visit, Vacation Plans

Despite our previous recommendation opposing work camps, Philadelphia has asked us to consider developing one in Austria. Friday, a few of us met to discuss a possible farm work camp near Klagenfurt this summer. Dr. Keller had planted the idea when I met him. He had said that there is a shortage of farm workers near his school and the farmers would welcome even the unskilled help. Mary thought a work camp there this summer would be great for the young people at the Community Center. The group could live at the school, which is in an old castle, and work on nearby farms. At any rate, our next move is to get in touch with Dr. Keller again and investigate conditions in his area. It will be a bit difficult to meet him as he spends most of his time at the school. I had just been lucky to find him in Vienna when I met him.

On Saturday morning, Steve Cary, one of the European Commissioners, arrived for a two-day visit. He is returning to the States this week and felt he should get a picture of our programs before returning. I spent most of day hosting him around Vienna and introducing him to all our members and their programs. We had a special staff meeting Sunday where he told a good bit about other AFSC European programs. Actually one group in Europe hears so little about other groups. He commiserated with us about the AFSC shortfall in budget. In Philadelphia, they find that their budget for October 1946 to October 1947 had been set $1,200,000 too high. Many programs are being downsized. When I took him to the Community Center, Mary cornered him about the possible summer work camp program. He was favorably inclined toward it if we could work it into our limited budget. Sunday night I took him to the opera to see *Aida*, one of the best operas I have ever seen. Some of our group had also seen it at the Met in New York and they say this one in Vienna is better. After the opera I hurried to take Steve to his train.

As Leigh is due to return Thursday from Innsbruck and our transportation problems have eased up a bit, I am planning to take two weeks of my allotted 30-day vacation now. I am planning to go to Italy to see Rome and to visit my old buddy from Iowa CPS days, Lee Lumpkin, who is with an AFSC program in Ortona.

But you can't just pick and go. There are all kinds of red tape that must be surmounted first. Last Wednesday afternoon I went to the Italian Embassy to find that it is open only from 10:00 to noon, weekdays. On going back Thursday morning, I was told that first I had to have travel orders. With travel orders signed by George, I went back Friday morning. This time I got many forms to fill out, get signed, and bring back another time. Back I went with the forms yesterday morning, but this time they wanted more money than I had with me. After one more trip this morning, I finally have an Italian visa.

Last Thursday I turned in a travel order request with the Army to provide transportation and food while in Italy. That request seemed to get lost so yesterday I hounded that office. Today they told me why I had not gotten it. It had been turned down because the Army is not letting anyone go to Italy as they are closing down their occupation there and have no food for people on leave. They finally agreed to give me travel orders in Austria to the Italian border and I can travel on into Italy on the strength of my passport and Italian visa.

I plan to leave this Thursday night on a British military train if I can get reservations. I am not going alone, Mary is also going. I doubt if we will see much of each other in Italy, as we will have different interests. We both wanted to see Italy and know that it is much easier for two people to beat out this business of red tape together rather than separately. So we will spend the night of March 6 (my 27th birthday) on a train headed west to Villach in Austria, and then over the border into Italy.

I forgot to mention two other items. First, at staff meeting yesterday I tentatively agreed to extend my term of service here three more months, from May 15 on to August 15. I guess I won't be doing any crop work at home on the farm this summer.

The other item could be a problem for us later on. Dr. Heiser's department at the Army has been closed out and we are to be turned over to the Civilian Supply Section. Rumor has it that they may order us to feed only in the American Zone of Austria and the American Sector of Vienna and may order some of our team to go home. Dr. Heiser has been a real friend to us and we will miss him. He too is thoroughly fed up with the Army, even though he has been part of it. For example, he is upset with the way the Army has handled Army dependents. None of the American children ever has any contact with Austrian children. They grow up thinking of Austrian children with a slur. Guess I am all full of anti-Army thoughts tonight. As the time draws nearer when the Army may leave Austria, they seem to get the idea of having more and more control. Now, let's forget about the Army. I'm off to Italy.

Italy

March 1947

March 9—On to Rome

Thursday night Bert took Mary and me to the train and sadly bade us farewell. (You see he and I have been kidding each other about Mary going to Italy with me and this saddened him a bit!) We had managed to get sleeper reservations on this British military train to Villach. When we arrived in Villach at 7:30 the next morning, we got off at the first of three stations that proved to be the wrong one. Fortunately for us, two other people made the same mistake. They turned out to be a 60-year-old couple, a British man and his wife. Together we hunted up a porter and headed on foot for the British occupied hotel, Hotel Post. The couple immediately seemed to take a liking to us and sort of chaperoned us the rest of the trip, for they too were going to Rome. The hotel tried to charge us $3.00 each for a couple of rooms just for the day, so the British couple, Mr. and Mrs. Mitchell, insisted we should use their room for cleaning up. Since Mary and I had no travel orders on from Villach to Rome, we went in search of the travel order office to get reservations to Rome. In error, we stumbled into a place for British women to put in their travel orders. Mrs. Mitchell showed her papers and got reservations for herself and her husband since he was a bit sick. Mary and I followed right behind and got reservations without showing any papers for we appeared to be with Mrs. Mitchell.

An hour before train time at 10:00 that night, a British truck called for the four of us at the hotel and took us to the train where we got on and got seats on the strength of the morning reservations. There were no sleepers anymore on the trip, so from there on we were always in a European style coach. Usually the train conductors check travel orders but the train was so strictly military that I guess the congenial conductor figured that everyone aboard must be legal. In a few minutes, we were called on to show our passports, and were in Italy. I was in a compartment with five British soldiers, as the British don't allow men and women to sit in the same compartments at night. I found those soldiers to be most interesting fellows. They had just returned from England and were telling how bad things were there in a material sense, but more importantly, they were worried about the moral decline there—"you just can't trust anyone in England anymore for no one there trusts you. It is almost as bad as in Germany and Italy!" The train slowly wound its way through the Tarvisio pass that by moonlight looked most fascinating not to mention dangerous. I wish I had been able to see it in daylight.

Morning dawned on a gray day without incident. When the train got to Padua, it stopped for an hour and a half for a meal. On going into the British mess, we found that we should have purchased meal tickets when we got our travel orders in Villach. The Mitchells for some reason didn't have any meal tickets either, although they had paid for them. When they told their story, they were allowed to eat anyway and since we seemed to be with them we could eat too, and even received packed lunches to take with us.

All day the train slowly wound its way down Italy over blown bridges and gutted countryside. The scenery was rather drab as it was level all day, since we were in the wide valley of the Po River. All the time I kept marveling at the differences between Austria and Italy. Every town was a beehive of activity with busy cement mixers, construction of all kinds in progress, and oranges for sale on every corner.

By evening we were in Rimini for our supper stop. At supper Mary heard we were only half a mile from the Adriatic and got all excited. We hurried over to the shore so she could see it and gather a few seashells. Suddenly I realized that the train was due to leave in 15 minutes so insisted we should hurry. I was still wearing long underwear, still on from the cold we had left behind in Austria. As we started trotting back to the train, the string on my underwear pants broke and they slid down inside my pants making it practically impossible to run. I was hardly in a position to do any-thing about it, so made the best of the situation and carried on. That half-mile was made in good time though my stride was something less graceful than that of an ostrich!

On through another night we went on that same train as it la-bored through Ancona and across the heart of Italy. At 5:00 a.m. this morn-ing, Sunday, we arrived in Rome. Before we could get off the train, a man came through offering to buy cigarettes for 200 lire a pack, about a quarter of the value of cigarettes in Vienna. After a last breakfast with the Mitchells, we walked out of the station and stood on a street corner in the heart of Rome, alone with our luggage, and not a word of Italian at the command of either of us.

March 11—The Eternal City

We boarded the first streetcar that came in our direction and spent the first money, six lire, since leaving Vienna. We had been fortunate in meeting the Mitchells. Due to their kindness, our whole trip so far had been paid by the British taxpayer. The streetcar shuttled us hurriedly around the city and all of a sudden, I recognized the famous Coliseum. Yes, we were really in Rome. We blurted out to the conductor the name of the street where the AFSC office was located and he helped us change to the proper streetcar, which we reached after walking across the Tiber. This new conductor knew exactly the street we wanted and asked for the house number. I gave it to him in French, and he understood! Contact had been made. Unfortunately, it was about the last we were to make with an Italian.

The AFSC headquarters in Rome is in sort of a monastery, or whatever you call a place where nuns hang out. It seems the building is for this sect where the nuns spend most of their time in prayer. The new nuns are put to work on dirty jobs like cooking and washing for the American Quakers who live here! At any rate, one of those soft-spoken individuals let us into the house and pointed out Bob Barrus' room. He is the AFSC leader in Rome. Since it was only 6:30 in the morning on Sunday, we hesitated to wake him. So we foraged around for ourselves and in due time found a place to clean up. By 8:00 when Bob awoke, the worn and weary travelers were all spruced up to meet the high and mighty potentate of Rome AFSC! I had called him the first of the week on the Army phone and our arrival was not entirely a surprise. We met his wife, Justin, and one other Quaker, George Fisher, whom I had known at Pendle Hill. It seems that there is no longer much AFSC work in Rome. This is just the central office for AFSC work over the rest of Italy.

After breakfast Bob dropped us off at a nearby Catholic Church that is famous for its chants. Mary and I spent an hour at a chanting Mass in the center of the Holy City. Afterwards we walked slowly back to the convent (I believe that is the word I want) through the parks, highways, and byways of Rome. I still could not believe I was really in Rome. It was a beautiful spring morning. The oranges were ripe on the trees, the grass was lush under foot, and the trees were in full bloom, particularly the olive trees.

It was such a different feeling from being in snow bound Vienna, which we had left three days before. Walking through one of the congested areas of the city, we were fascinated by the narrow winding streets, the crowds of dirty children playing underfoot, and in fact, by the complete living that seemed to go on in these streets of Rome. The people did not look like Austrians. They did not have the refined, cultured look, nor did they have the haunted, desolate look. Life seemed to be simple but happy for these Italians.

After lunch, Bob and Justin took us for a ride through Rome to help us get oriented. We later drove out of the city to the south onto the Appian Way. A large part of it is still the old Roman road of huge cobblestones lined with hundreds of monuments of various kinds, maybe a form of billboards, all built by the Romans. We clambered over the ruins of an old temple and then went on to go into one of the famous catacombs, where Peter and Paul were supposed to have been buried. Finally, by evening we came back into Rome and watched a beautiful sunset from one of the seven high hills of Rome.

During our absence that day, Doyle Porter arrived from the AFSC unit in Scauri to take a week's leave to show Mary and me around the country. He and Mary had been at Pendle Hill together. Doyle turned out to be a most likeable chap with almost the boundless energy of Mary.

Having had a general survey of Rome yesterday we were ready to start today on a more detailed point-by-point investigation of the city. Doyle had a jeep so we started out visiting this and that, reading guidebooks, and taking pictures. We visited all the usual things one generally sees, hurriedly but thoroughly seeing the Coliseum, the Roman Forum, the Roman baths, Hadrian's tomb, Trajan's column, the Palatine Hill, other famous sites, and finally, the Vatican to visit St. Peter's. We stood in awe at the huge cavern of a place that is so ornately decorated with all kinds of artwork, architecture, paintings, frescoes, mosaics, statues, and altars. It really is a most impressive place, but I am not yet a Catholic. It all seemed so much like an earthly palace of splendor and power dominating the lives of the poor people of Rome, Italy, and the world.

At noon Bainbridge Bunting, whom I had known slightly at Pendle Hill, arrived in Rome to join us on our tour. He is famous for his tours of Rome, for no other American knows Rome like he does, he being a rabid student of architecture. All afternoon Mary and I followed him around the streets of Rome visiting and seeing the fine points first of this palace and then of this church. I really learned the ins and outs of architecture this afternoon. Mary ate it up but I grew a bit bored with it all. Bainbridge was so intense with his descriptions and guiding. I think we were inside 20 churches this afternoon. My greatest impression of the day is a mental picture of Mary walking rapidly down first this street and that with a newly purchased guidebook in one hand, a notebook and pencil in the other. She would read about something in the book, look at it first hand, and then write it all down in her notebook. I was exhausted and felt I had had enough of this type of vacation.

March 14—Capri and Naples

Tuesday before leaving Rome, Doyle, Mary, and I spent the morning in the Vatican Museum seeing everything except the Sistine Chapel, which was closed for the week. After lunch we packed and started south with Doyle driving an AFSC Command Car, driving at first past one of the huge aqueducts leading into Rome. We drove past a beautiful volcanic lake, Albanik, through a dense fog, through the area of the Pontine Marshes, which Mussolini had drained and made into one of the richest parts of Italy. By night we had reached the little town of Scauri where one of the AFSC units is located.

It was good to see Dorrie Feise again (I had known her at Pendle Hill) and meet Peter Brown, an English chap. They are about to close out this unit but they had enough UNRRA food left to provide us with a good supper.

Wednesday morning, Doyle, Peter, Dorrie, Mary, and I drove inland to what was the town of Casino. It was positively ghastly. We didn't take time to climb the hill to the Abbey but we could see that it was completely ruined. We drove through what had been the town and saw not a building left. The town is slowly being rebuilt, but not on the old site. The gaunt reminders of that so recent destruction will stand a long time for the town is so destroyed that they will never rebuild on its old site. We drove on through other ruined villages in the warm afternoon, stopping to buy oranges at a farmstead where the women were carrying oranges in huge baskets on their heads, a most characteristic sight in Italy.

By midafternoon, we arrived in Naples. Physically the city did not seem badly damaged, not nearly as badly as Vienna. Yet I have heard there was considerable destruction in parts of it. Naples is a filthy city. Garbage is all over the streets, people are so dirty, cigarettes are on sale every 10 feet, and everything seems to be sold openly on the black market on the streets. We hurried on south from Naples under the shadow of Mt. Vesuvius around the Bay of Naples to the town of Sorrento where we parked the Command Car in a garage. Then taking a boat about half the size of the Island Queen in Cincinnati we put out to sea, the roughest sea I think I have ever experienced. However, we only had to sail about half an hour before we reached the famous Isle of Capri.

We hastily brushed aside the hundreds of porters that swarmed around us and took the "funicular" up the hill to the center of the island. At that point there were more porters and horse drawn carriages all striving their utmost to entice us to use their wares. We preferred to walk. That seemed to be the greatest possible insult to them and they practically fought with us to get us into their clutches. Still, we walked the mile carrying our own luggage. Two cab drivers however, persistently followed us the whole way throwing insults at us and pointing out how tired we were. (We were tired but we wouldn't have given in for anything!) At length we arrived on the south side of the island and found a very nice villa in which to stay, only a few hundred yards from the rocky coast. Expensive? Yes, to any ordinary tourist, but we stayed two nights and had five meals for $4.00 a person. The week before some English visitors had paid $25.00 for the same accommodations. How did we do it? A chap named Bill Congdon had been with the AFSC in Italy until this January. At the end of his term, he had come to Capri to live for six months while he was painting. He lives in a mansion belonging to a friend and had worked out the cheap arrangement for any of his friends who might happen along. We were his friends!

Before going to bed, we took a bit of a scamper by the sea to dream of days of yore when Tiberius used this isle for his summer retreat, or days when this island looked out across the Mediterranean to mighty Carthage, or to more recent times when it was a Nazi rest area. Now, here we were restfully reposing on this same Capri.

Thursday after breakfast, Doyle, Peter, and I doffed our clothes and went swimming in the morning surf, cool, invigorating, but not too cold. Just three days before, I had fought long underwear. Now I was swimming. Later Bill took us on a tour. Part of the estate on which he lives now includes a famous old grotto, high up in the rocks where tourists can't find it. We climbed a long time to reach it. It had once had been used as a Roman temple. The acoustics are very strange. Anyone speaking in the grotto can be heard hundreds of feet below at the water's edge. In fact, before the war the enterprising owner had arranged for a symphony orchestra to play in the grotto with the customers hearing the concert from a ship off shore. The concerts stopped, supposedly due to the war, but actually more because the bass viola players refused to carry their instruments up to the grotto! It is a fairly well established fact (as near fact as any legend can be) that it was from this grotto that the Sirens sang to Ulysses, trying to bring him and other wayfaring voyagers to land where the men of the island would promptly do away with them. We climbed higher until we came to an iron gate. I alone managed to squeeze through and hurriedly went to the top of the mountain over the grotto to find the ruins of a medieval summerhouse.

After lunch Larry, a friend of Bill's who lives with him, took us in his jeep to the western edge of Capri. Twenty years ago, there was no road, but thanks to Mussolini, we were able to drive the three miles in a matter of minutes. Parking the jeep, we started on another long hike, this time down for what seemed miles until we arrived at the water's edge near the famous Blue Grotto. Idle boatmen had seen us coming and clamored for our business at 60 lire a person. Bill said that was too high so after a good bit of dickering we started to climb back up the mountain. (Most visitors come the easy way by steamer. Very few ever climb down the mountain as we had done. Thus, the boatmen were surprised that we were willing to climb back without having been in the Grotto.) At any rate, before we had gone far they hailed us and agreed to Bill's figure of 40 lire! The ride wasn't too exciting, although interesting. You can see only a small hole in the side of the rocky mountain just at the water level. It is just big enough to allow a rowboat in, that is, if you lie down in the boat. Inside there is a huge cavern where the water is brilliant green. It is a very unusual phenomenon. Legend says that

Tiberius used it for his clandestine affairs and that he had it connected with his villa four miles away by a tunnel.

Then came the long climb back to the jeep. In a small café we indulged in some marvelous Italian coffee. (The best coffee I have ever had was in Italy. Even the streets smell of it. The coffee is good not because of the bean but because of the way it is prepared.) But we were not through hiking for the day. We headed up to the top of the highest point on Capri and reached it just after sunset. From there we could look west to a colorful sky and sea, north to the Bay of Naples and the mainland, east to where we are staying, and south straight down to the ocean. We were 2100-*something* above sea level; I wasn't sure if it was meters or feet. Common sense tells me it was feet but the climb seemed long enough to have been 2100 meters, 6500 feet. Then came the long stumble down the mountain in the dark to the jeep and back to our waiting supper.

Following the leisurely meal, we went to Bill's castle to look at his artwork. I suppose it was good, but then what do I know about painting. His room is about 100 feet above the breakers and I can well imagine it is a wonderful place in which to concentrate. He likes the place very much except for the fact that Gracie Fields is building a huge villa near by and her workers are muddying the blue ocean daily.

Today we were up at 5:30, packed, carried our luggage up the mountain to the funicular, and took it down to our waiting boat. A brisk boat ride took us back to Sorrento and soon the five of us were on our way in the Command Car. We did not head back to Naples just yet. We took the rocky ocean road on south and east and spent the whole morning driving leisurely over this tortuous road many hundreds of feet above the ocean directly below us. We passed through the towns of Praiano, Amalfi, Maiori, and finally by noon came into the level valley and beach upon which we saw the town of Solerno, next to its famous beachhead. We could not keep going south forever so we now headed inland and north toward Naples.

In a couple of hours, we found ourselves at the entrance to the famous city of Pompeii. Doyle and Pete had seen enough of it formerly, so just Dorrie, Mary and I took it in, all too briefly. Guides haunted us all through the place and being so well conditioned against them by this time we brushed them off without a thought. I had had no idea that the place was so large. One could wander for days and still find new things of interest. Yet in another sense, it was all the same, just old buildings. Still, it was an interesting place.

We had a rather dreary ride back to Naples, as the day was getting cloudy. The dark figure of Vesuvius loomed large and silent over us. It was enough to awe one into silence. What dark days of destruction might yet be hidden "neath that silent crown?" In Naples we put Pete on a boat that would take him back to Capri. Then we stopped at the railroad station for me to get a ticket for the train north tomorrow. I next found a hotel in which to spend the night. Finally, I said a hurried goodbye to Dorrie, Doyle, and Mary as they pulled out for Scauri where they are to spend the night and from where Mary would go back to Rome by train. I have had enough of seeing Roman Ruins. I am ready to strike out for something else.

One item bothers me this evening. Just before those three left, an Italian told Doyle that Russia had just broken diplomatic relations with the US, Britain, and France. That sounds ominous. Would Mary and I be able to get back to Vienna? Should we try? Maybe Austria has been completely taken over by the Soviets. I just don't know. No one I saw this evening spoke English and newspapers are Greek to me (or rather Italian!). Guess I will have to wait until tomorrow to find out. The rest of the evening I wandered the streets and was accosted any number of times. People either wanted to buy cigarettes or dollars or wanted to tell me where I could have a good time! After a quiet supper for 500 lire, I went to bed early in the room that cost me 300 lire. (Those prices are very high for Italians.)

March 16—Lee at Ortona

Yesterday morning I got up at 3:30 in order to catch my train. For the next four hours, I was on the only good train I saw in Italy. It was a two car electric train with comfortable seats, was not crowded, and made good time. After a comfortable doze I got off in the city of Foggia. I saw nothing of that town for at 8:45 the train I wanted came in.

After getting on it I struggled through three cars, almost batting people out of the way in order to walk the aisle. At length one compartment of Italians took pity on me and offered me a seat with them, six Italians and me on wooden benches in a cramped compartment. The train slowly limped along and at length we came in sight of the ocean, the Adriatic again. I had no map and not the slightest notion of how far I was going. All I knew was the name of the town I wanted, Ortona. None of the stations we passed seemed to have the town name displayed prominently, no conductor showed himself after the first perfunctory ticket punch, and no one spoke English. The train oozed itself along over temporary bridges, would run 10 minutes, then stop twenty, run 10 more and again stop twenty. At each stop cigarette hawkers and orange salesmen did a land office business with my fellow passengers. I had the idea that we should be in Ortona by noon. So from then on at each stop, I ran to the exit to see if it was Ortona. At 2:00, I had a suspicion that a town was really Ortona but was told it was not. Just as the train started, someone else said it was Ortona. I barely made it off the train.

Ortona was built on a high hill on a point of land extending into the Adriatic. I had to climb several hundred feet and carry that heavy Gladstone bag, which, many times on my trip, I wished I had not brought. As I topped the rise, I wondered how I would ever find the AFSC unit there. I had no address, just a faintly remembered telephone number. I wandered around a bit until I finally found the telephone office, wrote down the number for the girl, and in a minute I was talking with one of the men at the unit. He told me how to find their quarters, which turned out to be only a couple of minutes away, right in the center of town.

There at 2:30, on March 15, I finally found my old buddy from CPS days at Ames, Iowa, Lee Lumpkin. It was so good to see him again, and was he surprised. Since none of my letters had reached him he had no idea I was anywhere in Italy. The first thing I asked him was what the news about Russia was. It turns out that my information from the previous day, that Russia had broken diplomatic relations with the US, Britain, and France was wrong. Russia had just called in her ambassadors for consultation. It was not as serious as I had thought. After a long chat, he took me over to the project where they were working. It was sort of a work camp project in conjunction with the International Volunteer Service Program (IVSP). It consists of rebuilding a partially destroyed church, which when finished, will be used as a church school. Then we took a tour of the town.

For the first time in

Lee Lumpkin and I touring Rome

Italy, I was able to walk through a town without being stared at, for the people here are used to seeing these Quakers. By evening the rest of the scattered members of the AFSC, who were working in nearby towns, had returned to Ortona for supper and the night. Even Bob, the AFSC director, and his wife, Justin, arrived in a jeep from Rome. After supper, Lee and I walked around the town some more and got caught up on the past, the present, and even a bit on the future. It was so good to be able to recall the recent past of CPS 104 at Ames, Iowa with some one who knew it. We reveled in recollections of mutual experiences and friends.

This morning we walked and talked some more. I also met other members of the group, several of whom I had known at Pendle Hill. After lunch two jeep loads of us left Ortona to drive inland. One load was returning to Lanciano where they work. The other jeep included Bob, Justin, Lee, and me. Lee had decided to take a day off from work and go part way with us on our way to Rome, to be with me and also to see a part of the Italian program that he had never seen. Lanciano is a small town where a priest has started a school for homeless children. Four of our AFSC workers are living there helping run this school. We spent about three hours looking it over. Lee and I went out to a nearby farm where the school is thinking of putting in a few Church of the Brethren cows. They wanted Lee's advice about the farm as to whether he thought the farmer could take good care of the cows. Lee tells me he feels that Brethren cows for Europe are just not the right things for Italy. The average farmer just cannot afford to keep a cow. He does not have enough land to support one cow properly. Only farmers in the upper brackets would be able to care for them. He felt that the Brethren should be sending something smaller like chickens or goats instead of cows.

By midafternoon, we had pushed on from Lanciano and drove for about three hours into a cloudy evening. But it was not only dreary in the sky. Our route led up the Aventino valley. This valley was one of the famous lines in the war. The German Gustav line stretched across Italy from Ortona to Naples, more or less, and the Aventino valley was the site of some of the fiercest resistance and fighting. The valley itself is stupendous. As we drove along a narrow twisting road, we could look over the edge at the valley far below, almost as deep as the Grand Canyon, and see village after village snuggled in the narrow valley.

The villages were mere shells, completely bombed and now desolate. What new building was in process was always at some distance from the old destroyed village. Bob pointed out that considerable amount of this new building had been helped by AFSC and UNRRA workers. Finally, we pulled into the crowded, half-blasted stone village of Palena. This was the scene of the latest AFSC project in Italy. Old friend, Bob Adams, was there to greet me. His group had just moved into new quarters in a half-bombed building. They have no running water, no plumbing, no privacy, and no maid. They are living very primitively in relation to the luxury of our life in Vienna. We all pitched in and got supper, one person having to run off to the city fountain for our water. After supper we had a short tour of the town and saw rubble everywhere. Very little of it has been removed. Lee and I went around with this Bob for about three hours, ending up on a bridge over the river from where we could see most of the ruined spires of the town. A few Italians came up and talked with us, that is, with Bob.

For the first time in Italy, I felt at peace. It was the only place in AFSC Italian projects where I would be happy to work. The quiet, almost haunted, yet friendly atmosphere of Palena, the destruction surmounted by the will to rebuild attracted me. It was a memorable walk. Bob finally went to bed and Lee and I took another turn of the town, finishing our long delayed bull session and saying farewell, as he returns to Ortona tomorrow.

March 19—Rome, Florence, Venice

Monday, Bob, Justin, and I were up at 5:00 in order to leave in his jeep for Rome. We continued up the Aventino valley in the darkness and arrived at the head of the valley in the rosy hue of dawn. Every village had serious battle scars. A railroad that played hide and seek with us had most of its bridges blown and its tunnels were still mined. Most of the wooded hillsides on each side of the road are also still mined and will be unusable for years.

It was a beautiful drive over scenery the like of which I have never seen before. It included rugged slopes with scrub growth and a few fig trees, almost like my idea of Palestine. At noon we pulled into Rome at the AFSC office. I had been on the go for quite a time so I took time out here to really clean up, get a good meal, and wander around Rome a bit more. I was told that Mary had busily seen more of Rome in the last two days and on Sunday evening had taken a train to Florence.

At 9:00 that night, I bade farewell to Rome and took a train to Florence. I rode in a compartment of wooden benches made for six. There were 10 of us there. Two climbed onto the baggage racks and the rest of us were squeezed into the seats. On my right for the whole night was a very fat woman who snored furiously. On my left and across the aisle were two women who talked "like a mill a shellin" (a phrase my grandmother used to refer to the chatter of a grist mill grinding corn) in Italian the whole night through. Despite all this camaraderie, I managed to catch a bit of sleep.

Yesterday morning my train pulled into Florence into a beautiful and undamaged station. I had no idea where in Florence I could find Mary. Finally, I found an Army hotel and inquired where they thought an American might possibly stay. After a couple of false leads I actually found her. Since she had been there a day ahead of me, she suggested things I should see. I struck out alone and visited the main cathedral and the famous tower beside it with its odd coloring and designs.

You cannot go to any one place in Italy and say you have seen Italy. Florence seemed as different from Naples as day is from night. The people seemed orderly, relatively clean, with little black market, and the stores seemed to have a goodly supply of things. You felt as if you were in a city that had not been bothered by war. Then suddenly I came to the river and saw several blocks of utter destruction. However, it was all neatly cleaned up and piled up. I had not been aware that there had been any destruction in Florence until I stumbled into this area.

I was back at the hotel at noon for lunch with Mary. We spent the afternoon together trying to get into the art museum but eventually we found that it was not yet open. The Nazis had stolen most of the treasure and now that it has largely been returned they just do not have it set up yet for exhibition. Florence seemed to be a city of many famous statues. That man, Michelangelo, must have been a busy boy when he was alive. He left his mark all over Rome, particularly at St. Peters. His main emphasis in Florence seems to be in the statues he created. We spent some time in seeing his masterpiece, David. Florence is a delightful place to spend a lot of time seeing works of famous sculptors and painters, a place to forget the war, to relax in the feeling of the dignity of man and to feel his constant upward spiral. This feeling is most difficult to find in most of Europe at this time.

After supper I tried to persuade Mary to head north with me but she was determined to see some more churches. So I headed alone back to the railroad station, got aboard another of those monstrosities the Italians call trains, and crowded again into a wooden compartment. The people there were even worse company than those of the previous night. Finally, I left that second-class coach and went to a third class one. It was practically a cattle car with benches, but at least it was less crowded. At any rate, I was able to catch a little sleep.

In a couple of hours, we arrived in Bologna and somehow I found that I must change trains. I stumbled off and tried to find a sign showing me the way to the train to Venice. It was in vain; there were no signs. For a time the crowd pushed me but finally, in desperation, I tried a likely looking man in uniform. He indicated I was walking in exactly the wrong direction and that I had better hurry the other way. Finally, I came to another cattle car train and was made to understand it was the one I wanted. I went right to sleep on that wooden bench and the next thing I knew someone was shaking me and muttering something in Italian. I awoke to find that we were in some station and no one else was in the car. This was not Venice but Padua—I had to change trains again.

In about an hour, the train appeared to be heading out to sea, water on both sides. Shortly, we pulled into the station at Venice. For the first time since my arrival in Italy it was raining. I checked my heavy bag and took out onto the streets of that famous city. I knew that the British still had quarters in Venice so I headed for them. I saw one British sign and tried to follow it. There were no more signs and I walked and walked and walked in the rain, continually coming into blind alleys with a canal at the end. I never saw an American or a Brit in all that hour and a half that I walked. Finally, I fell into a large open space that turned out to be the center of the city, St. Mark's Square. I found a British office where they steered me around a corner to the hotel Danielle, just on the waterfront. Here, at this British officer hotel, I was able to arrange to spend the night. I then hurried back to the station to get my bag. Despite taking a short cut across the Grand Canal, I still spent an hour getting back to the station. After I retrieved my bag, I found out that there is a boat taxi service from the station to the hotel. So taking advantage of it I was back at the hotel in half an hour.

At last I was able to get out of my wet clothing, eat a British lunch, and relax. It continued to rain the entire day so I was unable to see much of Venice. I did go through the cathedral at St Mark's Square. It seemed hoary with age and tradition. The interior was the largest splurge of mosaic work I have ever seen. After supper, I tried to tour the town but the rain was too disturbing. Even so, I found evidences here and there of black market, more than I had seen in Florence. Maybe that is because there are more troops here than in Florence. Venice is a rest center for British troops. I dropped in at a British NAAFI (British Army café chain) for some coffee, took in a bad American movie in the British theater and went to be bed early. It has been three nights since I have slept in a bed!

March 23—Venice and Return to Vienna

Thursday, March 20, dawned clear again. The only rain of our trip was over. After breakfast I boated to the station, met the same train I had arrived on the day before, but could find no Mary. A half hour later, a military train arrived and there she was. She had talked her way onto it and had gotten a free ride from Florence. We decided to leave Venice that night at 9:00 for Austria so didn't bother to get her established in the hotel. We spent the day going into churches, climbing the tower in St. Mark's Square, wandering haphazardly through the streets, riding in a gondola for 500 lire for two hours, going through the National Art Gallery, and finally taking a boat over to the island of Lido. We found that the Lido had been turned into a US Army rest center. We wandered there on the beach where Mary indulged again in a favorite pastime of shell collecting. When we got back to Venice, we counted our remaining lire, figured our meal cost for that evening, kept enough for our transportation to the station, and went about town spending the rest of our lire for art pictures that Mary wanted.

At the hotel we inquired if a special boat left there to take us to the train. We discovered that there is no train at night. The only train leaves daily at 2:00 p.m. What to do? We had spent all our lire. Our military money was no good, as during our absence from Vienna the Army had issued new script to replace the old money. The cost of the hotel and two meals and lodging for each of us was 1000 lire ($2.50), but we didn't have 100 lire between us, let alone 2000 lire. I did have a $20 traveler's check but it was too late to cash it and besides we didn't want to spend all of it just for lodging.

At this point of need, we resorted to that means we have long condemned in Europeans, the black market. We offer no defense, we just did it. I took out the long carried carton of cigarettes and wandered through the back alleys of Venice. In 10 minutes, I was back at the hotel with 2000 lire fluttering in my hand. Despite our guilty feelings, we had a good night's rest and two solid British meals. After a final quick look at Venice we departed for the station and the 2:00 p.m. train. There we found that the British train did not leave directly from Venice but from the main line 10 miles inland from Venice at three. Paying 12 lire for that ride, we arrived before three at the junction with the main line.

Going boldly to the Rail Travel Office (RTO), we extended our military orders and asked to get seats on the train headed for Austria. The clerk was friendly but told us that it was absolutely impossible, as the train was fully booked. He also said our military travel orders were not sufficient to get us on even if there had been room. (They had been OK when we came down!) We had to get on that train! It was the last train we could take and arrive in Vienna before our Russian passes to go through the Russian Zone of Austria expired. The clerk expressed his regret but said there was nothing he could do. Just then, the train pulled in and to our surprise, the conductor proved to be the same British conductor who had been on our train from Villach into Italy. We told him our plight and he said, "Well, I'm full up but I don't see any reason, since I brought you down to Italy, why I can't take you back." With that, we were on the train!

At the supper stop at Udine, we managed to get another free British meal. Shortly after dark, we came to the Tarvisio valley and followed it for a couple of hours to the Austrian border where we passed inspection without difficulty. How good it was to hear German again from that Austrian official, after all the unintelligible Italian! In another hour we reached the end of the line, Villach. The next train to Vienna did not leave until the next night. We got rooms at the same hotel, Hotel Post, where we had stayed on our way down. And again, our lodging was on the British.

Yesterday we spent a quiet day in Villach. I hiked around the town a bit while Mary spent most of the day drawing up her notes on the architecture of King Alfredo's summerhouse in Rome, or something like that! I spent some time with a British soldier who was concerned about current life in England. He said Italians ate better than the British did. "Who won the war anyway?" Finally, it was evening and train time. The British conveniently called for us with a truck, took us to the station, and gave us sleepers for the night. This morning, March 23, we arrived back in Vienna at 6:00 a.m.

I have spent two very pleasant weeks in Italy. They were mentally restful although physically tiring at times. The cost was very little; I spent five dollars more in those two weeks in traveling, eating, and sleeping in Italy than I would, had I stayed on the job in Vienna. Of course, the British taxpayer paid a good bit of my bill. That is the tough lot of an AFSC worker in occupied Europe, having to let other people pay his bills!

In later years, I think three things will stand out in my memory about this trip. First, of course, will be Rome for its ancient history laid bare to the modern eye. Secondly, will be Capri for its restful escape from the weary world. Thirdly, will be the Italian eastern coast and the Aventino valley for the fellowship and contact with the boys there and the feeling in Palena that I was "at home." It was made more valuable by having someone along at least part of the time so as not to feel lost. In addition, the AFSC contacts helped so much in gaining insight into parts of Italian life, which I, a total stranger to the people and the language, could never have done alone.

Springtime in Vienna

April to June, 1947

April 1—Army Again, a Visitor, a New Member

As soon as I returned from Italy, I put in a large order with Ordnance for parts. I did this as I had found out that the Army had changed its mind again and was to cease its relationship with UNRRA on March 31, instead of July 1. Before I had left for Italy, I had taken two trucks to Ordnance for repair. Without that relationship, we would no longer have access to Ordnance. Our Army contact was now to be Civilian Supply. Leigh had tried to get Ordnance moving on repairing them, to no avail. I went to see my contact in Ordnance to try to persuade him to finish our trucks and fill that order even though the March 31 deadline was upon us. He said he would be glad to do so if I could get the proper authorization from his superior. On to this top man at Ordnance, and wouldn't you know, he turned out to be the brother-in-law of one of the AFSC workers in France. I got an extension long enough to get our trucks repaired and to fill my order! He told me that the Army is now in the process of setting up a Community Sales Office through which all orders for supplies must be channeled. However, it will provide us direct access to Ordnance instead of the old way of going first through UNRRA. Now we will have to pay in cash. I am not at all clear how that fits in with Civilian Supply. I'll just have to wait to see how this new arrangement works out.

Civilian Supply tells me that the Army has come down with a new ruling that they will sell gasoline only to agencies that work in the American Zone of Austria and the American Sector of Vienna. As we work not only in the American Zone of Austria but also in the British and French Zones as well as in all four Sectors of Vienna, his ruling would cut us off completely from Army gasoline. I shuttled back and forth between Civilian Supply, UNRRA, and G-4 (Deputy Chief of Staff Logistics) of the Army to try to resolve this quandary. Civilian Supply told me to sit back and let them try their channels. Meanwhile, I found they had given up on the Army and were hoping the Austrian government would provide gasoline to the relief agencies, 7500 gallons a month, but it could not do that. They don't even have that much gasoline. I started up the ladder at G-4 and finally ended with a Colonel at the top. He told me he was now reversing his decision and would let relief agencies have gasoline regardless in which part of Austria they worked. I reported this to the Civilian Supply and the man in charge couldn't believe it. We both went back to G-4 and got the new order in writing.

Friday, Irwin Graeber, the leader of the Innsbruck team, arrived for the weekend. Someone has to take the responsibility for entertaining these chaps when they come and this weekend I was it. Friday he trailed along with me in my work. That night we went folk dancing at the Community Center. On Saturday, he wanted to see Vienna so I made arrangements for a Red Cross tour of musicians' homes. Unfortunately, the bus went earlier than scheduled leaving us with only a bus tour of Vienna cemeteries. Instead, we took a tour of the catacombs in St. Stephens Cathedral followed by a climb to the top of the tower of St. Stephens. This took us to the highest point in Vienna and provided us with an outstanding view of the city. That evening we went to an Army movie theater and saw *Two Years before the Mast*. Sunday morning we went to a Philharmonic Symphony concert. That afternoon Leigh took care of Irwin so that I could drive a truck to take some 25 of our Community Center youth to another part of Vienna to put on a play in a reform school before a couple of hundred children. It certainly was an odd looking assortment of kids. There were some hopeful looking faces but many looked like junior criminals in the making. The school seemed to be a pretty good one but then I don't know much about reform schools in the States. Then last night I took Irwin to his train to go back to Innsbruck.

A new team member arrived today. Ed Wright will now be our oldest member. He must be over 50. I think we are all going to like him and I suspect he will be the most level headed in our group.

April 3—A Failed Project, Odds and Ends

Tuesday when I wrote, I forgot to tell you about another incident of last week. This is in regard to our plan to go to Klagenfurt to see Dr. Keller and look into the possibilities of a summer farm work camp. Between taking care of our Army problems, I spent a lot of time getting travel orders for Mary, Ed and me for the trip. First, I had to get USFA orders and then I needed British approval. This time I also needed Russian approval, something that usually takes a week, but through a friend in Russian Liaison I got them in one day. Wednesday I worked on getting a jeep all set for the trip. Finally, Wednesday night I called on Dr. Keller's wife to see if she had any message for me to take to her husband. She said she was sure he was coming back to Vienna the next day. At least that was the way I understood her. She said she was "fast sicher" that he was coming. That means she was almost certain he was coming, but I took it to mean she was completely certain, "ganz sicher," that he was coming. (I will never forget the difference between "fast" and "ganz.") If he were coming back to Vienna there was no need for us to go to Klagenfurt. I got both Mary and Ed out of bed to decide what to do and we came to the obvious conclusion it would be best not to go clear down to Klagenfurt to see him since he was coming to Vienna, so we didn't go. The next day I called and found that he was not coming this weekend at all. His wife had misunderstood him. (In fact, we never did get to see him and the farm work camp idea fell through, all because of my misunderstanding of the difference between "fast" and "ganz.")

Last Saturday Marlis and Comfort left in a jeep for Innsbruck to look over the situation there. Tuesday they called to say that the jeep had a broken transmission. They then came back by train and the jeep is still in Innsbruck. Tomorrow Leigh and the British chap, Percy, leave for Innsbruck to put a new motor in that truck we had pulled from Paris to Innsbruck in January. Yesterday Carlton left for Paris and from there on to the States as his term of service is over. We will miss him.

April 8—Easter Weekend

Friday night George and I took the Mozart, the American military train, to Salzburg where we changed to the Arlberg Express. This put us into Zell am See by 9:00 a.m. Not long after, we arrived at Fischhorn for the Easter weekend. Fischhorn, you may remember, is the castle belonging to Marlis and family. It was a rainy day and George and I spent most of it in the castle reading and sleeping. It was a restful Easter vacation, particularly helpful after the great push of the previous two weeks. That evening Marlis and Comfort arrived for a two-day skiing trip up in the mountains. We all just sat around and talked into the night.

Sunday morning, Easter morning, George and I managed to get up in time to make it to Mass at the Church in the nearby village of Bruck an der Glockner Strasse. The Church had that characteristic musty European Church odor despite the fact it was packed with people, a number of whom were not able even to find standing room. It seemed like a very nice service as masses go—the Priest taking time out to give a short sermon and ending with the thought that it might be a good idea for his listeners to come to Mass oftener than only every Easter! In the choir loft were a home talent orchestra and choir.

Just before the Mass ended, I noticed the wind instruments sneaking out the back way and I wondered what was up. At the end of Mass I found out. They had a band concert in the street 100 yards from the church—good old German band music, and even some good old time American marches. I listened some to the concert, noting that all the clarinets were the old difficult but richer sounding Albert system clarinets. Benny Goodman has been popularizing the Boehm system in the United States. Then I wandered to the war cemetery in front of the church. There were over a hundred graves from World War II, and Bruck is not as large as New Vienna, Ohio. As George and I walked back to Fischhorn, we noted many quaint costumes and relatively happy looking people. It was a beautiful spring morning and spirits couldn't help but be high. Bruck was very beautiful that morning, or rather the setting was beautiful with the warm sun in a valley surrounded by snow-capped mountains.

After dinner I struck out alone to climb the mountain behind the castle. First I walked through timber and over some hidden patches of snow. Then I hit more and more snow until, after I emerged above the timberline, I sank hip deep into the snow. I had to turn around without reaching the mountaintop. What a contrast—a month before I had been swimming in the Mediterranean!

After supper some of Marlis' Austrian and German friends arrived and we spent the evening talking—all of it in German. Much of it was in a dialect I just did not understand. One of them, Willy, talked most of the time telling about his war experiences when he was in the submarine division of the Germany navy. He had been in 15 different submarines, three of which were destroyed while he was in them, he being one of five who escaped from one sub, one of three from another, and he was the only survivor from another. He figures he helped sink some 300,000 tons of American shipping during the course of his war experience. Often at night, they would surface to see the New York harbor lights. I wish I could have understood more of his stories but he lapsed into a dialect that to me was all but unintelligible.

Yesterday morning I went on a bicycle trip with Marlis and Comfort to another part of the large farm. At 1:00 p.m., I walked alone to Bruck where I caught the afternoon local that took me in three hours to Salzburg. There I went to the Pitter hotel as per prior arrangement and met Barbara Mason, with whom I had dinner and spent a couple of hours. She was a classmate of mine at Westtown and I had all but forgotten her existence. Some months ago, she accidentally ran into Comfort and we became aware of the other's presence in Austria. She is an Army hostess and is thoroughly fed up with it. We had a pleasant session reminiscing about Westtown and bringing each other up to date. Then over to the Salzburg train station where I caught a sleeper back to Vienna. A delightful Easter weekend.

April 15—Transport and Other Events

We have had considerable discussion on how my job will be handled after my term is up on May 15. I will still be here until August 15, but will have other assignments including some vacation time. Leigh agreed to take over my job but we have known for some time that he is not too happy here and would much rather be in Innsbruck. If he stays here and takes my job, he could leave the garage job as we now have two good Austrian mechanics working there. Fortunately, I came up with another solution. I had heard that Howard Suits, whom I had known in Paris, would be available for a new job about the middle of June. I know he would be delighted to come here and he would be most capable. So yesterday after getting Paris approval for Howard's move, Staff Meeting approved Leigh's moving to Innsbruck. I will stay on my job into June until Howard can get here.

Tuesday night I went to an American-Austrian cultural club. The speaker didn't show up and eventually I was calling a square dance. It worked fairly well as most of them spoke some English.

On Wednesday, George talked me into going to hear a talk on pacifism by some Austrian professor, but he didn't show up and we had a dry talk on the history of Vienna. Why didn't the professor turn up to talk on pacifism? George pushed that question and the chairman was most embarrassed. It seems that the Austrian government had "suggested" that no such talk be given during the Four Powers conference in Moscow on a possible peace treaty. The government thought such a talk would undermine the unity of Austrian requests at the conference, for one thing Austria wants badly in the Treaty is permission to maintain a 50,000 man Army. The group at the club was rather ashamed of that rather flagrant abuse of free speech, which the Austrians are always saying the Allied governments do not give them!

Thursday George turned up with three tickets to the Swiss movie, *Last Chance*. He, Mary, and I went and decided it was one of the best movies any of us had ever seen. It really gives you the feeling of what it is like to be homeless in a world torn by war. One interesting thing about it is that everyone speaks in his own language, but it is all understandable. We could, of course, follow the English and the German. The other languages were helped by subtitles in German. I think everyone should see it, particularly Austrians and Germans. It would perhaps help them understand why so much of the world hates them.

Another Innsbruck team member, Owen Newlin showed up for the weekend. It seems as if we are just a vacation center for the Innsbruck team, but we do think it is a good idea for each of them to get here to see how things operate in Vienna. I did the hosting for him and this time we even drove across the Danube into the Russian Sector, both of us on our one and only motorcycle. This section of Vienna is a much poorer and more damaged section than where we live.

Saturday night Polly and I went to a Russian Orthodox Church Easter Service. The building, way off in the Third district in the Russian Sector, looked very odd with its almost Halloween-like lights. It began at 10 and went on all night. However, we stayed for only about an hour and a half. I liked the Church's interior, as it was much simpler than a Roman Catholic

Church. Since everything was in Russian, we understood not a word of it, but they did have a beautiful hidden choir. About two-thirds of the attendees were Russian soldiers.

At Staff Meeting, I presented an idea with which I had been playing. The group approved my plan to purchase a large amount of gasoline (10,000 gallons). This should supply us for some time, provide available gasoline for Budapest and Innsbruck, and insure us against either the pullout of the Army or the always-possible refusal of the Army to provide gasoline. Today George and I inspected an available storage area that we think will work out well for us even though it is in the Second District (Russian Sector). When I went to the Army to firm up our decision to purchase the gas the Lieutenant in charge turned out to be none other than the Judge against whom I had testified sometime ago. On my account, he was no longer a Judge. He either did not recognize me or else does not know I reported that incident about him and so he approved our purchase.

By rights, I should be spending more time in my letters commenting on the International situation, but really I don't know much about it. All we ever get is the Army newspaper, "The Stars and Stripes" and hard-to-read Austrian papers. Each occupying power controls an Austrian paper and you never expect to find the truth in any of them. You always know ahead of time what each will say about any given situation. About all I have read lately is that Henry Wallace leads the lunatic fringe and that George Marshall is the savior of humanity. I have a sneaking suspicion that neither of these statements is the whole truth.

Now, to one final item of the week. I have been asked to give a speech next Monday to the English teachers club at the University of Vienna. They want to learn farm machinery terms in English. I must get to work on an outline for that speech.

April 23—The Lieutenant and Other Activities

Last week I finished making the arrangements for storage of the gasoline we are buying from the Army. Then I went back to the Army to actually buy the gas. Again, I was to deal with this same Lieutenant about whom I have written before. We signed the proper papers and I agreed to pay $1331 for the 11,000 gallons of gasoline, but I had to wait a day to get the money from our office.

The next day before I could leave, this same Lieutenant and a Major came to our office, not about the gasoline but about the bribery charge of three months ago. The Major explained that this was a serious charge and if proven probably would mean dishonorable discharge for the Lieutenant! He then insisted that I testify on the spot about the charge and to do so in the presence of the accused. And here I was right in the middle of a gasoline deal with the Lieutenant! At any rate, I testified in good Quaker fashion, which seemed to satisfy the Major. The Lieutenant did not seem particularly upset by it all. In fact, we had a more or less friendly discussion on just what had happened that morning in February. Then later that day I went back to the Lieutenant's office and without any difficulty paid for the gasoline.

Last weekend we had another visitor, Bob Forthman, from the Innsbruck team, and as usual I was tapped to be his host. I am going to get to know this city well, the way I seem always to be the host for the Innsbruck team members. However, it won't go on forever. We just got a letter from Philadelphia saying that the Innsbruck program will have to close by July 1 because of the very tight financial picture. This word comes just when the Innsbruck team has pretty well overcome its obstacles and is really getting rolling. Philadelphia tells us that the AFSC is more than a million dollars over budgeted for this year. Contributors in the States must have forgotten about war-torn Europe completely.

Saturday afternoon I went to the Red Cross library to look for material on farm machinery, but as I feared, I found nothing. However, I did get interested in Henry Wallace's book, *Corn Growing and Breeding*, or something like that. Then Monday afternoon I went to Dr Kober's home and the two of us went to the meeting of the English teachers' club. There were about 15 teachers present and they all listened attentively as I told something of farming in America. I wanted to tell them more of the life and values of it but they wanted me to go into the machinery angle, as they are English teachers in technical schools. I told them about plows, threshing machines, etc. Most of it was new to them and they seemed to enjoy it.

Travel items. George has gone to Trieste to investigate shipping possibilities through that port. We currently get all our supplies through Antwerp, which necessitates a long overland haul. At one point last week, I had expected to be going to Mannheim this week for a supply of parts that were coming there from Paris. But on Sunday, I talked with our unit in Ludwigshafen to be told that someone was coming all the way here from Paris to bring them in. I called Paris and could not seem to get any definite answer, so the whole affair is up in the air. However, I doubt that I will go for there are several people in Paris who want an excuse to visit here.

April 28—Finances

Part of the last few days I have been working with the new Army Community Sales Office, which services civilian employees of the Army. While working out this purchasing process two items of contention came up. The first is the discovery of the high cost of our past Army services. Up to now we have never paid a cent for all the work we have had done at Army Ordnance. All work was recorded and the bills sent to Army HQ in Frankfurt. From there the bills were supposed to go to UNRRA in Washington from where in turn they might to be sent to the AFSC, Philadelphia. We were assured that probably the Army or at least UNRRA might just eat the bills. That was not the problem as we had expected to pay them eventually. The problem was that they were so big and that they want them paid now in Vienna. For example, last winter Ordnance had told me that each motor would cost us $115. Now the bill they were preparing for UNRRA showed a charge of $350 for each one. It seems that the last figure is the catalogue price, but for all Army people they give a 2/3 rebate for an old motor. They also have a directive from the top saying that they cannot discount anything to private organizations, so for the motors and other charges, I had run up a bill of between $3000 to $4000 when I thought it should be between $1500 and $2000. I have fought this matter all week but it looks like we will have to pay the whole thing in cash.

The second problem is that both the Army and UNRRA are each billing us this nearly $4000 figure. I went to both offices where I was told by both to disregard the other and just pay them. There is something wrong here but I haven't gotten any satisfaction from anyone. At the Army I have been from a Sergeant to the top Colonel but still have no clear answer. They simply say to pay the bill in cash or we will be cut off from all services by May 20. And don't pay UNRRA. I surely will be able to get UNRRA to drop that double billing. On top of all this, last week the Army billed us for all the rooms we have occupied since we arrived, over $1000. Then I just spent a day working over old coal bills, as they asked me to turn in a statement on how much coal we had received so they could bill us. Unfortunately I played honest on that and we are due for another big bill any day. To add to our financial woes Frederick, one of our Austrian drivers, returned from Salzburg last week with six ruined truck tires. The replacements cost $30 a piece. It turned out that this was not his fault as a bent axle caused the excessive wear. With all these sudden expenses, Philadelphia may label me a spendthrift!

April 30—Extracurricular Activities

Although my job here is Transport, I do manage to combine it with other activities. For example, today under the leadership of some of our Community Center Austrian Youth we took two loads of about 60 Volksdeutsch children under age 12 from their camp for an outing in the Vienna woods. We plan to do this with different Volksdeutsch children every Wednesday.

Friday, John Eliot, the last of the Innsbruck team, arrived here for the weekend. As usual, I took him to the Friday night folk dancing group at the Community Center. Saturday evening I continued my "friendship over boundaries" plan by taking one of the Austrian University girls to an opera. I had wanted to go out with an Austrian girl for some time but Mary had said I was not to do it with any of our Community Center group. She said I must remain aloof and not show any partiality. I just broke down and took this girl to *Don Giovanni* anyway. We had a nice evening, absorbing some ice cream after the opera and just talking. It was a very pleasant evening to be remembered for the fact that it was the first time I had so spent an evening with a girl who speaks no English.

Then Sunday, Mary and I went to the edge of the city where we met Austrians of the Friday night group and spent all day hiking in the hills beyond the Vienna Woods. It was in the Russian Zone, but we went anyway over the protest of some of our American group and the approval of others. Unfortunately, the weather was cloudy and cold, so we spent two or three hours in a Gasthaus eating our meager sandwiches and folk dancing. It was a very friendly, restful day just trying to be as Austrian as possible. It was a nice feeling to be in that Gasthaus and be thought of by all as an Austrian student.

May 1—May Day

Today was an Austrian holiday, as big as Christmas and Easter in the sense that everyone takes the day off. The streetcars stopped for half the day as well. You may have seen the papers telling of May Day celebrations all over Europe. Well, Vienna had its share of glory. Literally hundreds of thousands of Viennese took part in the parades. The Socialist party started at 7:30 this morning, parading past the City Hall with manpowered floats, German bands, placards, etc.

At 10:30, the parade was still passing the City Hall. The large City Hall square was jammed with people the whole time. At 11:00 the Communist parade took over. There was some fear that there might be clashes between the two groups but the police managed to control everything. The Communists had a platform in front of the Parliament Building next to the main street and I wormed my way to the street in front of the platform. I spent an hour or so there, going the wrong way in the parade in order to stay even with the platform.

The Communist parade was about half motored floats, the Russians having furnished the gasoline for the trucks. Many of the trucks were filled with little children under the age of six, waving flags and shouting "Freiheit und Brot" (Freedom and bread). As each group neared the stand, they raised a clenched fist and shouted "Freiheit" (Freedom). One of their big banner slogans was a demand for a national election now while the Russian are still in Austria. However, a large number of the party members are probably not wholehearted in support. No one in the party would dare renounce its program for fear he might just disappear some morning.

Crowds in front of the Rathaus (City Hall)

In the election of 1946 (a secret election), although 25% of the people belonged to the Communist Party, it pulled only 5% of the vote. The third party, the Volkspartei, the government party, did not take part in the parade. It is the Conservative Party and draws much of its strength from rural Austria. They had a quiet meeting somewhere else in Vienna. Their slogan for the day is "Enough of marching, let's sit down and talk things over." If and when another election comes off, the Volkspartei will probably lose to the Socialists. The Communists recognize this and are talking big about a union of the Socialists and the Communists so that they can be in a position to control the major party. However, the Socialists won't have any of this particularly since they see too much of Russia behind the move. At any rate, it was an interesting day for all. As one paper put it, "The Socialists had the numbers, the Communists put on the show, and onlookers had the fun." I was an onlooker.

Communist platform

Communist motorized float

May 3—A Wedding

Freddy, our young Austrian mechanic, invited me to go to his wedding today in a nearby Catholic Church. He then hesitantly asked me if I would be willing to take care of his and the bride's two-year-old son at the wedding. I was a little taken aback at the request but agreed to baby sit the boy at the wedding. The boy turned out to be very polite and was quiet throughout the long Catholic service. The wedding went off without a hitch.

May 5—Staff Meeting

At our weekly staff meeting, George read a cable he had received from Philadelphia, a cable that was hard to understand. It seems that because of the financial crisis, all units including ours in Vienna, will have to cut down on our work and numbers immediately. The financial crisis is so bad in Philadelphia that we can't even finish out our present commitments for this fiscal year even though we have already cut our costs to the bone. The cable says, "Letter follows giving details for personnel shifts." So we are all up in the air at the meaning of all this. Looks like I'll really be in the dog-house with all these repair bills I have incurred for AFSC at this moment.

Despite our uncertainty we went ahead and re-elected George Coordinator for the next four months. And, as Comfort leaves for home this week, we named Marlis as George's assistant. We are cutting back on personnel slightly as Leigh left for Innsbruck last week for good. I will now have to find more time to spend in the garage supervising the two Austrian mechanics. I think this will work out all right but the language is a bit of a problem since the older mechanic speaks with an almost unintelligible dialect. I don't, at the moment, see how I am going to get through the next month what with keeping track of everything in the garage, planning their work, keeping our two drivers busy, dealing with the Army, keeping Innsbruck and Budapest happy, etc. I wish Howard were already on his way here, but he is not due for another month.

May 6—Strike

Yesterday afternoon I went over to the ÖGB building to talk with Herr Novotny about trucking. As I arrived, I found the streets filled with several thousand Communist demonstrators. Apparently, a strike was about to be called, due to the lowered food ration enforced over the past three weeks. None of the heavy workers' cards had been honored and they were demanding that the ÖGB, as their trade union, call a national strike against the government. (This was despite the fact that the government had no more food to give.)

The labor leaders were in the building, meeting with ÖGB leaders when I arrived. The mob was in an ugly mood as I forced my way through the crowd to the door. One Austrian, seeing me in my Quaker uniform shouted, "Oh a Quaker. They are in cahoots with the conservative leaders of our Union," and he tried to turn me back.

Others saw what he was doing and said, "Oh Quakers, they are all right, they don't play one party against another," and they helped me through the crowd.

Herr Novotny spied me through the window and shouted to me to get inside. The staff inside was trying to hold the door against the mob but managed to squeeze me in.

The mob was craving action. They rammed the door and about 50 of them rushed in before the Austrian Police could form a barrier. Again my uniform caused a reaction; this time, some of the mob thought I was an American Military Policeman and reacted angrily that I was protecting the ÖGB. Fortunately, the ÖGB workers had locked all the typewriters in safes and hidden all important paperwork. The crowd began to shout, "Break the windows," but nothing was actually broken. Still, I stayed as far from the windows as possible!

Finally, the Conference ended. It was a tense moment as the crowd waited to hear the result. If the ÖGB gave in and agreed to call a strike, they would be doing so under pressure and not on the authority of a majority of all workers. If they didn't give in, well we didn't know just what would happen.

The Communist member of the ÖGB appeared on a balcony and made a 10-minute speech that was frequently interrupted by catcalls. Still, he managed to mollify the crowd. He announced that the Conference had agreed to hold an election of all workers in two or three days to see if a majority really wanted to have a national strike. He said the ÖGB would not call a strike any other way. The fact that this spokesman of theirs at the Conference was a Communist and yet had agreed to the ÖGB terms seemed to satisfy most of them. Many angry shouts were heard but the crowd gave in and gradually left.

It really hadn't been all that dangerous, but it was the angriest crowd I had ever seen. In a sense, it was just a small picture of some of the great scenes of violence that went on here during the time the Nazis were trying to get into power in Austria. You could just see those memories come flooding back in the minds of our friends in the ÖGB. Would such mob violence always have such power in Europe? Yes, as long as the whole populace is near starvation—it is on just such conditions that Communism thrives.

May 8—Rumors

Last week Vienna put on another celebration. This was a farewell to General Clark, the Commander of the US Forces in Austria. He was about the best-loved soldier of occupation in Austria. Austrian rumors say he is being sent back to the States because he spoke out too strongly for Austria at the Moscow Conference and thereby embarrassed General Marshall. Another rumor going the rounds is that 60,000 Soviet troops have come into Austria in the last week. I understand it isn't true but no one seems to know for sure. Another rumor is that the Americans are going to with-draw from Vienna and move headquarters to Salzburg, thus leaving Vienna entirely to the Russians. General Clark emphatically denied it but still there is the rumor. There is a bitter feeling about the Moscow Conference. For now it looks as if the occupation will continue indefinitely, despite the war's end promise of freedom.

May 10—Mother's Day

This afternoon Bert, George, and I went up to the restaurant on the Kahlenberg (in the Vienna woods) for a Mother's Day celebration put on by the government. They had chosen 300 mothers over the age of 70 and had invited them for an afternoon of entertainment and food. We sat more or less by mistake at the main table. The Austrian Chancellor, Leopold Figl

was at the head of the table and pre-sided over the affair. At one point he shook hands with all at the head ta-ble. We were thus similarly honored. They had speeches, a band, a magi-cian, etc. The ladies were in tears of joy at being so honored. I heard a couple of them say it was the greatest day of their lives. That did indeed seem odd to me but I suppose after having been neglected, forgotten, and oppressed for years such honor and attention did impress them. The AFSC had furnished some of the food for the occasion.

Austrian Chancellor Leopold Figl

May 12—Details

Every day something seems to go wrong that requires my at-tention. Last Wednesday the Army dumped five tons of coal for us into the wrong bin. That required nearly a day's work tracking down the right coal men to get it moved to our bin. The next day the elevator in our garage refused to operate—for the rest of the week we could not retrieve any of our supplies or an extra jeep from the basement. At least today I got someone to repair it.

One evening last week Bert and I did relax by going to an Austrian stage production, *Figaro gets a Divorce.* We actually understood it enough to enjoy it. Friday night most of us went to the Westbahnhof (West

Railway Station) to see Comfort off for Paris from where she will sail for the States in a couple of weeks. We are all going to miss her, as she has been practically the kingpin in our organization.

Today I went back to the English Teachers Club to explain the names of Austrian farm implements and their use in English. A plan to broadcast my presentation fell through. However, the English teachers seemed to appreciate it and I enjoyed it too. I think I got a bit more insight into Austrian schools.

May 13—Finances Again

Yesterday the long awaited letter came from Philadelphia telling us that there probably won't be enough money to feed anyone in Europe next winter. The AFSC budget for 1947 was $7,000,000. They are now estimating the budget for the year beginning in October 1947 as $1,200,000. It seems that contributions have practically ceased, so we must begin to plan to drastically change our whole future work in Vienna. They say that most of us will have to go home by fall. That is all right for me as I am going then anyway, but it is hard on others of our group who had not so planned.

Next winter may well be the worst yet known in Austria. No UNRRA, no AFSC, probably no better crops yet, and Austria is still under the boot of the occupation. This budget shortfall makes my current Army bill seem even more of a problem. So today, George and I went to several Army offices to try to get these Army bills reduced. The best suggestion we got was for George to write a letter to General Keyes, the replacement for General Clark. Now all we can do is wait for a reply from the General.

May 14—Accidents

Last week Marlis smashed into a truck with our best jeep, ruining the front end so that it took considerable time to get it to our garage for Freddie, our young Austrian mechanic, to repair. Of course it took me nearly all of Friday to deal with the insurance part of it. Freddie got the jeep all fixed Monday, but when he took it for a test-drive an Army truck hit him hard and threw him free of the jeep. He wasn't hurt but the jeep was ready for another repair job. By working all day yesterday and today, he got it back in good shape. It was important to get it done today, as it is one of two jeeps we are taking tomorrow for a long weekend in Prague. We have to take this jeep as our Russian permit has it listed for our trip and there wouldn't be time to do the paper work for another jeep.

A few of us decided that since Prague is only 200 miles from Vienna we should use some less busy weekend like this one to go have a look. George, Mary, Ned Weaver (a new addition to our team sometime back), Jean, Bert, two other Mennonites, and I will be going. I even got a supply of Army K rations to eat along the way.

May 18—Prague

Thursday we got away by 9:30 a.m. and with special permits, drove past the American airport at Tulln on through the Russian Zone of Austria until we reached the Czech border by noon. The Russians held us up for a long time on the Austrian side by claiming we couldn't go through the border with the 10 cans of gas we had brought. At last, they relented and we then passed through the Czech border with no difficulty. We soon stopped to eat lunch on a rolling hillside. The countryside was peaceful and looked productive. All farmers live huddled together in small towns and there are practically no houses on the individual farms. At one point we could see seven towns dotting the landscape with no houses isolated on the land. We arrived in Prague by 7:00 p.m., got settled in a hotel, had supper and it was time for bed.

Entering Russian Zone from Vienna

Friday morning several of the group wanted to go shopping so I struck off alone and just wandered around the city window shopping, looking at the people, and trying to talk a little with them. The stores certainly didn't seem like Austrian stores. Just about anything you could want was there for sale. One store I went into was almost identical with five and dime stores back home. Prices are about on a par with prewar American prices. Gasoline, however, was an exception, as it cost about a dollar a gallon. I bought gas in Vienna from the Army for $0.11 per gallon! The quality of many things didn't seem to be up to the American standard. However, the point is that these things are available.

The people looked to be in fairly good health. They, of course, all spoke Czech but practically everyone understood German. Still, you didn't dare start talking German, as it is a most hated language. You always had to ask first if they understood English and sometimes they did. At least when they saw you were not German, they would be willing to speak it.

I talked to three or four people who told me that there was no longer an acute food shortage here. There is a form of rationing but the only real rationing is the price, for although by our standards the prices were not high, they were steep by Czech standards. The average clerk or teacher gets around $35 a month whereas the prices, as I said, are on a US par. So people really have to pinch pennies.

Some of us planned to take a tour of the city after lunch but all of a sudden, the brakes on our now infamous jeep gave out. The repair job, as usual, fell to me. I spent most of the afternoon on that project. I discovered that the brake fluid had leaked out due to a loose tap. Fortunately, my German vocabulary included the word for brake fluid (Bremsflüssigkeit). After visiting a number of stores, I finally found one with brake fluid for sale. Then after a long search of our tool kit, I found the right wrench with which to bleed the brakes. We were back in business!

That evening we all had dinner with a Czech Quaker, Dr. Myslik. Afterwards we went to the home of a member of the FOR (Fellowship of Reconciliation, an international organization dedicated to resolving international disputes). He told us interesting but sad stories of life in Prague during the war. It was a rather moving session—hearing the hatreds and horrors of the war in Prague. Everything there was either black or white. There was no middle ground.

Saturday morning several of us took a conducted tour of Prague in order to see the more important buildings and castles. Most of the city was only a little damaged by the war, except the Center Square was badly hit. Most of the damage occurred between May 5 and May 8, 1945 in the so-called Revolution. The Czechs turned on their German occupiers because they thought the American Army was coming into Prague this time. However, the American Army stopped its advance for three days by agreement with the Russians, and many Czechs died in the interim. That evening we all went to the Prague Concert hall. The Prague Philharmonic played Debussy and two French composers. The audience certainly appreciated the music.

Dr. Myslik

This morning Jean and I picked up Dr. Myslik and drove some 40 miles southwest of Prague to a very famous old castle. Karlstein turned out to be some castle. Charles IV built it in the 14th century. It is one of the few castles completely standing (due partly to a rebuilding program in the 18th century). It rained most of the morning but that only added to the ghostly impression of the castle through which a professional Czech guide took us. Dr. Myslik translated his tales of the history of the castle into English. Then back to Prague for a quick lunch and we were off by 2:00. After an uneventful trip, we arrived "home" in Vienna by 8:00 this evening. I had never had a great desire to go to Prague but finding it so easy to go there and to have a group going for a long weekend made it all seem feasible. At least I now have tasted a bit of the flavor of another country.

May 19—Back to Work

At Staff Meeting this morning, we decided to release Marlis to go to Germany to set up a program for DPs. Ed Wright is also leaving temporarily for Rome to see about doing the same there. After lengthy discussion about the serious budget cut from Philadelphia, we decided to stop the feeding of the 25,000 old people and the 9,000 apprentices in Vienna. By so doing, we may have enough funds to continue with the TB cases and the ÖGB recuperation homes through the fiscal year and maybe up until Christmas.

Yesterday, Del brought a broken down jeep from the team in Budapest. Today he went on by train for a vacation in Switzerland. I took his jeep to Ordnance for a complete overhaul and then spent the rest of the day on that old Army bill at various Army offices. My visits proved futile. The deadline for paying that bill is tomorrow. Since George had not received a reply from his letter to the General, I just brashly went to the General's office and actually got an appointment for George to see him Friday. The payment can wait for the outcome of that meeting.

May 21—A Typical (?) Day

I thought I would tell you what a day's schedule now is for me. Every day is different but this may give you a slight idea of my work. Up at 7:00 and off to the garage (it is just around the block) to see that the day's work is well started there; off to breakfast at the Eiles Café, which is downtown; then to the office for paper work and coordination of transport needs for the day; by 10:00, off either on foot or by jeep to go to various offices, US Army and Austrian ones in search of some needed item; pick up the mail at the Army post office at noon; lunch back at the Eiles; a quick trip to the garage to see how things are going there; take the truckload of Volksdeutsch children to the Vienna woods (Wednesday only); help Richard, one of our Austrian drivers, load up a truck at the ÖGB for his 600-mile trip to recuperation homes tomorrow; supper with George, Bert, and Miss Baehr, another Mennonite, at the home of the Switzers, an American couple, working in Vienna for the Brethren; then a call from Richard that his loaded truck had sprung a leak in the gas tank; off to the garage to install another gas tank on that truck. This let me go home to bed at midnight.

Did I call this typical? Every day is different.

May 23—That Army Bill Again

This morning I took George to his appointment with General Keyes and ran some errands while he was there. It turned out that General Keyes was sympathetic to our problem but felt we should pick up at least part of the costs we had incurred. He and George came to a compromise and agreed to lower the bill to $2300. Then this afternoon I went to the Army Finance Office to pay the bill. It should have been an easy task but like all other dealings with the Army, there were complications. There, I ran into a new Army ruling. Every time you spend a 10-dollar bill there, you have to record its serial number and sign your name. As military money is not printed in anything larger than 10-dollar bills, I had to write down numbers and sign my name to 230 10-dollar bills. At least this Army problem is behind us now.

May 24—The Police

Early in the week, a distraught Austrian woman came to our office and was shunted to me. She claimed that one of our trucks had hit her eight-year-old daughter on May 14 causing concussion of the brain. To dramatize her story she brought in a strand of the child's hair to which was still tied a bloodstained blue ribbon. Erika, one of our Austrian secretaries, and I spent several hours trying to determine the truth of her story. We found that the Austrian police had turned in a highly undocumented report of the accident based on the statement of a sole witness. However, neither the police nor we could locate this witness. Therefore, I spent more time with our insurance agent to see to what extent we might be liable. One problem is that we cannot find any of our staff who thinks they were near the accident spot on May 14.

Last night on my way home from the Friday night folk dance group, I was picked up by an Austrian Policeman and taken to an Austrian Police Station. The charge was that I didn't have the proper title for my jeep with me. The Captain in charge, however, seemed rather embarrassed to find that his Lieutenant had brought in an American and he was most relieved when I finally discovered a slip of paper in my pocket bearing the proper license number, although the paper had no official status. This really is a sign of returning normalcy! It is the first time any of us have found an Austrian Policeman daring to take an American to court for anything.

May 25—Future Plans

I do hope I can take a little time off in the next few days in order to spend more time with Austrians. I have been too much tied down with transport. I fear there won't be much release until Howard gets here. Jean is trying to get me to help her run the work camp she has scheduled in Tyrol from July 11 to September 5. I don't think I will. That would mean no leisure moments in Vienna and no time to see other parts of Europe and England if I am to get home in early fall. Before I leave Austria, I hope to work a bit more with the ÖGB recuperation homes and in Vienna there are still a number of things I want to do, such as seeing the great Austrian musicians' homes.

Sometimes there is the temptation to postpone going home for a long time. I might even get a job here with the State Department or some similar organization and spend my life jumping from here to there. Such a life would have its fascinations and the pull in that direction is strong. I know I must resist it, for I know it would not prove to be a satisfactory existence. There is a continual void in that future, even with the busy life here now. It is just that there a number of things I dread to return to now. I will be oppressed by some of the narrowness of home in America. I will be oppressed by the intense desire for continuation of the status quo there. I must go back nonetheless. The good life I speak of here is not a genuine thing. Being a foreigner in a position of power (food is power) gives one a false sense of values. Life in Europe seems fascinating. Yet it would not be, were I to turn to living as the Europeans do. I must dig in somewhere in America and New Vienna, Ohio or at least the Middle West can be that place. Perhaps there that longing, for I know not what, can be satisfied. "I have traveled to the ends of the earth in search of treasure—but can only find it in my own back yard" might describe it.

June 3—Always Busy

There never seems to be a dull moment. A jeep wanted here; a jeep wanted there; a truck needed to haul beds for the ÖGB; some dissatisfaction with the Austrian drivers; Leigh's friend, Steffy, left her car in our garage too long; attempts to trace details of the accident with the Austrian girl; and continued problems with the Army. The latest Army problem was over our use of Army phone lines. On a call I was making to Paris, I was interrupted by the Army operator and told we were no longer authorized to use Army lines. In fact, he said our authorization had ended on May 8 and I had used them several times since then not knowing I wasn't supposed to. Del, who had come from Budapest for parts, had called Budapest, Bert had called Basel and I had talked with Paris, Ludwigshafen, Regensburg, and Innsbruck. Today I tried to find out more about this new ruling. It turns out that if we call in a certain way (proper sequence) we call still use the lines. That certainly is better than taking the problem to higher authorities.

Grit Elsner

Every morning I feel just like I used to before going to an exam at college. Only here it is every day. But I love it. I am beginning to find time to have a bit of social life. Sunday evening I took Grit Elsner, an Austrian girl in our Friday night group, to see Offenbach's opera, *Orpheus in the Underworld*. It turned out to be more of an operetta than an opera and we both thoroughly enjoyed it. She told me that during the intensive fighting as the Russians invaded Vienna she had hidden for nine days in a cellar and even then was slightly injured by falling debris.

June 4—Another Movie

Today Del and I loaded his truck with all the parts he needed to take back to Budapest. We finished about 6:00 and felt like celebrating. We called the Swedish "Save the Children" group and got a couple of dates. He knew a Swedish girl there a bit and I took a Canadian girl who also works there. We went to a movie, *It's a Wonderful Life*, with James Stewart. It turned out to be the first American movie I have seen in Europe that I really enjoyed. It was so good it almost made me homesick.

June 5—Russian Contact

This morning before getting Del off for Budapest, I took him downtown on an errand. As I waited for him in the jeep I noticed a Russian soldier driving a jeep slowly past me and eyeing me as he went. In a few minutes he returned and stopped. Hesitantly he asked me if I could speak German. Finding that I could he explained that he was badly in need of a timing chain for his other jeep but could not get one through his Russian channels. Was there any possibility I could get one for him? I suppose, usually, I would have turned him down, but here was my first chance of doing something for a Russian so I said that maybe I could help him. I had him follow me to our office where I alerted George and had him come with me. I knew he would have his camera with him and true to form, he got some pictures of the deal. We drove to Ordnance where I had the Russian park a block away. I easily obtained the chain and gave it to the beaming Russian. He then paid me for the chain and was amazed at the low price I charged him. I charged him in Austrian schillings at the official exchange rate whereas he wanted to pay me in the black market rate. This Russian was very friendly and most appreciative. I suppose I can now be accused of arming the enemy for the next war!

June 8—Black Market

Last night I took the Austrian girl with whom I had gone to that Ball last winter to supper. I had not called her since that Ball, but by now I had forgotten what a rotten time I had had. I won't forget again. She spent most of the evening pouting because I hadn't called her since then!

After supper she asked if I would take her to a warehouse to get some meat for her uncle's restaurant. The warehouse proved to be in the Russian Sector. The meat turned out to be a whole quarter of beef, which we managed to load into the jeep and take to her uncle's restaurant in the center of Vienna. It was my first visit to a real black market restaurant. The furniture was all new mahogany. Fancy mirrors and chandeliers adorned the place. Good meals were being served, ration-free. The only catch was that the prices were in the 150-shilling ($15) range.

This was the first time that any of us had known that it was possible to buy food in Vienna ration-free. I asked her if it wasn't just plain black market but she sort of shrugged that off and said it was just good business to give people of discretion what they wanted and could pay for. There are precious few people in Austria who could pay for that sort of thing when a high salary is 400 schillings a month. As I implied before, this will be my last date with this girl.

June 9—Sunday Activities

Sunday afternoon I talked again with Paris about the imminent Innsbruck closure. Near the end of the conversation I had a curt interruption from an Army operator who ordered me not to use Army lines any more. Oh, my, not again, I thought. At least I found out that Howard has all his papers and is ready to leave Paris for Vienna as soon as the French railway strike is over. After that, Ed and I went to the Vienna Quaker Meeting that meets every other week at 4:00 in the afternoon. It was not a particularly friendly group. I had not been there for some time as they often meet in different homes, often in the Russian Zone, where we can't go. Some time ago, Ed had applied for a Russian permit to go to an all day conference of Viennese Quakers meeting in the Russian Zone. They turned him down.

June 12—Always the Army

Two Army officers turned up at the garage this morning while I was there. They had come to arrange with us to turn over our garage to them. This game has been going on for months. This afternoon I followed up on it and found out they had come this morning due to a bookkeeping mistake! So we are safe from the Army for another unknown period. Then I did get some good news from the Army. I went to the military head of Army telephones and actually got our telephone problem straightened out. We are now authorized to use military lines in Europe at no cost! To add to the confusion at the garage this morning while the officers were there Leigh and Irwin showed up from Innsbruck looking for drums in which to haul gasoline to Innsbruck. What a madhouse I live in.

June 17—Musicians Tour, Tires, Frederick

At last on Saturday I felt I had time to take the long delayed musicians' tour. I finally arranged a tour for Irwin and me with the Red Cross, which runs a bus tour of musicians' homes every Saturday. After making the arrangements, I learned that last week the Army cut off some of the supply of gas for the Red Cross, so the Red Cross cancelled the bus for the tour. However, since only an Army girl, Irwin and I showed up for the cancelled tour, we talked the Austrian guide into going with us in our jeep. In one sense it wasn't particularly interesting. We just kept going to various houses where Mozart, Schubert, and Beethoven had slept, houses, which I have passed a hundred times without knowing who had slept there! However, I guess some of my mother did creep into me and I found myself beginning to enjoy the tour with some enthusiasm. We lingered in the house where Schubert was born. Then we went to Heiligenstadt (a suburb of Vienna) and visited three houses where Beethoven had lived. We were told that he had lived in 27 different homes in Vienna during his lifetime. These three homes were just like the other houses in the area and are now occupied by the present day poorer classes of Viennese. The only distinguishing mark was that on each house was a plaque erected by the city some twenty years ago commemorating the spot. At times one could almost feel like one was back in those days of yore. We visited the church where Schubert attended as a youth.

We then went into the inner city and went inside the ruined State Opera House. The story goes that American bombers hit the city in the very last days of the War in the belief that it was the Nazi headquarters. Finally, we went to the Central Cemetery where the musicians are buried side by side, Beethoven, Schubert, Mozart, Brahms, and other lesser-known musicians.

Yesterday I went back to Ordnance to try to close a deal to buy 15 truck tires. I had gone there Friday on the rumor that a new shipment of tires had arrived in Vienna but the Lieutenant in charge of them had not been in that day. While the Lieutenant agreed to sell me eight tires, I first had to go the Community Sales Office to get an authorization for the tires and then go back to Ordnance to actually get the tires.

When I went to the ÖGB to talk over transport plans I ran into another problem. Frederick, one of our Austrian drivers who had been hauling food to the ÖGB recuperation homes, was reported drunk and had been passing food out of his truck to friends in a bar. He arrived back in Vienna with a good alibi but we have a police report on his escapades. Guess we will have to let him go and I will have to find a new driver.

June 24—Howard Arrives, Vacation Plans, A Refugee

Friday morning I got up early to meet Howard, who was scheduled to arrive from Paris at the Westbahnhof. No Howard could I find until I arrived at the office at 9:00—there he was! He had come in at midnight with only George's phone number, but George was out of town. He hunted up an Army billet and spent the night there! My replacement was here! I could leave. Well it isn't that simple but I did have that feeling.

In fact, life is much easier now—just his presence here and the knowledge that all the work is not on my shoulders. I spent Friday and the whole weekend getting Howard documented and acclimated to Vienna. It turned out to be a very restful weekend even with the arrival from Innsbruck of Leigh for the last time before he goes home. He brought a truck from Innsbruck, as the unit there will be closing soon.

I feel a pang of regret to think that my days here are numbered. Today, Howard and I spent most of our time in the garage getting him acquainted with everything there. At noon, Del arrived again from Budapest to get a load of gasoline and spare parts. Then this evening I took Howard to an orientation meeting for all Austrians who are going to the work camp that Jean is going to lead at Brixlegg near Innsbruck later this summer. He is getting acquainted rapidly!

Today a German refugee showed up at our office seeking help to get to Germany. At the end of the war he was stranded in Romania and managed to get out on May 25. Since then he has been walking and getting across borders illegally as he has no papers. He seemed to be a most worthy chap so we agreed to keep him a few days in our apartment until something can be worked out to help him travel further.

Del, Bert, George, and I are talking about taking a trip to Sweden, leaving here about July 15. This would be my scheduled vacation. After the trip I would come back to Austria to spend a couple of weeks at the work camp, a few days in Vienna and then head for Switzerland, England, and then home. It is all very tentative yet depending on a number of factors to be cleared up.

July 1—Vacation Decision

This past week has been hectic trying to decide on vacation plans. Last week we received a request to transport 10 Austrian students to a month's conference beginning on July 3 in Copenhagen. Owen, from Innsbruck, had been planning to go to Copenhagen about July 1 to look into the possibility of going to an agricultural school. He had planned to go by train but decided to help us by driving a truck with the 10 Austrian students instead. He could then drive the truck back to Brixlegg after he studies the agricultural school possibilities. He arrived in Vienna Saturday to be available to go from here.

George and I decided Sunday to go to Scandinavia in the truck with him and the students for several reasons. First, it would be cheaper than the train. Second, we would much prefer to drive through Germany than to rush through on a train. Third, Howard has been here a week and has gotten the rudiments of my job down pat. He really was not doing much, since as long as I was around everyone kept coming to me with transport worries. Finally, Marlis will be here for another three weeks now and George can get away better while she is still here.

Bert and Del had planned to go with us but are now out of the picture. Del just can't leave this soon, and Bert left last week for a private Scandinavian trip with Mary. (I wouldn't be surprised to hear of an engagement when they return!) Yesterday morning in Staff Meeting George and I announced our intentions of leaving tomorrow with the students and Owen.

After we got Staff approval, I called the leader of the Austrian students to confirm our travel with them. I was told that the trip was off as they had not been able to get Danish visas and had been so informed just a few minutes earlier. Staff then decided that George, Owen, and I should take a jeep and proceed with our trip. It is against our policy to take jeeps on vacation jaunts across Europe and while I was against it, Staff decided that we owed Owen something for his coming here from Innsbruck and delaying his trip.

Another reason for our going ahead was that since two Danish students are going to the work camp in Brixlegg Owen could transport them in the jeep from Copenhagen to Brixlegg. The final clincher for taking a jeep was that it would save the AFSC about a hundred dollars over going by train. So, today I feverishly went about getting Danish and Dutch visas, German transit permits, and Russian exit permits out of Vienna, not to speak of getting the jeep ready and giving Howard last minute pointers on transport problems here. Now we are packed and will leave tomorrow, July 2.

Northern European Trip

July 1947

July 2—Into Germany

Owen, George, the German refugee, and I left Vienna about 8:30 a.m. and traveled through the Russian Zone without incident. In fact, we managed to talk the Russian control into letting our refugee through! We dropped him in Linz as he felt he could get into Germany on his own better than with us. We then drove up the Danube valley. It was a very scenic drive and one I had never taken before. We drove into Germany as far as Passau where we managed to talk the manager of an officers' hotel into putting us up for the night. At supper we ran into a CIC (Army Counter Intelligence Corps) man who was taking the lead in the town in forming boy's clubs for German youth. It seems that from all the occupation troops in Passau he was the only one who was willing to be bothered with associating with Germans. We met several of the boys. One of them showed us around the town and you could see he thought the world of our CIC friend. This man was the only representative of America in Passau who was doing anything to show these German boys what American democracy means. And he was a Jew!

Passau itself is a most interesting town at the junction of three rivers. It sits on a high plateau and there seemed to be old castles everywhere. We walked around a lot and talked with several local people. The town is near the junction of Germany, Austria, and Czechoslovakia. Everyone we talked with thought that the lowest people on earth were Czechs and Austrians. The hatreds engendered by war seem to go on in a never-ending cycle.

July 3—More of Germany

We bounced along over rough roads into Regensburg where we stopped long enough to take a few pictures and eat lunch. Then by the middle of the afternoon, we arrived in Nürnberg. I thought I had seen destruction before but Nürnberg topped the list. It had been a top example of a medieval city. It used to have a unique center. We tried to drive through it but found it practically impossible to do. One lone street had been partially cleared of rubble. The whole inner city was just impossible and not a thing had been done yet toward clearing it. I just can't describe it. American bombers had wiped it out but had done little damage to the industrial area on the edge of the city!

Then as the weather cleared up, we drove on to Würzburg where we ate supper in a beautiful officers' R&R center. Since we hadn't made many miles we drove on into the gathering dusk and arrived in Frankfurt in the dark. Frankfurt is the headquarters of the American occupation, so we absolutely could find no rooms. We pushed on another 15 miles to a little town called Höchst where by midnight we managed to get rooms. Our whole trip is being made more difficult by the fact that in Austria since July 1, the Army will no longer issue travel orders. Without them you are not entitled to any Army privileges! We just had to talk our way in.

Nürnberg destruction

July 4—The Rhine, A German Quaker

Today turned out to be a beautiful day. As far as scenery goes, I would say this was the high point of our trip so far. We drove over the Rhine, into the French Zone of occupation and on through Mainz. Then all morning we drove down the Rhine hugging its left bank. This is the world famous Rhine journey with high overhanging bluffs, terraced farming, and many castles and ruins of castles. The road played hide and seek with a railroad for about 100 miles, crossing it every five miles or so! We got caught early in the day at one crossing by a long freight train. Then we would speed up to arrive at the next crossing only to find them shutting the gates for a 10 minute wait for that train to come and pass. We did that for eleven crossings and were never able to get across the tracks first.

At noon, we arrived in Koblenz where there is an AFSC unit. After considerable searching we managed to find the group and had an enjoyable two-hour "talkfest" with them. They were taking the day off as they reminded us that this was July 4. We ate lunch with them in the French Army mess across the Rhine, got some gasoline from them, and by mid afternoon were on our way further down the Rhine. The terrain leveled out gradually and by evening, we had arrived in level country from where the Rhine goes on to the sea in level repose via Holland. Arriving in Cologne we managed to find the British Quaker office where we got instructions on where we might stay and eat this evening. Cologne is in the British zone so we were quite surprised to find the Army transit hotel and restaurant being run by Belgian soldiers! It seems that this area of Germany near Belgium, although a British zone, is operated by Belgian troops of occupation. However, the British foot the bill.

Rhine Bridge at Cologne

After supper I drove around the city and finally found the home of Asta Brügelman, a German Quaker. Aunt Elsie had urged me to visit her if I were ever in Cologne. She turned out to be a most gracious hostess and I spent over three hours with her. The front of her house appeared ruined beyond repair, while there were a number of rooms in the rear that were in good shape. She hastened to point out that she and her family were not living like typical Germans at all but that they were much better off than the average. She had unbounded enthusiasm for her work. She is head of the German Fellowship of Reconciliation (FOR). However, at the moment, her energies are turned more toward a movement in Germany for women against war. She reminded me a good bit of Aunt Elsie in her enthusiasm and energy for her work and I could indeed see how they have become such good friends. She seems to think that the greatest need now is for Germans to admit their guilt and renounce war. This would put them in the center of the East-West tug of war and perhaps be a means for bringing America and Russia together. She also is carrying on her own relief program, or rather the FOR program. She has a storeroom nearly filled with Swedish shoes bought with money contributed by the FOR in the States. She gives out the shoes to each local FOR group in proportion to their numbers. According to AFSC guidelines, this was not good relief procedure. The AFSC would not countenance giving relief to members of a single group. Perhaps AFSC standards aren't always the best in all circumstances.

I left her home by 11:00 p.m. and drove back through the center of the city to our hotel. This center is just as bad as Nürnberg only larger. This was the first time I was frightened in Germany, driving through that area at night. It was completely black, the headlights picked out rubble upon rubble and people staring stupidly at me. It was really ghoulish. By day we had visited the area and decided that Cologne was the worst we had seen.

July 6—Northern Germany

Yesterday we crossed the Rhine again and headed northeast intent on getting some miles behind us on our way to Denmark. It was slow driving on a most hazardous winding road. We passed through the Ruhr district at last and by noon were on one of the good superhighways of Germany. Here we were able to make good time. We stopped for a spot of tea at a British wayside inn. The British always seem to put a lot of milk in their tea!

We began to notice a change in the farming scene. Cows seemed to be the main business and generally, they were Holsteins. For the first time in Germany, we began to notice that each farm was neatly surrounded by fences. In the south, fences are unknown and they are not common in Austria. The land was gently rolling and the villages with their German red tile roofs looked most picturesque—that is, those that had not been damaged. We regretted that we were so early in the season, as the wheat was just beginning to ripen and was not yet ready for harvest.

By evening we came to the Hannover railroad station and found the place swarming with disconsolate looking Germans. Hannover is the mouth of the funnel out of the Russian zone and Berlin. Berlin is some 150 to 200 miles away. These Germans were, in a sense, refugees, people moving west and trying to get out of the Russian zone. They had finally succeeded but now had no idea where to go or what to do. Estimates are that some 2000 people a day are passing out of the Russian zone. Now they are in Hannover with poor clothes, no food, and no place to go. The city and the government are doing all they can to move the people on to less congested areas. It was a pitiful scene. Black market was rampant. Everything was offered for the gold of the land—cigarettes. One chap came up with a pair of silk hose, which he wanted to trade for cigarettes. Officially the mark

(German currency) is valued at ten to one dollar. One cigarette is worth six to seven marks! In Austria it is worth only one schilling. Thus you can see how worthless a mark is.

This morning, after breakfast, we drove on through and out of Hannover. We noted its destruction but felt it was not nearly as bad as Cologne. We stopped at a British gas station and managed to talk our way into a free tank of gas for the second time. We had no British coupons and were not entitled to draw any British gas. However, the word "Quaker" works wonders with British soldiers and we received over 40 free gallons from the British by the time we reached Denmark. The British are really good chaps. One could never do that in the American zone without proper credentials.

We stopped for a time in Hamburg to see the docks. I had always heard that there was great destruction there but we just didn't see it. It is bad, yes, but not as bad as Vienna and far better than Cologne. On north we went to Kiel, where we temporarily got lost when we got on the wrong side of the Kiel Canal. We finally righted ourselves and ended up by evening at the border town of Flensburg, five miles from the Danish border. We spent a comfortable night in a British hotel and accidentally ran into four Quakers, three British, and one American. I had known the American a bit at Pendle Hill. They are working in Schleswig, some thirty miles to the south. One of the British chaps turned out to be the same fellow I had spent a couple of hours talking with in Ortona in Italy last March when I visited Lee there.

July 7—Denmark At Last

At the Danish border we found the customs to be as bad as elsewhere. It took us over two hours to work our way through. The first control was the British as we left Germany. Then half a mile further was the Danish control. We had to exchange money, declare all other money, insure the jeep, get food ration stamps, and get gas coupons. At last, we were in Denmark. And what a difference we saw from Germany. The landscape was about the same, the cows were about the same, but the buildings were all painted and in good repair. The people seemed different. In the first place, we saw many who are really fat, an unknown sight in Germany or Austria. And they were so friendly. We met hundreds of people on bicycles and everyone waved and shouted greetings to us. It was unbelievable how friendly they were to three strangers in a jeep.

By noon we reached Kolding where we had lunch, and what a lunch. We each had a large platter of steak smothered with eggs and a quart of milk, and this cost us $1.25. The storefronts indicated an unbelievable amount of goods for sale. At least it seemed that way compared to Austria and Germany.

We drove over a huge bridge to the island of Fyn and finally arrived at the port of Nyborg where we drove onto a large ferryboat and in an hour and a half, we were on the island of Sjaelland. By 6:00, we found ourselves driving into the heart of Copenhagen. We made immediately for the Danish Quaker office for that was where Owen was to pick up the two Danes to return to Brixlegg. We were greeted by the leading Danish Quaker, Elise Thompsen, and were established for the night. For some reason I had lost my appetite so the other chaps got a bite to eat without me. In the middle of the night I woke up rather nauseated and soon the steak I had eaten at noon and I parted company.

July 9—Copenhagen

Yesterday I had rather a rough day, as I could not eat a thing. However, I did take a tour with George to Helsingor where we went through the Kroneburg castle. This castle was supposed to have been the castle that inspired Shakespeare to write Hamlet. It is always referred to as Hamlet's castle. In fact, in the courtyard a stage was being erected for a presentation of Hamlet in a couple of nights. This castle may have inspired Shakespeare, but only in his dreams. History tells us that Shakespeare probably was never in Denmark. This castle seems to be very dear to the hearts of the Danes. We were then taken on a tour of a genuine smorgasbord lunch and I couldn't eat a bite! When we got back to Copenhagen, I went right to bed for the rest of the day. George and Owen went to the Tivoli, a very famous playground and park, perhaps something like Coney Island.

Since I felt much better today, I went with Owen on his visit to the Agricultural College of the University of Copenhagen. He had wanted to go to Iowa State College this fall but heard that they were full. He thought that since he was in Europe he should investigate the possibility of enrolling here in Copenhagen. We first talked to two Ag professors, one the head of the dairy husbandry and the other of swine breeding. Only one spoke English but the other at least spoke German. Then an assistant took us on a tour of the College. Only a few students were here as this is summer vacation. We saw fertilizer experiments with alfalfa, clover, and other legumes, moisture movement in soil experiments, and other Agronomy experiments. We then visited the college dairy and the Ag Engineering department. All looked modern except for the Ag Engineering department where there were only a few binders such as you might have seen twenty years ago at some State Fair in the US. On the campus we saw many mounds that had been built as air raid shelters. There seems to have been very little destruction in

Denmark. Nearly everyone we talked to roundly hated the Germans but admitted that for an occupied country Denmark had suffered relatively little. The recovery of the country to a foreigner's eye seemed nothing short of remarkable. After supper at the Quaker Center we took a boat ride through the city.

July 13—Sweden

Since Owen is heading back to Brixlegg with the jeep, George and I will spend the rest of our trip on trains. Thursday morning I met George at the station where we tried to buy tickets to Stockholm. However, since the Danish currency is not as good as the Swedish currency we could only buy tickets to the border. We rode the train the three miles to the port and then spent an hour and a half getting through Danish customs. Then, after an hour and a half boat ride, we arrived in Sweden at the town of Malmö. We thought we had time to make the train to Stockholm, but little did we know.

We had not counted on the Swedish customs. This time they were thorough and called me on the carton of cigarettes I had brought. (Why had I brought them? I don't rightly know except for the fact that I remembered how handy they had been one night in Venice last spring). The Swedes have a rule that you are not allowed to import more than 50 cigarettes without paying a high duty of the equivalent of one dollar per pack. George was also caught by this rule as he had brought cigarettes to smoke. Customs would only accept Swedish money of which we had none as yet. We were told to check our luggage, walk up town to a bank, get money, come back, and pay our fee. I just was not interested. I was too mad to give those cigarettes to the customs officials, so I said I was going to throw them into the ocean and started to do so. That got everyone's attention. Then George offered to give the official one pack if he would let us through with the others. That offer plus my threat to throw them all into the sea did the trick. We had successfully bribed our way through Swedish customs and I am almost sorry to say it worked.

We then hurried for the local bus that took us to the train station. We arrived there with just a few minutes to spare until the next train to Stockholm. Still we had no Swedish money and no train tickets. I got in a long line for the ticket window and George ran into town to find a bank to change a traveler's check. At that point, the train conductor came along asking who was going to Stockholm. When I said yes, he took me to the front of the line at the ticket window as the others were buying tickets for local trains. I cashed a traveler's check on the spot, got the tickets, and was ready to catch the train thanks to the conductor. Where was George? The conductor urged me to hurry and I couldn't get him to understand I had a friend. Finally, he gave up in disgust and said he couldn't hold the train any longer. I ran out into the town hunting George. It was pouring rain but I ran on and found him in the first bank three blocks away. We ran back to the station to see the last car of the train disappearing in the distance! However, we found that there was another train in three hours so decided to check our bags and see Malmö. We waited in line exactly one hour and four minutes to get our bags checked. So we didn't see much of Malmö—just enough time to get some lunch and come back to stand in line half an hour to get our bags out of storage. At last, we were on the Stockholm-bound train.

The scenery was not spectacular. At first it was just like Denmark—gently rolling with well cared for land. Gradually the farmland began to diminish and woods took its place with trees and rocks. Occasionally lakes appeared between wooded areas and I could imagine being in Maine. We were riding third class but the car and the seats were as good as any first class section I had seen elsewhere in Europe. We had a good supper in the diner car and realized that although the train was moving as fast as any I had ever ridden in, it was very smooth. We found few people with whom to talk, as most did not speak English. Danish too had not been understandable but the Danish written language looked a good bit like a combination of English and German. Swedish, although very similar to Danish, was unintelligible to us.

At last about 9:00 p.m. we pulled into Stockholm where, we had been warned, it would be impossible to find rooms. We went across the street from the station and into a small hotel and got rooms on the spot. Later other Swedes told us we had been exceedingly fortunate. We took a brief walk up the street. It was unlike anything I have seen in Europe. Neon lights were all over the place but in an orderly array. It was New York at night without all the glaring contrasts. On every corner was a hot dog stand—hot dogs without bread, but good.

Friday we found a Howard Johnson-like place for breakfast, where we have eaten every morning as they have eggs and milk. Then a leisurely walk across town to the address of the AFSC office, where we spent two hours talking with Carl Levine and his wife about Stockholm. I left George and went to the office of Swedish Save the Children, for I had the name of one of the girls who works there. She turned out to be a most charming Swede who spoke acceptable English. We made an arrangement whereby that evening we were to get together. After lunch George and I took two city tours, one by bus and one by boat. Stockholm is like no other city I have ever seen. There are no slums here. Everything looks modern and utilitarian. Everyone looks healthy.

The people were not overly friendly. Everyone seemed to be going about his or her private business and everyone else could go to blazes. Three or four times I got bumped off the sidewalk by Swedes who didn't appear to even see me. In Denmark everyone had been so happy to help a poor stranger, but not so in Sweden. It was practically impossible to strike up an acquaintance here. I was just fortunate in having the name and address of this girl. After a delicious supper with George, which cost us each $1.75 and used up our entire meat ration coupons, I hurried to meet her. We went out to the City Park that is a combination zoo, park, and open-air concert area. It was a beautiful place where the evening sunshine on the palisades across the river reflected golden gleams. We listened first to a band playing the apparent favorite, semi-military band music. Then we listened for a time to a quartet singing popular songs, too many of which were American. We walked around the zoo and stumbled onto a folk dance. There were around 500 young Swedes there in native costume doing folk dancing to a caller with an accordion. It is a weekly affair to which many people come. My "date" did not care for it particularly. Otherwise I would have joined the group.

It turned out that this girl, Margaretta Bjorkman, was not really a Swede at all but had only come to Sweden in 1944 from her home in Finland. So from talking with her I learned more about life in Finland than in Sweden! At 10:00, we went to the Academy of Arts for a Chamber Music concert but since we arrived so late we had to sit on the steps. Most of the music was Swedish but at least one piece was Bach. We ran into her roommate who is also Finnish. After the music I walked them both home and learned more about life in both Sweden and Finland.

Yesterday I spent all morning on red tape, something I am well used to by now. First, I had to go through a line and fill out forms only in Swedish in order to get more meat coupons, then to the Norwegian Embassy for Norwegian visas. Because of the housing shortage in Oslo, we couldn't get visas without a prearranged housing address there. Off I went to the AFSC office for help. Someone there had the name and address of a Norwegian family in Oslo, and with this name I was able to get visas on the possibility of our staying with this family in Oslo.

Then I spent the rest of the morning on a rather interesting expedition. Internationally Sweden is one of the leaders of the co-op movement. I went to the co-op office and went from office to office until I found an official ready and willing to give me some of the story of Swedish co-ops as well as some literature on them. The consumers' co-op includes over a third of all consumers' goods in Sweden. The producers' co-op is also rather strong. I had lunch with Margaretta after which we spent the afternoon wandering the streets of Stockholm. She filled me in more on life here.

This morning George and I went to what we thought was a Catholic Church, but George, a Catholic himself, could see no signs that it was Catholic. It appeared to be more like a Lutheran Church. We never did find out for sure. This evening we had supper with the Levines. At 10:00, we boarded a train for Oslo. Again, it was a good train even though we were in third class. As night gradually came on, we realized how short the nights are. It never did get completely dark. The sun disappeared about 10:00. At midnight it was darkest but still a warm glow in the sky. At a little past 2:00 the sun appeared again. Margaretta had told me that in Stockholm on June 21 the sun was gone for only two hours!

July 16—Norway

After arriving in Oslo Monday at 9:00 a.m., we spent two hours hunting for a room. We finally found one in a run down water front hotel that had no charm but at least it had a bed. The next problem was food. We walked down the main street for an hour an a half until we found one restaurant where all they had were so called sandwiches, just one piece of bread with fish on top.

We were so tired we decided to go back to the hotel and take a nap before taking a city tour. We slept until three, so we were too late for any tours. Instead, we took a bus to the Peoples' Museum, which consisted of a large outdoor collection of three and four hundred year old Norwegian homes. In a nearby museum we saw three Viking ships built about 800. They seemed to be only overgrown bathtubs and I don't see how they ever floated across the Atlantic. Then back we went to our grand hotel for dinner, which turned out to be very good for $1.75.

Tuesday we took our anticipated bus tour of Oslo. Somehow, the city didn't impress us as much as Stockholm had. Copenhagen has about one million residents, Stockholm about 600,000 and Oslo about 250,000. Copenhagen seemed big and sprawling; Stockholm, clean and utilitarian and Oslo seemed like a frontier city. Our tour went up into the hills around Oslo and passed a very famous ski jump. We stopped in several museums, one of which contained Amundsen's ship. After lunch we boarded a boat about the size of the Island Queen in Cincinnati and headed south toward the sea. We had planned to sail all afternoon through the good scenery and spend the night in Tonsburg. We got acquainted with a young Norwegian sailor who suggested we get off one stop before Tonsburg at a hidden resort. His friend met us with a motorboat and took us the three miles up an inlet to a hotel. We were the only Americans who had been there this summer and we found the hotel very pleasing. After supper we lolled around the dock talking to the fishermen and sailors in English and German. About

10:00, we went to a dance hall that was filled to capacity. Fellows and girls go separately or together, as they like.

Today we were up at 6:30 a.m. to catch the boat back to Oslo. We could rouse no one about the place to pay our bill so just left an estimate. Hope they found it! In the afternoon as we were going back to our hotel to get ready to leave, a 50-year-old woman came up to us, said she saw we were Quakers, and asked if we would listen to her story. We of course agreed and took her to supper and talked with her up until the last minute before our train was to leave Oslo. She had been in prison until last month as a Nazi and had only just been released on parole. She said she was still a Nazi and would always be, but not in the German sense, rather in the Quaker sense! Figure that one out if you can. At any rate, her story was of brutality and cruelty in this prison to the some 60,000 Norwegians who had been Nazi party members. Her story sounded just as bad as any I had ever heard against the Nazis during the war. The Norwegian government is to blame for it all according to her. All she wanted was for someone to investigate these prisons and publish the truth. Perhaps then the government would allow food to be sent to these prisoners. Her story went on and on. Part of the trouble, she said, was that many of the officials in the government had been helping the Nazis during the war but had managed to save themselves in the change, and were now persecuting the Nazis unbearably. The woman was in a state of near hysteria. She says every movement is watched and that the government will know tomorrow that she has talked to foreigners and she may go back to prison for it. What could we do? We promised to report it to the AFSC Commissioners in Paris.

July 17—Copenhagen Stopover

It seems all we do on this trip is go through customs. After getting on the train last night in Oslo, we went through the Norwegian customs. Then in half an hour we went through Swedish customs. We were in a third class sleeper so we got some sleep. Then this morning in Helsingborg, we again went through Swedish customs. Then the train was driven on a ferryboat and we were soon in Denmark at Helsingor for another set of customs. In Copenhagen we were supposed to change trains after a half an hour lay over. I hurried upstairs, bought some milk and sandwiches, and went back to the train to find that we had been misinformed. Our train did not leave at 10:00 in the morning but at 11:00 at night, so we must spend the day again in Copenhagen. And we had only eight kronen between us. We managed to sell two packs of cigarettes at the standard rate of $0.40 per pack in order to have a little more Danish money. We took in a movie, at 4:00 went to a dairy store, and bought four quarts of milk, a loaf of bread and plenty of butter.

All of it cost two kronen, or $0.50. It was the best meal we have had! Finally, we went back to the Quaker office where preparations were on for a farewell party this evening for Elise who is sailing for the States next week to go to the Third FWCC Committee Meeting in Richmond, Indiana. It will be the first time for her in the States and she was very excited. At any rate we got in on the little party, most of which was in Danish, but she made a point of making us feel at home. At last, we were off to the train and were able to say farewell to Copenhagen.

July 21—Holland

Friday morning our train brought us to the Danish-German frontier where we stopped an hour for customs. Then five miles further we went through British customs putting us back into Germany. We rode all day, first through Hamburg, and then through Bremen. There was a Dutch diner on the train but they would take only hard currency and all we had were travelers' checks. Finally, a US Captain took pity on us and gave us 15 Danish kronen, which bought us a fair lunch. We were eating as we pulled into the station in Bremen. Out the window we saw hordes of hungry Germans. Their watching us eat made us feel bad. Mid afternoon brought us to the Dutch border where we spent more time going first through the British customs and then through the Dutch customs. Our ride on into Amsterdam was not spectacular. The country was very level and looked like land between Martinsville and Blanchester, Ohio. I didn't see a single windmill.

Saturday morning we spent getting a bit oriented in Amsterdam, arranging for tours, and arranging for a train back to Germany. In the afternoon we took a boat trip through the city. Many of the streets are water, something like Venice, although not so picturesque and not so much water. Last evening we ran into a large parade, which was demonstrating for official action against the dictator in Spain. The parade was communist controlled. I thought it was indicative of the state of affairs in Holland that the only thing the communists could think of to parade about was something in far off Spain—nothing in Holland.

Yesterday we spent the whole day on a tour up the Ijssel Sea. It used to be called the Zeider Sea. We visited two picturesque towns, Volendam and Marken. Only in these two towns did I see the old Dutch costumes and homes. Even there I saw only one windmill. In Amsterdam I was told, most people in Holland dress like they do in New York. Only in these two little towns do they preserve the old ways. I have a suspicion they do so mostly for the sake of the tourist trade. Last evening we took a walking tour through Amsterdam and found it to be the rawest city we had been in.

I would say it was somewhat like Chester, Pa. Every other store was a bar for sailors and the crowds seemed rough and ready. Amsterdam seems like the typical idea of a US sailor city.

Today we took a bus tour, which lasted most of the day. The guide spent too much time pointing out how the Dutch had been slaughtered by the Germans and how hateful the Germans are. By this time we were almost out of Dutch money so bought milk and sandwiches for supper. We caught the night train for Frankfurt. But guess what? We still had two sets of customs officials to go through. This make 16 times we have gone through customs on this trip.

July 23—Back Home (Vienna)

After a sleepless night from Holland, we arrived yesterday in Frankfurt. We immediately caught a military train to Munich. Last night at 7:00, we took another military train to Vienna. After the train was under way, we were told we were not authorized to be on the train. So in Salzburg we had to get off. However, we were fortunate to be there at the right time to catch the civilian Arlberg Express. This put us back in Vienna this morning just three weeks to the day since we left. It has been too hurried a trip. We tried to do too much, but maybe that is the best way to get a bird's eye view of those countries. And the trip was not expensive. I spent a total of $120 of which $75 was paid by AFSC. While we were traveling about the only news we heard was the potential of a possible Marshall Plan. In all four countries we visited, there was a lot of enthusiasm about it. The big question is, will Congress pass it? It seems to be billed as the last great hope for Europe. However, we have the feeling that these four countries have the least need of any help. In Sweden, for example, they already seem to have the good things of life—milk, nylons, etc. Denmark, Norway, and Holland seem to be making rapid strides toward recovery from the war years.

Final Weeks in Austria

August to September, 1947

August 5—Quick Trip to Switzerland

Upon my arrival in Vienna on July 23, I found myself involved in all kinds of details of my old job. The first thing I discovered was a pleasant surprise. That Austrian girl with the concussion supposedly caused by one of our jeeps is not only recovering nicely but the police have now determined that it was not our jeep that struck her! Howard and Marlis left on the 24th taking two trucks to Germany. Marlis is then driving on to Poland and Howard is coming back here with a load of tires. In his absence his work, of course, falls to me and I had to locate new housing for Howard and Bert. As of August 1 we had to vacate all Army housing and therefore had to find housing with Austrians. I didn't have to find housing for myself, only for Bert and Howard, as I will not be much longer in Vienna. In fact, I left Vienna for a time on July 28. Let me explain.

Hugh Moore, from the fund raising staff in Philadelphia, is now in Europe to get a clear picture of AFSC work in Europe. Of course, he needed to include Austria in his visit but he was stuck in Switzerland with no pass to get into Austria. We easily got a pass for him in Vienna but it would have taken a week for him to get it by mail. I was elected to deliver that pass to him in person in Switzerland.

On July 28, I drove to Jean's work camp in Brixlegg, not far from Innsbruck. After spending the night there, I drove on to Grins near Landeck where Irwin and Walter Pearson are helping the town in a rebuilding project. Last year a fire destroyed part of the town when the fire department in Landeck was unable to cut the French army occupation red tape in time to put out the fire. From Grins, I caught a train, which put me into Bern where I met up with Hugh and by evening of the 30th, we were back in

Grins. After seeing the transport work of Irwin and Walter and meeting all the proper Grins officials, we drove in my jeep back to the work camp in Brixlegg where we spent a couple of days so Hugh could get acquainted with the project. Next, we visited the ÖGB recuperation home at Frankenmarkt near Salzburg, the same one where I had last year picked up a load of apples.

Hugh Moore, Walter Pearson, Irwin Graeber,
Dr. Nöbel, the Grins Mayor

Then we stopped for a time at Gross Raming, near Enns to learn of Ed Frederick's industrial project assistance in the construction of a dam. Finally, today we arrived in Vienna where Hugh will stay for three days before going on to Prague and Stockholm. Saturday I will be taking a train to the work camp in Brixlegg where I will join the group for a couple of weeks.

I should make one comment here about the news. The Marshall Plan about which we had heard on our northern trip is all the talk here in Austria now. Secretary of State George Marshall has proposed a 20 billion-dollar assistance program for war-torn nations. You can hear everything here about it. Still, what you hear is mostly party line depending where your heart lies with the East or West. The Marshall Plan is the salvation of Europe or else it is just another example of the grabbing interests of dollar-seeking America who is trying to take over all of Europe by making the countries in debt to her. Russia is coming through with a counter plan for her countries. Yesterday, the Communist paper stated that Stalin had announced he would release all Austrian prisoners of war in Russia by January. Both factions are certainly courting Austria. It seems that Austria is the key to the future. He who holds Austria holds Europe.

August 23—Work Camp

I have spent the last two weeks at the work camp in Brixlegg. The group consists of a number of Austrian youth, mostly from the Community Center in Vienna, as well as three other Austrians, three Americans, and three or four students from Denmark, Sweden, and England for a total of about 20 people. The work consists primarily of manual labor to rebuild three homes that had been destroyed in the bombing. I have been shoveling sand, hauling bricks, mixing cement, and hauling cement in wheel barrels. The work has not been too fasci-

Brixlegg Work Campers

nating but the group was most congenial. I forgot to mention that one of the campers, Chandra, is from India. He was really the life of the party.

One evening we had a general meeting lasting until midnight in which I managed to stick my neck out too often. I have felt that Jean was not running things too well and she and I had several differences of opinion that evening. In my opinion, she just isn't sensitive enough to peoples' different feelings. She has been claiming that the camp was running democratically, but she seemed to be making all the decisions.

Pouring a cement floor

Chandra in foreground, Ed Wright in background at Brixlegg Work Camp

For example, we spent over on hour in that meeting deciding whether to take a two-day hike over the weekend. The decision was to do so. Then later we found out that she had invited guests for Saturday when we as a camp would be obligated to stay to host them. Thus the camp was forced to give up its democratically arrived at decision.

As a result of all this, a new program committee was chosen on which I found myself to be a member. We are functioning well and if I do say so I think doing better than the way things were handled previously.

Friday was an Austrian holiday (Ascension of Mary). Instead of working, we took a one-day trip into the heart of the Tyrolean Alps to a village called Hintertux. There we divided into two groups, a fast and a slow group for a day of Alpine hiking.

Gerti Mader

I started out with the fast group and climbed for over three hours, taking time out in a mountain pasture to snap a picture of Gerti Mader, one of our Viennese campers. We soon reached an Almhütte where we had lunch. Then, even though we had reached the 2500-meter (8000-foot) level, we even went a bit further onto an honest-to-goodness glacier, my first. It had been very hot in the morning but on the glacier, we found a delightful cool breeze. We went further up the glacier until we came to the beginning of crevasses. I joined the slow group, which had caught up with us at lunch, to return to our truck in Hintertux. The fast group went by a circuitous route to reach a distant peak and promised to join us at the truck by 7:30 p.m.

My first glacier experience

By 8:00, since the fast group had not returned, Jean decided we could wait no longer and told us all to get in the truck and leave without the fast group. Fortunately Owen and I were some distance from the truck and didn't hear her order for a time. When we finally did, we were aghast at her plan to leave for Brixlegg 50 miles away without the fast group.

She was adamant that we leave but Owen and I were even more adamantly against it. At 8:30 p.m., the fast group finally arrived and we were immediately happily on our way home. It really had been a wonderful day climbing in the Alps. If for any reason I ever leave the States, I am heading straight to live in the Tyrolean Alps with a mountain cabin and a few cows! It does look wonderful to this outsider, at least.

A work camp is not only about interacting with different cultures and providing labor for a project. The Camp also has to provide labor to support itself. One member is qualified to be the cook for the camp but Tina, the camper who does most of our cooking, needs help. All campers share in that duty on a rotating basis. My three-day term began last Saturday. It meant getting up before 6:00 a.m. to get the coal range fired up to cook cereal. After breakfast came the dish washing followed by sweeping out Castle Matzen (yes, we were living in a castle). Then, help Tina prepare dinner. Then, do dishes. The kitchen clean up does not end until about 9:00 p.m. And always the unexpected happens. For example, Sunday afternoon Marlis and George showed up with about 10 of Marlis' relatives. That meant last minute padding of the dinner to make enough for all.

Yesterday, even though it was raining a bit, we finished the roof of one of the houses. We managed to get the tile up to the roof by using the old-fashioned technique of the bucket brigade. Last evening we had a celebration. Whenever a roof is finished here, a celebration is called for. First, a small fir tree the size of a Christmas tree is raised on the roof. Then, a feast is prepared for all the workers. We feasted in a local Gasthaus, although most of the food came from our Quaker storehouse.

Campers raising roof tile up a ladder

The group here at the camp is most varied and interesting. I have grown especially fond of the two English chaps but each person has something positive to recommend him or her. This is the real purpose of a work camp—to bring people from different countries and cultures together. Jean keeps drawing lines along national backgrounds but I keep finding that the differences in the group are not along national lines as much as along individual differences. This camp has been very cross-cultural, challenging, and enjoyable. I may have criticized Jean too much. In general, she has done an excellent job as camp director. My criticism is probably a reflection of our different viewpoints.

August 25—Heidi Land Interlude

Saturday, the camp took another day's outing in the Alps, hiking from one valley to another to be met on the other side by Ed Wright and the truck. On the way home, I left the group at Wörgl and took a train west to Landeck where at about 12:30 a.m. I was met by Walter who took me back to Grins for the rest of the night. We were up at 6:00 a.m. to begin a two-day trip up into the mountains to the place where the town of Grins pastures its cows for the summer, a place known as an Alm. Four young people from Grins went with Walter and me in a jeep.

We first went down to Landeck from where we drove east to Imst and Lermoos from where we had an excellent view of the famous Zugspitze. Then on to Reutte and then west up the Lechtal valley. We stopped for lunch at a Gasthaus in Holzgau and spent about three hours as one of the Grins chaps had a girlfriend there. It was a beautiful Sunday afternoon and I sat and chatted with the proprietor for quite some time. Finally, we went on west to the town of Steeg from where we turned south up the Almejur valley. The road was just a path climbing steeply. Often it was just a cut in the mountain with a 1000-foot drop practically straight down and with no guardrail. I was driving and just didn't bother to look over the edge but kept my eyes on the road! Eventually we came to the end of the road at a little hut called Kaisers Almhütte.

"Mother" at the Almhütte

From there we proceeded on foot. We climbed steadily for about two and a half hours until we neared the head of the valley, having seen no Almhütten or homes all that way.

At last, we could see our destination, the Almhütte. Actually, it was not a real Almhütte as it was not set up for casual visitors but was more of a working farm building. It was a relatively modern building, perhaps only 15 years old. Still it was built in the old style. We first went into the kitchen where there was a dirt floor and a huge copper kettle for cheese making. Then we went into a front room, which had a huge stone stove. Here we were welcomed by the "Mother" of the group. She served us a delicious supper of milk, cheese, bread, and butter. Then out we went to see the cows coming home. There was no living thing within miles of us except the seven men and one woman living in the Almhütte plus the 80 cows.

It was a beautiful sight to see the men gathering the cows in from all sides of the mountain slopes, and to hear the alpine bells tinkling musically from the cows necks. Now it was milking time in the stables. This was a large area with a capacity of 120 cows and it was just adjacent to the kitchen.

Cows at the Almhütte

Perhaps I should say a word here about this Alm. Each family in Grins has a cow or two. All the available pastureland near the village must be put into hay for winter feed, so about June 1, all the cows are driven over the mountain to this Alm, which belongs to the Federal Government. However, for about 400 years the people of Grins have been using this land as their private pasture in the summer. All the cow owners are members of a cooperative. The coop hires the crew for the summer and turns over all the cows to these men, all from Grins.

The day on the Alm starts at 3:30 a.m. in the first half of the summer when the cows are producing well (10 liters a day). The seven men milk the 80 cows in about two hours. Then at 6:00 a.m., the cows are turned out for the day to wander more or less at will over the mountain slopes. However, three men go with the scattered groups to keep them from the steeper precipices. One man spends the day cleaning out the stables. Two more churn the cream into butter or make the milk into cheese. The butter is cooked enough so it will keep and cheese keeps anyway. At 4:00 in the afternoon, the men begin rounding up the cows and have them in the stables by 6:00 p.m. Then two more hours of milking and the day's work is done. This goes on from about from June 10 to September 20. Meanwhile, the farmers back home are storing up hay for the winter use. In midsummer, the cheese and butter are backpacked out of the Alm to Grins. Again it is done at the end of the season. This Almhütte was modern enough to have electricity for night-lights since they had a small light plant operated by a small turbine, as waterpower is most plentiful.

About dark, the rest of our group left to grope their way back to the jeep to get back to Steeg for a dance. Walter and I decided to stay and shortly thereafter climbed up to the loft above and were soon fast asleep in the hay. There was no such thing as a real bed, but the hay made a wonderful bed. We didn't wake up the next morning in time for milking but were up just in time to see the cows turned out and the sun peek over the mountain range to the East. I never saw so rapid a sunrise. One moment I was in shadow and then suddenly I was in sun. I could not run down the mountain as quickly as the shadow receded. It was a wonderful picture, the morning sun on the dewy slopes as the cows departed for their day of grazing.

We hiked a bit more around the mountains but returned as scheduled to Steeg by 1:00 p.m. No jeep was to be found. We waited until 4:00 and found the jeep and the group not 300 yards away on another street!

We now concluded our trip by driving further west to the Flexen pass and descending into the province of Vorarlberg on a long curving road from which we had another magnificent view. Sheds to protect the road in winter from snow slides covered most of the road. Soon we turned back east to climb over the Arlberg pass and within an hour we arrived back in Grins. We had made a complete circuit of the Lechtaler Mountains and had seen some of the most beautiful mountains of Austria. The entire Alm experience reminded me so much of my mental picture from the story of Heidi and her mountains.

August 29—A Mountain on a Motorcycle

Tuesday, Irwin had a hauling job some 10 miles up the Paznauntal valley. I took the motorcycle and met him there. Then, while others loaded his truck, he and I continued on the motorcycle up the valley, heading southwest from Landeck.

We drove for an hour and a half and then the road finally ran out. However, there was still an old cart wagon trail, very rocky but passable for a motorcycle. We drove on above the timberline into this strange valley, which seemed to be used as a horse ranch. Finally, we arrived at Bielerhöhe, next to the Silvretta Stausee, a large artificial lake. It was dammed from the valley we were in and from the valley leading off northwestward. In the distance to the south, we saw glacier-covered mountains, which we knew to be Switzerland.

The whole area was completely deserted except for one workman. He told us the dam was built during the war as a source of waterpower for electricity and that further down the Vorarlberg side was the power plant. We noticed a French flag flying above the dam and wondered about it. He said it was just an outpost of the French military occupation. Both dams had been built during the war without having a single railroad or road built into the place. It had all been built by carrying the material up on a cable car.

We then hurried back to Irwin's truck and on into Grins for supper. Then I caught a train, which put me back in Brixlegg by 12:30 a.m. I am leaving Brixlegg for good tonight. Even though I have been here only three days, this time I found myself getting mixed up in the camp politics. But enough of that. I left Brixlegg this evening by taking the train at Wörgl. Later on, a prearranged meeting on the train with Steve Cary, a Commissioner from Paris, worked out well.

September 1—Travels With Steve

Friday night Steve and I rode the train to Villach where Mel and Ned Weaver met us at midnight. Then Saturday, we visited two of the ÖGB recuperation homes, first the one for girls in Mittewald and then to the one for boys at Tamsweg. The purpose of the trip was to show Steve more about AFSC's Austrian programs. I had never been to Mittewald and was glad of the chance to visit it.

Sunday we drove on to nearly Salzburg where we took a slight detour to Germany to visit Hitler's Berghof villa near Berchtesgaden. It was just a shell of a building as it had been badly bombed at the war's end. Then

Remaining roof of Hitler's Berghof villa, August 31, 1947

back we came to Austria to spend the night in the ÖGB recuperation home in Frankenmarkt. Today we left Ned and Steve at Gross Raming to visit the dam project while Mel and I came on back to Vienna.

September 7—Indecision

Since getting back to Vienna, I find that the team as well as Steve has offered me the opportunity to stay six more months in Vienna. They feel there is a real need for a second community center and they think I would be right for the job. I must say I was sorely tempted. Yesterday morning we had a full morning's staff meeting to discuss this possibility. Then yesterday afternoon, I spent discussing the matter with several Austrian friends. Then last evening, I went over the pros and cons with Mela Zvacek. Everyone was most positive about my staying. However, this afternoon I told Steve and George that I had decided to go home. Steve accepted my decision as my decision but George was pretty upset by it. Now the die is cast and I must bid farewell to friends and get packed. At least I do have a boat reservation for September 27 from Southampton.

September 19—Farewell to Austria

I don't know where the time has gone for the last two weeks. I have been so busy in tying up loose ends, helping Howard, and visiting the many Austrians with whom I have become acquainted. In addition, I have been hosting several AFSC VIPs who showed up to see our Vienna work.

Finally, on Wednesday I boarded the train at the Westbahnhof at 5:00 p.m. after waving farewell to over a dozen well-wishers who had come to see me off. Yesterday morning I got off at Innsbruck and stayed until this afternoon at the home of one of the campers from Brixlegg. This evening, I took the train for Paris, and now I am about to leave Austria as we are going into the sunset near the Arlberg Pass.

A favorite scene from Austria, the "Silent Soldier" haystacks

September 21—Glimpse of Paris and the Channel

I spent yesterday in Paris getting my luggage properly moved from station to station and getting my ticket in order for the channel crossing. Then, I hunted in vain to find any of the few friends I know in Paris. At least I knew people at the AFSC center where I spent the night. Again, I had a very good chat with Steve, who happened to be passing through Paris at the same time. This morning I went with Jack Hollister to the station. He is in charge of the German desk in Philadelphia and is returning on the same ship with me.

At Dieppe we boarded a channel ferry for the three-hour crossing to England. It turned out to be a very rough crossing. Although I didn't get sick from the motion of the boat, most of the other passengers were violently sick and the boat was too crowded for any semblance of cleanliness to be maintained. At any rate we made it to England, caught a train, and are spending the night in London at the Hotel Royal in Russell Square.

September 27—First Visit to England

I have been having a great time in England. One day I went 30 miles south of London to spend the night with Percy's parents. Percy is the English chap who has been working in Vienna for the British Quakers. Another night I spent north of London with Percy and his charming Austrian wife. Then I did some of the touristy things. I went through St. James Park, Westminster Abbey, the Tower of London, and saw the changing of the guard at Buckingham Palace. And, of course, I visited in Friends House. One day, I took a train to Birmingham and spent the night with your old English friends, Sewell and Helen Harris. The next day I stopped off both in Stratford and Oxford for a brief glimpse of two famous towns. At last, today, we were off at 9:23 a.m. by train for Southampton. Finally, this afternoon I was aboard the Marine Tiger as it sailed out of England for New York where we should arrive on October 5. My year and a half of service with the AFSC is over. I hope my service in Europe was of some value to people. I certainly can say that it has certainly been the high point of my life so far.

Farm Life in Ohio

October 1947 to October 1948

October 1947 to October 1948—Readjustment

(This is not a letter, as I was home with my parents. It is my recollection of events during this period.)

At first, it was good to be home again. For a few weeks, I was sort of a celebrity in the neighborhood. I was asked to speak at umpteen meetings about my experiences. I began to take part in the normal activities of rural America. I attended Fairview, my local Friends Church, taking part in its many activities. I went to Farm Bureau meetings, local Advisory Council meetings, Grange meetings, and Agricultural Extension Seminars to name a few. I began to get the hang of farm work and management again.

These were all the things I had been looking forward to from Vienna, the treasure in my home garden. Yet, somehow it was not enough. I grew restless with the relative isolation of farm life. Further, after being my own person in college, CPS, and AFSC in Europe, I chaffed at being too much under the direction of my parents. In quiet moments, I wondered if I had made a mistake by coming home. I tortured myself with questions. Had I given enough in my AFSC work? Was there more for me to do in Vienna? Should I have stayed and taken over that Community Center project? Was farming all I was meant to do? Despite the turmoil, I kept these questions to myself and vowed to make the best of my decision to come home.

Two things happened, both testing my decision. First, a letter arrived from Germany, months after it's German postmark. I was astounded that it had found it's way to me, at who sent it, and even more at its content. The letter was from Helmut, one of the German PWs I met in le Pouliguen, France so very long ago.

January, 1947

> *Dear Robert,*
> *You will be astonished to receive a letter from me in Germany. In the fall I finally received the first news from my family. That was a great joy, but it was also very sad. We have lost all, our house in Danzig was destroyed and everything was stolen by the Russians. My wife and my three children had to take to the open fields for three weeks without daily food. She, being German, had to leave Danzig and go to Germany as a DP. But it took her nearly a year to find transportation. When she and the children got to Germany near Hanover, she found everything worse. She finally found a room with no furniture and as a DP, she is treated like dirt. She is out in the country where the people did not lose so much*

during the war and they do not understand the fate of the DPs.

In the meantime, I found that I could be released from being a PW if I would agree to stay and work for a year in France. I am now released and am taking a one month leave from my job—the same job I had as a PW in le Pouliguen—to visit my family in Germany. My job is not sufficient to support my family in France, so I hope to go to America as soon as possible.

The letter continued with his wife's addition:

I have heard so much about your group in le Pouliguen and how nice you all were to my husband. Helmut had hoped we would join him for his year in France, but we just cannot finance the move and stay there. So we hope to go to America if we can work out the details. We must get out of Germany, for here there is nothing to look forward to. There is nothing to buy, nothing to wear, only hunger and need.

> *Your friend,*
> *Helmut*

While I was relieved to know he was safe and free at last, the hardships he and his family had already faced and those still ahead haunted my thoughts. It was a blow to know that people I knew were still left in such desperate circumstances. While I fretted about farm chores and over-involved parents, Helmut wondered how he would feed, clothe, and shelter his wife and children. Doubts about my choice to come home, those I had chosen to suppress, resumed their relentless circling in my thoughts.

The second event testing my resolve to farm came in July, when Mela Zvacek, the director of the Austrian apprentice program of the ÖGB, visited America. After discussing a plan with the AFSC in Philadelphia, she came with Mel, one of the Vienna team members, to Ohio to visit me. Her primary mission was to offer me an opportunity to return to Vienna. Since April 1946, the AFSC has been supporting the apprentice recuperation home program of the ÖGB with food. She and the AFSC had agreed that it was time for the AFSC to do more in these recuperation homes than just provide food. They wanted to embark on an educational and recreational program.

At Mela's suggestion, the AFSC agreed that I might be just the right person to take on such a project. Elise Tomino, from the AFSC staff in Philadelphia, then sent me a letter outlining the AFSC attitude toward this project as follows: "This educational and recreational program (EDREC) will be a wonderful opportunity to bring to hundreds of young Austrian apprentices something more than material relief. Today as we review our work abroad, we believe that AFSC still has a very important role in Europe. After the emergency relief needs have been met, Friends' emphasis should be placed on the educational and spiritual aspects of work in the international field."

One of the European Commissioners had written, "AFSC should stay in Europe to help demonstrate a world of friendship and an attitude of fellowship with the people, to counteract the attitude which official Americans take and to help build the understanding that the world needs."

After discussing this opportunity with friends and parents, and considering my unending internal debate, I decided to take on the project. As soon as the corn harvest was completed in October, I would head back to Austria for a year or so.

To my relief, my father indicated he could hire temporary help on the farm in my absence. Not only was he willing to see me go again,

Me with Mela and my father on our farm

he seemed happy for me. I was confused by this, until he relayed his own tale of turmoil regarding service after World War I. While he had been accepted by the AFSC to go to France in 1918, his local draft board refused to let him go, telling him his only options were to join the Army or stay on the farm. He stayed on the farm, and regretted all his life not being able to go to France. He saw my previous and further work with the AFSC as partial fulfillment of his own dream.

Whatever doubts I had about returning to service were dispelled by the story of his denial and disappointment, and while I was a farmer at heart, I once again looked forward to planting seeds of another type, back in Europe.

New Job Preparation

November 1948 to February 1949

November—Beginning Contacts

I've been busy as a beaver ever since getting to Philadelphia about November 5. First, I had to get the usual equipment, clothing, and incidentals that all AFSC workers take to Europe. In addition, I have purchased a 16mm sound projector, a record player, records, handicraft sets and have begun the search for films. I have also been visiting a number of agencies, some in the search for films, and others to get myself acquainted with the apprentice programs of the unions and of the US Department of Labor. In this search, I first visited the Philadelphia Board of Education and talked with the board member in charge of vocational education. Next, I visited the Wharton school library as well as the Swarthmore College library to learn more about apprentice programs.

Margaret Jones, at the AFSC, is in charge of the Austrian desk. She lined up a number of interviews for me in Washington, D.C. and New York. Therefore, two weeks ago I spent three days in Washington, D.C. visiting several offices. I started off by seeing a Mr. Kauffman of the Forestry Association. He sent me to the USDA Department of Forestry where I managed to pick up a film on forestry. Then, I went to the film division of the USDA. They sent me to the State Department who told me they could do nothing, as this would be an overseas service in occupied countries. They suggested I go to the Information Service Branch of Civil Affairs of the US Army in New York. Then, I visited the American Motion Picture Association in vain. Finally, that day in Washington, I went to the Austrian Embassy where I had half an hour's talk with the ambassador himself. At least he is now more aware of the AFSC in Austria and with my job assignment.

One day I visited the Bureau of Apprenticeship of the US Department of Labor. They agreed to raise money in Washington for my recently purchased projector and promised to cooperate in getting correspondence started between apprentices in the US and Austria. I then visited the apprentice division of the AFL (American Federation of Labor) and talked with the apprentice overseas division at the CIO (Congress of Industrial Organizations). Another day I had lunch with Joseph Roland of the State Department who was already familiar with AFSC work. All these visits helped me to better understand the apprentice programs in the US, in case I needed to answer questions the Austrians might have.

Last week I spent three days in New York interviewing a number of different groups. I continued my search for film sources, mostly in vain. At least I am finding a number of connections in Europe to help me with my program, including the Austrian Information Office, Church World Service, American Rescue and Relief, and the National Catholic Welfare.

In addition to visiting a number of offices in the three cities, I did have a chance to see some old friends. I was particularly delighted to meet George and Bert who had just arrived in Philadelphia from Europe. We drove around the Philadelphia area showing Bert places he had never seen such as Pendle Hill, Haverford College, Swarthmore College, and Westtown School. It was a delightful reunion.

One Sunday morning, I gave a talk to the high school age group of the Swarthmore Meeting about AFSC work. Last Monday, George and I were honored by being invited to sit on the facing bench at the weekly AFSC staff meeting. We were introduced and George gave a little speech. One evening, Margaret and her colleague, Elise Tomino, took me to the home of the Roberts family in New Jersey. Their daughter, Alice, an Earlham graduate in 1946, is now with the World YMCA-YWCA in southern Austria.

The "orientation" back into the AFSC family has been a delightful time. I was scheduled to sail today on the Queen Elizabeth from New York, but a strike has stopped all shipping to Europe from the US. So tomorrow, I will take a train from Philadelphia to New York and on to Montreal on the way to Halifax where the AFSC was able to get a reservation for me on a Dutch boat. The strike does not affect it as it goes from Canada.

November 26—Train to Halifax

I had a very pleasant two-night train ride to Halifax. All I saw of Montreal were the railroad yards. The scenery on to Halifax was just rugged, rolling, rocky landscape. I arrived in Halifax at three this afternoon and was able to get on board the ship immediately. We are scheduled to sail at midnight tonight.

December 4—Ocean Crossing

Our ship was a combination passenger and cargo ship. For this trip there was no cargo and only 169 passengers. Thus, we bounced all across the ocean like a cork. Many people were seasick but I only got sick with a cold! My fellow passengers were mostly English businessmen. There were only a dozen Americans on board, including six Mormons going to England to do mission work there. We have had movies every day and in the evening, we were entertained by a good string quartet. Oh, I forgot to mention that when I came on board in Halifax I received a telegram, "We love you," signed by George Mathues, Comfort Cary, Elise Tomino, Barbara Moffett, Margaret Jones, and her secretary, Florence. Nice send off. We arrived this evening in Liverpool and will disembark tomorrow morning.

December 13—On To Vienna

A week ago Saturday, I took the train from Liverpool to London where I stayed until Wednesday. I made one trip out of London, this time to Cambridge. I had visited Oxford last year. Then Wednesday I took the train, then the channel ferry and again a train into Paris. There it took a couple of days to get properly documented to travel on through Germany to get to Vienna. In Paris, I had a nice chat with Earl Fowler, a classmate of mine from Earlham College days. This afternoon, my train brought me back "home" to Vienna. I was warmly welcomed at the Westbahnhof by Mela, her husband Fritz, Mel, and the new AFSC head of mission in Vienna, George Little.

December 23—Settling In

The first couple of nights after I arrived in Vienna I had to sleep on a cot in the new Quaker office at Jauresgasse, as no hotel room had been reserved for me. Then for a few nights, I had a room at the Hotel Austria. I spent quite a bit of time last and this week hunting for a place to call home. I finally found one that seems quite satisfactory, even though it is on Landstrasse Hauptstrasse some two or three miles out from the center of Vienna. I managed to find a free parking place for my jeep across the street in a British military compound. My room is quite large with adequate closet space. It even has a grand piano in one corner. One minor drawback is that I must heat it myself using a huge American made coal stove. The room costs the AFSC 150 schillings a month. Officially that is $15, but if you figured it on the black market rate (which we do not do), it would be $5 a month!

During the week, I spent considerable time at the ÖGB. Mela made sure I met all the proper officials and particularly the men who will be helping me. Karl Novotny (Noverl) will be with me the most, which pleases me, as I had known him reasonably well last year. Herr Rohm is an older man who will be most helpful to me in my speaking to and talking with the apprentices. He speaks no English but he can follow my fractured German very well. Finally, there is Herr Bartel who will be helping us more in the transport area. The ÖGB has just moved into new offices on Hohenstauffengasse, all newly constructed because the original building had been bombed. Noverl and I have been given one of the new rooms. It has two complete office desks, a telephone, some cupboards, central heating (almost unheard of in Vienna), and our names on the door! I am now Herr Colleague Bob. Thursday I was able to move my office material from the Quaker office to my new room at the ÖGB. It will be good to have this new office, as the Quaker office is so crowded that there is no place there to work.

This morning Mel, Mela, Noverl, George, and I drove outside Vienna a short way to Hueber House, which houses one of the training schools for the recuperation home leaders. We went to see the arrangements that had been made to give a three-day Christmas celebration to orphaned apprentice workers who are poor. Hueber House is up just a bit above Vienna and there was actually a bit of snow there, giving it all the beauty of a genuine Austrian winter hillside scene.

December 27—Christmas Activities

Christmas began for us on Thursday night, December 23, at the Quaker Center. This was a party for all the young people from the old and new Community Center. We all had place cards, sat around tables, and talked. There were several little programs and we had a bit to eat. Gifts were given out and I even got a few, primarily from Inge Peinlich, Ericka Protsch and Grit Elsner, all Austrian girls I had known last year. . After the party, Paul Driesbach, a new team member, and I went to the International Club that Arthur still runs in the same old grand style.

Friday morning, December 24, at breakfast I met Alice Roberts, who is spending Christmas in Vienna. I had visited her parents just recently in their home in New Jersey when I was in Philadelphia. She is working with the World YMCA-YWCA program in southern Austria. She graduated from Earlham in 1946 and I had known her brother when I was there. She wants to work with us in Vienna, but at the moment, there is no opening for her. So, for the next three days I acted as her guide. That afternoon I took her in a jeep up to the Kahlenberg from where we both admired the scenery as well as views of the Danube and of Vienna.

That evening was the big time in Vienna. I think Christmas Eve is more important here than Christmas Day. We were invited to come at 8:00 p.m. to the home of an Austrian family that is receiving food and clothing from your women's club in Ohio. Knowing it was at 8:00, we figured it was not for supper, so we went to a Mennonite party at the Bristol hotel and had a big supper at 7:00. Upon arriving at the Ruzickas, we found a table all beautifully prepared for Christmas Eve supper. This was the same room where a year and a half ago I had eaten apple dumpling "if they could find the three apples." Well, we had apple dumpling, soup, fish schnitzel, bread, and a tasty assortment of pastries. All of this was on top of the Bristol meal. They couldn't understand why our appetites were not better! They had a nice little tree on a table by the window and just before we sat down to eat, they lighted the candles on the tree. These were not electric candles but genuine wax candles to burn. At 11:30 p.m. we got in two jeeps and drove to the Hietzing church. It so happened that none of us are Catholics, but that made no difference as every one goes to Mass on Christmas Eve. The Church was jammed full and I never did get to see the altar. We stood until 1:30 a.m. through the Catholic ritual, through a half hour story of the fourth Wise Man, a number of hymns, and finally all four verses of Silent Night. Although the evening didn't make me into a Catholic, it was very impressive.

Christmas Day noon the AFSC team joined the five Mennonites for Christmas dinner at the Cottage Hotel. Later we went to George and Virginia Little's home for sort of an open house. Then we took in a second open house at the residence of Dick Engstrom, another team member. Alice and I capped off the day by going to the Theatre-an-der Wien for my first opera of this year, *Rosenkavalier.*

Sunday, someone else entertained Alice. For the evening Sven Heikka, a new team member from Sweden, Louise Powelson, also a new team member, and Grit, an Austrian girl, joined me in accepting an invitation to the home of one of the other Austrian Community Center girls. It turned out this was also for supper, which included a number of Viennese dainties as well as the standard apple strudel. She also had a beautiful Christmas tree with candles.

Since today, Monday, was a holiday in Austria it was also a declared holiday for us. However, the US Army was working, so I went to the Army Information Service Bureau and began to search for films for my program. Later I went to some electric shops to try to get the transformer, which I had bought in Philadelphia, adjusted for Austrian current. US current works on 60 cycles while Austrian is 50. That makes too much difference in the speed a phonograph player runs so I must get an adjuster for that discrepancy. Then this evening, I took Alice to an Austrian movie before I took her to her train to Klagenfurt. It has been a lovely Christmas and so far, I am most happy to have come back to Austria.

December 31—Christmas Week

I have spent a good deal of time this week looking up people whose names and addresses had been given me in the US. It was a very enjoyable exercise, that is, when I could find the people at home. The best visit I had was with a family whose name had been given to me by Muriel Specht. I spent some time helping wrap gift packages for 50 DP children. Thursday evening I took Gerti Feifar, an Austrian girl, to the Volksoper to see *The Magic Flute*. Of course, I spent some time at the ÖGB getting better acquainted with the personnel there and getting more ideas for my planned trips to the recuperation homes. For New Year's Eve, Sven and I arranged to take Ericka Protsch and Grit Elsner, two Austrian girls, out for the evening. I picked up the girls and we went to a bus station to meet Sven. We waited an hour for him in vain so I then took the girls to a café where the three of us spent the evening in eating, chatting, and dancing. Without Sven, I had to do double duty with the dancing. It turns out that Sven had simply missed his bus back to Vienna.

January 1, 1949—Military Ceremony

After sleeping late this morning, I took a stroll through the first or center district of Vienna. This area is controlled jointly by all four powers, the Russians, the French, the British, and the Americans. The top command for the district rotates every month from one power to the next. At noon, I stumbled onto the first of the month changing of command from the Russians to the Americans.

In front of the Allied Control Headquarters came marching a Russian military band followed by one hundred soldiers with fixed bayonets. They stationed themselves smartly to one side of the square. Then, from the other direction came the American military band and one hundred soldiers with fixed bayonets. They took position just opposite the Russians. The two leaders presented arms to each other very smartly. The Russian and American generals then marched out of the building. The Russian band played the Russian national anthem while everyone saluted. The American band then played the Star Spangled Banner and everyone saluted again. The Russian flag on top of the building was replaced by the Stars and Stripes. After the troops marched away, the Russian and American Generals shook hands and the ceremony was over.

It was very impressive, particularly when you realized that nowhere else in the world could something like this take place. In Vienna, people are so used to seeing both Russians and Americans that they think nothing of it.

Changing of guard from Russian to American

In a sense, it is odd how calm everyone seems to be here about the possibility of a Russian-American conflict. I heard much more talk in Wilmington, Ohio of the possibility of war soon than I have heard here. As I left the ceremony, I walked down the Ringstrasse and past an imposing building where the pictures and the star on the front left little doubt whose headquarters it was.

Russian occupation headquarters

January 6—Film Search

As one of the main parts of my EDREC program will be showing movies, I have been and will be spending a good bit of trying to get the proper films, not an easy task. I had been told in Philadelphia that the AFSC office in Munich might have a few films. So Monday night I took the train to Munich, and even managed to get a sleeper.

The AFSC unit in Munich is under the direction of Marlis from our original AFSC group in Vienna. Marlis' unit is working under the UN's International Relief Organization (IRO) in an orientation program for DPs. The DPs have been homeless for three or four years and are hoping to go to the States under the recently congressionally passed DP bill. Very few have made it so far, as they must first have assurances of a job in the States.

As well as getting a few films from the Munich AFSC, I was able to get a few leads from them of other possible sources of films. Tuesday, I visited the JDC and several other organizations in Munich. All I managed to get were more leads. Yesterday, I visited the educational division of the US Army on the suggestion of General McClure, whom I had seen in New

York. The man I talked with said that he had jurisdiction only in Bavaria and that I should go to Nürnberg to talk with the man in charge of education in all of Germany. He made an appointment for me to see that man today. I borrowed a jeep from the AFSC and drove the hundred miles to Nürnberg. There the very friendly officer in charge of education for all of Germany told me that he had no authority to give out films. That could only come from the office I had just visited in Munich! In addition, since I wanted to use the films in Austria, I would have to get them in Vienna. However, I already knew that this Army division in Vienna didn't have any of the films I wanted. Run around, run around.

January 7—Other Errands

Apparently, my reputation as a former transport officer in Vienna has stayed with me. Marlis drafted me to drive a jeep 40 miles south to Bad Aibling, just to get it there.

The camp there works only with DP children. The AFSC responsibility is just for education as the camp is under the direction of the IRO. When the AFSC started to set up classes there, they discovered that IRO hadn't provided any beds for the children. In other words, the IRO just fell down on the job. So instead of starting the education program, the AFSC has spent most of its time getting the physical setup usable. It was most discouraging for them to see such carelessness exhibited by IRO. It seems that too much of IRO is just one big graft after another. Many of the top people are ex-UNRRA workers who were looking for a soft berth. However, there are some good people and it is absolutely necessary for it to continue, bad as it is. No one knows what would happen to the DP children without it.

I forgot to tell you earlier that in Austria we no longer have free use of Army phone lines, so I made quite a few calls from Munich for the Vienna group. Part of the calls concerned with another little errand I was asked to do while in Germany. Next week, the ÖGB is sending 200 children, aged six to 10, from Vienna to Denmark where they will live in and eat in Danish trade union homes for a month. However, they are not able to get any food while traveling through Germany either from the railroad or from the occupying powers. While in Nürnberg, I arranged with the wife of one of the Nürnberg Judges for an American wives' group to provide soup for the children when the train stops in Nürnberg. I called our AFSC unit in Brunswick, near Hannover, and they agreed to feed the children when the train stops there. Of course, I called Vienna to report all this, as you can call into Austria even through you can't call out.

Last evening one of the AFSC members and I went to a Russian Orthodox Church to hear the Christmas music. January 6 is the Russian Christmas. We stayed for about an hour and a half of Christmas music from many lands—Hungary, Rumania, Greece, Lithuania, Latvia, Estonia, Poland, Finland, Ukraine, and finally Germany. It was beautiful but was it cold!

January 10—Weekend Excursion

I had intended to return to Vienna from Munich Friday night. However, since Margaret Williston, one of the Munich team members, was going to Garmisch and Oberammergau, I decided to go with her. We drove through the night to Garmisch where I went into the billeting office to arrange for rooms.

As I was about to leave the clerk pointed to the door and told me that the man standing there was Charles Lindbergh. He was talking to two of the top military brass of the area and the contrast was indeed great, these two ordinary looking officers talking with this tall civilian. I would have liked to have talked to him but was only able to speak the following, "May I get through to the door?"

Lindbergh said in reply, "Oh, pardon me, of course."

We spent the night in a nice hotel out in the country in a beautiful valley completely surrounded by mountains. It was an absolutely clear night and the snow lay all about. These were the Alps—wonderful. We were at the foot of the highest mountain in Germany, the Zugspitze.

The next morning we drove the 15 miles or so up a narrow mountain road to Oberammergau, a lovely Bavarian town filled with winding streets and picturesque homes. We went to the Passionstheater, which was locked, but the caretaker was about and spent over half an hour taking us through. The auditorium seats something like 6000 people. We went back stage, saw all the techniques for changing scenery, saw most of the costumes as he took us from costume room to costume room, saw the swords, spears, shields, crosses, crown of thorns, etc. It was a very impressive half hour. The play will begin (they hope) on May 1, 1950.

One would think that such a town in which most of the people take some part in the play would really be a town of good will. However, in Obergammergau there is a camp of Germans who are now DPs because their homes were given to Poland after the war. What would you expect the people of Oberammergau to do for them? The locals spend their lives portraying the life of Christ and you would expect them to be kind to their fellow Germans. Yet they do absolutely nothing for them. They will not hire a single one for any kind of job. They treat them as untouchables and are outraged at the Americans for thrusting these people into their midst. Why won't they help?

The people of Oberammergau are south Germans, Bavarians. The DP Germans are Prussians. As such, they will have nothing to do with them. I saw another example of this in Munich. A German girl working as a secretary for the AFSC is very well qualified to teach high school. She has had all the training and is an outstanding person but cannot get a job in Munich. Why? She is from Berlin and is therefore a Prussian.

From Oberammergau we drove to Mittenwald to another DP camp where the AFSC works. Since it was Saturday afternoon we found no one at home. Then back we went to the base of the Zugspitze. We parked the Volkswagen and took the cog railroad up the mountain. The first hour of the ride was a beautiful steep climb up the lower regions of the mountain. The last half was in complete darkness as the train goes into the heart of the mountain and comes out near the top on the far side. There we found ourselves at a large resort hotel, which has been entirely taken over by the US Army. We had a good meal there and arranged for rooms for the night. We were looking forward to an excellent mountain view the next day. That night there was a typical Tyrolean show all in costume and with Bavarian dances.

Sunday came with no view; it was snowing. We took a cable car to the peak from where you could see into five countries on a clear day—we could see almost nothing.

Back at the hotel we found a tunnel that goes for about ¾ mile through the mountain to the other entrance in Austria where there was a hotel with no soldiers. We decided to go there for lunch, but the border guards on the German side would not let me through. They said I didn't have the right papers to go to Austria! We finally got in by promising to come back. We went for a half hour walk through a winding, climbing tunnel into Austria. After a typical Austrian meal, we went outside. I noticed a low place in the ridge a couple of hundred yards away. I took off on that last climb in foot deep snow to the peak of the Zugspitze. At that moment, the snowing stopped and the sun came out. I stood in the snow, supported by a little wooden post announcing the German-Austria border, with a most exciting view of the whole mountain scene. Here there was no border patrol at all!

Back we went down through the tunnel to Germany, down the cog railway to Garmisch, in the car to Munich in an hour and a half, and onto the Vienna-bound train, which put me into Vienna at 6:00 this morning where there was no sign of snow.

January 17—EDREC Preparation

EDREC (Educational Recreational) is the official name of my program with the ÖGB. During the last 10 days, I have been working to get it well organized. Even though I have managed to find some appropriate films for use in my program, I am still looking for more. In addition to the easily found short comedies, I am looking for films with an international flavor to help the boys know there is a wider world out there beyond Austria. I am also always on the search for films that at least hint at the possibility of a peaceful world. I have finally managed to find some appropriate films for use in my program. The four organizations that have been most helpful from the many I have visited were the Information Service Bureau (ISB) of the US Army, the JDC, the British Film Service, and the IRO.

I spent many hours in my office at the ÖGB previewing the films in search of the best. Mela, Mel, and Noverl have helped in the previewing. I have also spent considerable time with my equipment. I found a portable screen that cost me 120 schillings. Then, a bearing went out on my projector. After getting it fixed, a belt on the projector broke. It is such a task to find replacement parts that will fit my machines. Breaking equipment reminds me of my work in the garage two years ago!

January 19—Extra Curricular Activities

I may be busy on my EDREC program during the day but my evenings are free for fun activities. One evening I took Nancy Foster, who is visiting here from Ohio, to see *The Marriage of Figaro*. Another night I visited Arthur's International Club. Friday I went out with Mel, Mela, and her husband, Fritz, for dinner. We had very good goulash for 2½ schillings ($0.25). Saturday night was a folk dancing at the Youth Center. Sunday night Gerti Feifar and I went to the hospital to visit Paul Driesbach, one of our team members. When I arrived in Vienna he dropped one end of my trunk on his feet and they subsequently became infected. He should be out of the hospital shortly.

Tuesday night was one of my most productive nights since returning to Vienna. I put on a program of my films for about 25 Austrians at our Youth

Connie Madgen and Austrian fianceé, Rudi Kosohorsky

Center and it went over very well with them. Another night a small group of us had a farewell party for Connie Madgen, an English girl, who is leaving our team to return to England. We had dinner at the Rathauskeller. I think it was the best meal I have had yet and it cost us 23 schilling ($2.30) each.

January 20—Vienna Condition Today

It is positively amazing at what a different Vienna I find now from what I left over a year ago. People generally can get food now. If one member of a family is a wage earner, the family can eat sparingly. If two members are wage earners they can eat fairly well, and if three members are wage earners, the family can begin to catch up on such things as shoes, window glass, new plumbing, etc. The shop windows are full of consumer goods, but much of that is because most people don't have the money to buy these goods in the windows.

It is dreadful to see the contrast between life here and the life of the people in Munich. Munich is now similar to my memories of Vienna two years ago. In Munich 10 people scramble for every cigarette butt whereas now in Vienna you may find a number of butts left on the sidewalk—a crude illustration I know, but graphic. Two years ago, everyone in Vienna was in need. Now only some of the people are in need. The areas of desperation have been much reduced.

January 23—Another EDREC Dry Run

Friday, Sven and I each drove a truck to one of the ÖGB recuperation homes, Sigmundsberg bei Maria Zell. We took 25 Austrians from our Youth Center for a weekend of skiing. The recuperation homes are all closed in January so it was possible for the youth group to go there now. Both evenings were turned over to me to put on some of my projected programs that I am getting ready for the recuperation homes in February. I was heartened by the response, as everyone was most positive.

Saturday afternoon I got up enough courage to go skiing. It began to snow and became hard to see. The rest of the group left me to head back to the recuperation home. In a few minutes, I followed but got up so much speed that I could see absolutely nothing. So I just shut my eyes and kept going. About five minutes later, the hill leveled out and there was the rest of the group. I hadn't fallen once. Maybe I can ski a little better now.

This afternoon we drove back up the mountain slope, over the divide through drifts as high as a car. Fortunately, the road had all been plowed out. By 8:00 this evening we were back in Vienna where there is no snow.

February 3—Patiently Waiting

I just can't get started yet on my EDREC program as the recuperation homes only open next week. Meanwhile, I have continued getting ready for my first trip. It is just as well I haven't started, as last week my projector broke again. I spent almost a day hunting down a repair shop. The shop, where I had already had some contact, only works on radios. He gave me another address. But as they do no repair work, they gave me another address. This place only works on 35mm projectors and mine is a 16mm one. They referred me further. But the next place only works on Austrian projectors. Then at last, I found a shop that agreed to help me. A bearing had burned out. He said I had not oiled it enough. Two days later the other bearing burned out. This time he found that the tubes leading from the oil spout to the bearings had been compressed in the original assembly of the machine and thus the bearings never had been oiled. But at least it is now operational. The record player is now in running order and I have a number of good records to use.

One other essential item is now ready—a truck. Some time ago, the AFSC had acquired an enclosed van from the US Army. It is just right for my program particularly since it seems to be in good shape. The ÖGB has had it for some weeks getting it painted a light gray and painting a large sign on each side. The sign says, "INTERESSANTES AUS ALLER WELT BRINGT DIE JUGENDFÜRSORGEAKTION DES ÖGB, BEIGESTELLT VON DER AMERIKANISHEN QUÄKER HILFE" (The Youth Department of the Austrian Trade Union Organization presents interesting programs from around the world, as provided by the AFSC).

February 5—Personnel Problems

A good chunk of my time has lately been taken up with team problems. First, Dick has been asked to leave the team against his will. He is very likeable, but George feels he is just not an efficient worker. He is leaving to go to Paris in search of another AFSC assignment there. Then, some of us have been trying to convince the authorities that a slot should be found here for Alice, but so far to no avail. I have had many long conversations with various team members about personnel problems that really are none of my business. Our team is not one unit in spirit at all but is a much-divided group, nothing like the old group, which we had two years ago. It is most unfortunate and it deprives us of a lot of our efficiency when we have to fight every inch of the way to make sure that some members are not trying to pull something over on the others. It is most un-Quakerly, I must say.

I must also say that I almost enjoy it. With all the problems, I feel like I am a stabilizing influence. I know I have helped Dick through his difficult time. In some instances, Dick was perceived as not as satisfactory in his work as some wished. In response, the Paris office was asked to offer him a job in Germany. When it was offered, he said he would rather stay here. To get him to move, pressure was applied under the pretext that the other job was more urgent. Before he could get away, it turned out there was no job in Germany. It seems now that they wanted to get rid of him, not so much because of his perceived inefficiency as just due to personality conflicts. Our chief, George, is not my idea of a good director. He is more efficient than George Mathues was, but he seems to lack warmth, understanding, and the human approach. I think he is basically all right but more of the trouble is with his wife. They came here last June. When they arrived, they announced she was going to have a baby. They both claimed they were not aware of her pregnancy in June even though the baby arrived in November. If the AFSC had known of her pregnancy in June, she probably would not have been permitted to come. George may not have known it but no one believes her. There are also a number of minor problems about which we probably should write Philadelphia. However, we hesitate to put them in a letter that might be misunderstood. I guess we will just worry it out here. However, as I have said, I must leave the problems of the Vienna unit to others and concentrate on my EDREC job.

February 7—More Evening Fun

It seems that every night some activity presents a diversion for me. One night I took Gerti Feifar to see *Hamlet*, the last night it was on the stage in Vienna. Then, despite my misgivings of two years ago about Balls I did break down and go to not one, but five. Last Saturday at noon, Sven was talking on the phone with one of our Youth Program girls. It turns out he was just declining her invitation to go to a Ball that evening. She then asked me to go as her escort, as she was to take part in some of the opening dances. Remembering my experience two years ago, I at first declined, but after lengthy persuasion I accepted. It turned out to be a masked Ball with all kinds of interesting costumes. For me it was a much gayer evening that the one two years ago. The girl was nice enough. Her father is a painter and had just painted the walls of the hall. We danced but little. Most of the time we sat and talked. About all I had to say from 1:00 to 5:00 a.m. was yes, no, and maybe! The second Ball was not a masked Ball. It was attended by about 15 from our Youth group and that made for a lot of fun. The music was good. There were two bands in this huge ballroom, one a modern dance band, and the other an old time monarchial band that played only Viennese waltzes and marches. This Ball was a beautiful sight to see. Dick and I were the only Americans in attendance, as far as we could tell.

Another evening we stopped in at an official government Ball for an hour or so. Several government officials including the Chancellor were there. A couple of us looked in on other nights at two other Balls, the Technical Ball and the Artists' Ball. Every night in February there is a big Ball that lasts until 5:00 in the morning when the streetcars start up. One of our Youth group members said she had been up every night the last week until 5:00 at a Ball. Then she had to go to work at 8:00 a.m. every day. It just seems like too much of a good thing.

February 12—My Bosses

Your letter today reminded me of all the people to whom I am responsible. Let me try to list them. First, I want to keep you as informed as much as possible on my life here. Then, I feel responsible to keep Fairview, my home Meeting, informed. Then, there is the AFSC in Philadelphia, the AFSC in Paris, the Quaker Team here in Vienna, the ÖGB, the USDL in Washington (they bought my projector), the many organizations from whom I have borrowed films, and of course, the people here whom I represent in the realms of ideas in the current difficulties of the unit. This list does not even mention all my personal friends who want to hear from me about my program. Life is hectic, busy, and satisfying.

EDREC in Action

February to April, 1949

February 19—At Last EDREC Begins

I spent a good bit of time this week in orienting Herr Rohm to my planned program. I had done most of my planning with Noverl, one of the ÖGB Central Office employees. Herr Rohm, another employee of Mela's, will be with me often. Although he does not drive, he will be an asset to me as he is a good speaker and can help me with my speaking. He will augment my program by giving a sex lecture to the apprentices.

Thursday, Herr Rohm and I left Vienna about 10:00 a.m. and arrived at 4:00 p.m. at my first home, Sigmundsberg bei Mariazell. It was not quite the complete plunge into the unknown I expected, since I had gotten acquainted with the director, Frau Bayer, a month ago on the Quaker House outing. Even so, it was not without some feelings of hesitancy and perhaps even inadequacy, that I began my first program Thursday night. Herr Rohm started by explaining about the Youth Division of the ÖGB, about AFSC work in Austria, about Quaker philosophy, and then introduced me. I uttered a few sentences of that "fluent German" ascribed to me by an AFSC newsletter last fall, and then began the visual education program, films.

Yesterday morning, I attempted what is known as "informal Quaker interpretation" by talking informally with the boys. The extent of my success can best be gauged by the following: 1) I now know how to play Bauernschnapsen (a crude card game), and 2) I gained the confidence of the boys enough for one of them to ask me a question. Mind you, this is the first question put to the Quakers in the beginning of this great educational program, the EDREC program. The question was "How can I join the US Army in Vienna?" Following that, I did get more involved with them, mostly answering questions about life in the US. Then last night I felt more at ease in presenting a second evening of films.

February 26—Real Job Under Way

Last Saturday we moved to my second recuperation home, Spital am Semmering, and stayed three days, leaving on Tuesday for my third home, Moosham bei Tamsweg, where we stayed until yesterday, Friday, before returning to Vienna. My old nemesis, truck problems, hit us both on Tuesday and on Friday. First, the truck began to hesitate now and then. For four hours we hobbled along, stopping every few minutes to investigate another theory we had developed on what was wrong. Eventually the truck died completely. Fortunately, we were right in front of a British Recovery Post. In this eastern outpost of the British Empire, I managed to find a most cooperative Englishman who in a couple of hours had us back on the road in good style.

Then Friday, when we returned from Moosham to Vienna, we had to go through Salzburg onto the American road through the Russian zone as my Russian pass over the Semmering had expired. We had difficulty going over the Tauern Pass as it had been snowing all night, which made the road very slippery. Soon the truck began to limp along again. We made it to Wels where it completely died in front of a US Army QM (Quarter Master) dump. By doing some first class pleading, we managed to get help and got a new gas line. Without further problems, we got back to Vienna that night.

Back to the recuperation homes. You may be surprised that we visited only three homes. We had planned to go on to Mittewald but it had just closed due to a scarlet fever epidemic and won't be open for another couple of weeks. A fifth home is at present under construction at Cap Wörth am Wörthersee. The Central Office is negotiating for a sixth home in Tyrol. These last two should be in operation by May or June. The other recuperation homes of the ÖGB are in the Russian zone and thus off limits to me.

I considered this trip as rather an experiment to find out just what I could do that would appeal to the boys. Each night of the trip, I put on movies, narrating those that were not in German. On this trip they were as follows:

- Evening #1
  - Comedy
  - *Scottish Wool,* a film on wool manufacturing
  - *Reaktion Positive*, a German film on syphilis
  - Comedy
  - *Geography of the Earth*, proving barriers are only in men's minds
  - *Hindu Dances*
  - Comedy
- Evening #2
  - Film strips on the panorama of the US
  - *Clear Track Ahead*, a film on US railroads
  - Comedy
  - *Ohio Farming*, a film I made last year in Ohio
  - *Portage*, a film on how Indians built canoes
  - Comedy

- Evening #3

    - *Achtung Mücken*, a German film on malaria and mosquitoes

    - *The Eighth Plague*, about Grasshopper plagues in Africa

    - Comedy

    - *Searchlight on the Nations*, a film about the United Nations

    - Comedy

At first I was rather hesitant about the US films, as they might be perceived as being perhaps too much overt US propaganda. I find that I must be careful not to overbalance the program with them but as the boys are intensely interested in almost every phase of American life and as my own experience is naturally mostly from the US, one evening entirely devoted to US films is not too much. They particularly seemed to enjoy my film on Ohio farming! Using film strips was most acceptable even though it does put more of a strain on my German

In the first two homes, because of lack of time on their part, I gave no other formal programs. However, in each home, Herr Rohm held a two-hour lecture and discussion with the boys on sexual problems. They put unsigned questions into a box and he then led a discussion on each question. In every home the following question always arose, "What is a kiss?" Herr Rohm answered it in part as follows: "In one sense a kiss is a civilized form of greeting. To some peoples of the earth it is a very comical form of greeting. But then we think of some other forms of greeting as comical. The Eskimos rub noses in greeting. A few years ago there arose a most comical form of greeting in Middle Europe. When two friends met instead of simply greeting each other they would always drag a third party into it by raising the right hand and saying 'Heil Hitler.' " That always brought down the house. In the course of questions, there were always a number about America and with Herr Rohm's help, I did my best to address them.

In Moosham where we had more time, there developed an obvious interest in my other prepared program, music. One afternoon about 70 of the 150 boys in camp gathered for an hour and a half of record playing. About their only knowledge of American music is jazz. I chose to use a program I had developed on folk music. I would informally tell something of the background of each record before playing it. I had been dubious as to the reaction I would get but was most happy to find that the boys took to it very well. After the formal program was over, they gathered informally to ask other questions about music and to listen to some classical music I had with me. I believe this type of program offers more opportunity for direct contact with the boys than the films do.

In general, I spent time in each home showing movies, playing records, going on hikes with the boys, playing cards with them, talking with them on about any subject, and yes, fumblingly playing a little soccer. The camp had only one soccer ball. It seems to me that one method of improving the program is through the group leaders. To the apprentices, I am only an outsider who presents programs and ideas and then is gone. The group leaders will be there every time I visit a camp. They are young fellows between 18 and 28. The leaders have ongoing contact with the apprentices. At Moosham, the 150 boys are divided into four groups, each under one group leader. On this trip I found that the group leaders were more interested in discussing basic problems of the groups in the camps—the world, democracy, communism, Quakerism, unionism, etc.—than the boys themselves were. I hope that in the course of time I will be able to really get to know these group leaders, their problems, their hopes, and their fears. Through them, perhaps I can have a more lasting influence with the apprentices. My hope is that during the course of the month some of the ideas presented by my program and my presence will give rise to continued discussions between the apprentices and group leaders.

The last evening in Moosham proved to be a most satisfying one. After the last film was shown, a group of apprentices presented a short program for me consisting of a number of folk songs and a speech of thanks and farewell. Then one of the boys presented me with a charcoal drawing of the camp that he had made. It was a most touching ceremony symbolizing to me the fact that there can be as great or greater hunger of the mind than of the body. Those boys really appreciated the fact that their relatively dull vacation had become interesting because of the EDREC visit. They were entertained, they were given food for thought, and in my opinion, what is most important is that they had a chance to exchange ideas and experiences with an Ausländer (foreigner).

Upon returning to Vienna, I made a report to Mela. She asked me how the boys reacted to the program. I told her what I had heard the boys say, "Leiwand, leiwand. Es war sehr Klass." I hadn't actually understood what that meant. It is not good German but is Viennese slang. Mela didn't tell me either, but she said if that was the reaction she was quite satisfied. Well, we with the EDREC program are at last under way, feebly at first, but it is started. By we, I mean a lot of people, Mela, Mel, Noverl, Herr Rohm, the Vienna AFSC, and AFSC support in Philadelphia. Philadelphia writes that there is a lot of interest there in the EDREC program. I can now report to them that the whole ÖGB is taking an interest in it too.

March 7—Another Skiing Attempt

Friday night, Walter Adrian of the Mennonites and I took the train to Salzburg. Then Saturday morning, we went on an Army bus to Berchtesgaden in Germany where we met Elaine, Wendy Elliott, and Alice, all of the Munich team. Alice had just recently left the YM-YW work in Austria to join the AFSC in Munich. We spent the weekend in this Army hotel and worked at skiing during the daylight hours. An operating ski tow helped a lot. I actually got a little better than before under the skillful teaching of Alice, who was the only experienced skier of the group.

After dinner Saturday night, the five of us were sitting around the dinner table, drinking coffee, and talking in German. A German waiter came in bringing a military policeman who told Alice she had to leave the hotel immediately. I demanded to know from the MP why he was trying to eject her. He said the waiter told him that he had heard us talking and though it was obvious the four of us were American, Alice's speech gave her away as being a German and Germans were not allowed to be served there. Alice then broke into her normal English and the MP apologized profusely. I think Alice was quite pleased with the incident. This had been quite a festive meal for me as it was my 29th birthday.

March 21—Odds and Ends

I have been busy the last two weeks doing a lot of housekeeping in Vienna. One weekend we entertained the Munich team. I needed to start the application for a Russian pass for my next trip out. One weekend was parents' weekend at the Community Center where our Austrian young people did programs for their parents. Afterwards I led some folk and square dancing.

I had trouble with the heating in my apartment. I had a huge American stove that had no draft and always

Community Center program for parents

smoked up the curtains. I got a new stove that is so small you can't feel the heat three feet away, so I spend as little time as possible in my apartment.

One morning I spent "in conference" with Mrs. Wesley P. Cook, whose husband is the new trade union representative on the Marshall plan in Austria. She has done a lot of workers' education work and was most helpful to me in planning additions to the EDREC program. Tuesday, Noverl and I went to Sigmundberg and Thursday to Spital am Semmering for two short EDREC program visits. Noverl does not make speeches to the boys; he just becomes one of them.

This past week I was able to get a visa from the Hungarians along with entrance and exit permits from the Russians in order to attend a Fair in Budapest. This may be my last chance to go there as the AFSC was expelled from Hungary last week. I don't care about the Fair and probably won't even go. I have the names and addresses of several people whom I will try to visit. At any rate, I left Vienna on the train at 5:30 this evening. There were many people on the train as we left Vienna, but by the time we reached the border there were only five left to go through to Hungary. Even so, it took us an hour to go through customs. The officials were most friendly. At one time seven of them, all Hungarian soldiers, gathered around to look at my camera and inquire how much it cost and how available it was for the average worker. I arrived in Budapest at 11:30 p.m., but did not know how to find the hotel where I had a reservation. I couldn't make anything out from the signs as they were, of course, all in Hungarian. Finally, I found a Hungarian soldier who knew some German. He took me to the proper streetcar and before letting me get on, found another soldier to go with me. So, being handed over from one to the other I made it here to the hotel.

March 23—Budapest

I think I wrote that I never did make it to the Fair, but spent the whole time in visiting people. Dr. Loren Hadley of Ohio had given me the address of the first family I visited. He had been in Europe with the AFSC after World War I. For the past two years, he has been in correspondence with this family as they had found his name in one of the coats distributed by the AFSC. The last letter they wrote to him said that things were not going so well in Budapest, but said no more. Would I just drop over to Budapest sometime and visit them? He had given me two addresses for the Ory family. Upon going to one of them, I found it to be a building with many apartments but no nameplates. A policeman standing in the hall wanted to know whom I wished to see. However, a sixth sense told me not to tell him for whom I was looking. I went to the other address and found the right apartment without difficulty and without help. I knocked and presently a woman some 60 years old came to the door but did not open it. She asked in Hungarian what I wanted (I suppose she did, as I know no Hungarian). I asked her if she could speak German. The door opened a crack and she asked me in German what I wanted. I told her I was from the Quaker team in Vienna and was looking for the Ory family. At that the door swung wide and I found myself seated in the parlor before more was said. I explained I was visiting them at the request of Dr. Hadley and would be particularly interested in talking with her son, Alex.

At that, she burst into tears. After a couple of minutes, she managed to regain control of herself enough to say, "You came to see Alex, but you are just one day too late. THEY took him yesterday!" He had left home in the morning and later two policemen came to the door demanding to search for him. She asked why he was wanted and they said it was none of her business. As soon as they were convinced he was not at home, they left. He did not return home last night. And if he had gone into hiding, he would have sent word. None came and they know what that means—he has been taken. Been taken? What does that mean? She said that it is now the systematic policy of the government to take all Hungarians who were officers during the war and who were in American prisoner of war camps. In the final stages of the war, the officers had the choice of heading east or west for capture. He had gone west. And that was enough of a crime.

What happens now, I asked? Of course that means he is now in Andrassy Ut 60, the political prison in the center of the city. The women who do the washing report that every day the clothes that come out to be washed are blood stained. So his being there probably means torture and death.

The whole family had made plans to escape Hungary. On the Sunday before, Alex had been to the border. He reported that the whole border between Austrian and Hungary was mined and guarded by bloodhounds. Anyone caught trying to escape disappears completely. He found that the border of Yugoslavia was not as well guarded, and had planned to leave that way the following week. Now it was too late. Frau Ory, her husband, and their daughter had also made plans to escape. A friend of theirs has a friend who works in the American Legation (American presence in Budapest, but not an Embassy) who claimed that for 6000 forints per person he would put them aboard American Army trucks taking textiles out to Vienna. Pinning their hopes on this, they had sold everything in order to get the necessary 18,000 forints. However, they did not trust this so-called friend, and were fearful they might be betrayed.

She wondered if I, as an American, could discreetly inquire at the Legation to find out if such a transport really existed. I am afraid I had to draw the line on that one. You can imagine me going to the Legation and inquiring at the information desk where to get in touch with the department operating an illegal smuggling ring to get people out to Austria. Here was the only way I could help them and I couldn't even do that!

The fears went on for three and a half hours. Story after story of the brutality and inhuman controls of a police state were cited. I was getting a glimpse almost back to the days of Nazi Germany. The Ory family feels they are marked for extinction because they are and have been members of the middle class. They know that any day now the husband will lose his job at the State Museum where he is a famous taxidermist. Each of them has been grilled a number of times to determine their connection with the West. They have refused to do Party work such as checking attendance at church. A record is kept of everyone who attends.

Presently, I met the husband and daughter, frightened, hysterical, and yet amazingly brave despite it all. They told me how fortunate it was that I had not asked the policeman where they lived, for the mere fact of a visit by an American could spell disaster for anyone. They realized that my presence was a danger but in spite of it they thanked me again and again for visiting them and giving them a chance to see that there are still people "of good will" in the world and that there are countries in which one can yet live in peace. The only thing I was able to do for them in a tangible way was to bring some letters out of the country for them. One of the letters was from the daughter to her fiancé in Germany whom she has not seen for four years. Let me quote part of it:

"Everything here is a lie. It is a terrible situation. War with all its horrors would be preferable to this situation in which we live. We cannot sleep peacefully anymore since the Party has marked us off. Even should the travel permits come, we would not now be allowed to leave the country by any legal means. We are simply locked in a prison! Do not believe any of the Hungarian reports in the papers. They are 100% lies. It is this terrible Russian situation, which will determine whether or not we will ever again see each other. It would take a miracle and in such I can no longer believe. Only God can help!"

There was one other thing I could have done for this girl. While the family did not outright ask it of me, they hinted very broadly that I should marry the daughter for a few days and make it possible for her to legally leave Hungary. Fortunately for me, I didn't have to make a decision on this as my Hungarian visa and Russian pass were only good for two days and the marriage paper work would have taken several more.

Let me tell you of some other visits I made. I visited with Kato, a Hungarian girl, who had worked with the AFSC team in Budapest prior to their expulsion from Hungary last week. She feels that she is in a very desperate situation. Having worked for the Americans, she cannot get any work now in Hungary. She sees no future for herself in Hungary and is searching for every possibility to get out. She was also concerned about one of her fellow Hungarians who had worked with the Quakers. She was convinced that he had been selling out the rest of the Hungarian Quaker workers in order to insure his own position.

I called on a 35-year-old woman who had lived in Vienna for a couple of years after the war and had come to Arthur's International Club there. She is a violinist and plays over the radio. Arthur told me she probably would talk frankly about the situation. She much prefers living in Budapest today to Vienna! She says the government takes care of artists. They get enough salary so they do not have to worry about their daily bread.

I asked her if she didn't feel hemmed in by the police state. She said no, life was very pleasant in Budapest. Although she is not a member of the Party and does not approve of some of the things they do, she has absolute freedom to come and go as she pleases, to play what she wants. Of course, you must be discreet. You don't say anything against the government, you have no associations with Americans, your record must be clear of Nazism, and you must not have been a member of the middle class. Aside from those minor restrictions that don't bother her, everything is rosy in Hungary!

My next visit to a Reformed Church Minister was not very satisfactory. Almost before we had exchanged greetings some member of the church who spoke English insisted on translating from Hungarian rather than letting the Pastor and me talk directly in German. He said that today the Reformed Church has no difficulties at all with the government. The Church is growing, life in Budapest is wonderful. Later, the Mennonite in Vienna, who had given me the Pastor's name, told me that relatively speaking, this might all be true. In former days, the Reformed Church could hardly make a move because of the oppression by the Catholic Church. He thinks they may have a really new found freedom, but one that will not last long. Like me, he mistrusts this eager beaver translator.

Last Saturday, an article appeared in one of the Budapest papers about the departure of the Quakers. I saw it myself but of course had to have Kato translate it. It said something like this: "The American Quakers have completed their mission in Hungary and are now returning to America. As the leader of the mission, Albert Simon, was leaving he stated that in his opinion there was complete freedom of religion in Hungary today." Albert

Simon may have very well said that when he left Budapest but since he left Hungary a year and a half ago it certainly doesn't apply today. The leader of the mission who left last week was our own Ed Wright from Vienna.

Now let me say a word as to my reactions as a tourist. The border officials were courteous as could be. On my return, they were no more difficult than the border officials between the US and Canada. In Budapest on the streets, I found everyone to whom I tried to talk most helpful in giving me directions. About every third person could speak German but often their German was not good enough to recognize me as an American! On two different occasions on the streetcars, an identical conversation took place. The conductor wanted to know how far I was going. But she never spoke German. I would only answer with "Können Sie Deutsch?" (Do you speak German?), until some kind passenger would help. In both cases after I paid the conductor the passenger sat down with me and in low tones asked if I was from Germany. Upon hearing that I was from Vienna, they asked in plaintive tones, "Well, how are things on the OUTSIDE anyway?"

People seemed to be fairly well dressed. However, I could see but little difference in the dress and in the shop windows from Vienna. Prices were nearly identical in relationship to the actual wages in each country. I was surprised to notice the American display of books in the window of each bookshop. They always had Sinclair Lewis, "Strange Fruit," "Inside USA," and no other author. In addition, when I say Sinclair Lewis, I mean everything that I ever heard he wrote. My only bit of sightseeing was to walk up to Andrassy Ut 60, morbid curiosity I suppose. Having worked myself up into a state of righteous indignation at the government by that time, I could just feel the horrors going on behind those walls. Outside was something real. Troop after troop of soldiers were marching around the whole prison, 55 in a troop, 100 feet between each troop. Each troop was singing in perfect rhythm some weird chant.

What do I think of this whole business now that the communists have taken over Hungary and I have had a glimpse of it? It would take a better man than I not to be horribly confused by the whole affair. I do know that I saw some of the terror that a police state can instill in the hearts of some of its citizens. It may have been a justified terror, or it might have been only imagined. But to the Ory family it was real. Time and again from all who would talk, I heard it said that there was no hope from within Hungary. The only hope lies with the outside. They are longing for the day America intervenes and drives the Russians out. Is it enough for me to tell them that war is never the answer to stopping injustices? They now see only the injustices and have already forgotten the horrors of war. Then at last, this evening it was a relief to take the train back to Vienna where life seems to be worth living for more and more people.

March 27—The Recuperation Home for Girls

After getting back from Budapest Wednesday night, I took off right away on Thursday with Herr Rohm for Mittewald bei Villach. This was my first visit with the EDREC program to the recuperation home for girls, all 110 of them. They are housed in a more permanent structure than the barracks at most of the other homes.

The news of our coming and some hint of our planned programs for them must have preceded us for we were photographed and welcomed most heartily.

ÖGB Home at Mittewald

Home Director Elli Schubert on left, and assistants

We put on a similar program to the one we had given at the last boys' home. I found the girls to be more responsive to our program. They didn't hesitate to raise questions that seemed to be more thoughtful than those raised by the boys.

I also found that it is better to stay longer in a home. The first day is spent in just getting acquainted and helping the apprentices get over their fear of talking with a stranger. Today, my only formal program was one on music. The rest of the time was spent in informally answering questions and carrying on discussions with the girls.

I was pleasantly surprised to find a number of them genuinely interested in Quakers. As you know, I am not one to go to the homes and attempt to proselytize. On the other hand, when someone is really interested to know why we are here, I don't turn down an opportunity to expound.

Apprentices welcoming us

Presenting my program

Music program

Audience to my program

One of the girls who was particularly interested in hearing about Quakers, was a girl from Berndorf. She said she had been curious ever since 1946 as to just who the Quakers were. She had heard of them from her grandmother, who had gotten some clothes from them. She had never had any personal contact with them until I turned up in Mittewald. She was not only interested in the relief aspect of the AFSC, but also wanted to know what Quakerism in America was like. Now do tell, which aspect of Quakerism does one explain—Philadelphia Yearly Meeting, Five Years Meeting, Oregon Yearly Meeting, or what?

March 30—A New Recuperation Home

Monday, we drove on west through Lienz up the Glocknerstrasse to a little town of Kieferhof. We found it to be one of the most beautiful regions of Austria, in the East Tyrol. We had to walk the last mile, as the narrow road was still too icy to drive over. This home had been run by the Carinthian division of the ÖGB for the past two years, but had just been taken over by the central office in Vienna. No one from the Central office had ever been there so Mela asked us to include it in our itinerary. The director and the one group leader (there were only 27 boys in the home) were totally unaware of the fact that the local ÖGB had turned over the home to the Central office. At first, they were naturally a bit reserved toward us, but then they just about fell over themselves trying to make a good impression on us, for they felt the security of their jobs depended on our report.

I can report favorably on the director but the group leader was an entirely different matter. The first hint of difficulty was during the first evening's program. The boys simply did not react to anything. They didn't even laugh at my most amusing comedy. Herr Rohm was as much surprised as I at the lack of reactions. The next day I put on the program of music, but this time I was alone with the boys and they were normal again. Then, in off-hours we talked with the group leader. As a result of it all and of a number of other observations, we found that this leader was the essence of strict discipline. The boys hardly dared breath without his approval. It made for an orderly camp but it is hardly the sort of atmosphere that AFSC would care to support. In the course of this long discussion, it turned out that this leader is what one might call an un-regenerated Nazi. He had been in Finmark during the war and was with the retreating Germans as they laid waste the countryside. A number of revealing comments came forth from him. Hitler didn't go far enough on the Jews. America made the great mistake of getting on the wrong side in the war. He expressed great regret that Dewey was not elected, as everyone knows the Republicans would have taken a strong stand against Russia. This chap is a keen one with a number of obvious blind spots. The situation was all the more surprising because I have not found a similar one in any of the homes operated by the Central Office. In fact, I am continually amazed at the high quality of the personnel in the homes.

This brings up the question as to how far I should take an active interest in the affairs of the homes. Should I report my reactions or not? There is always the danger that I have misunderstood or misinterpreted. On this particular issue, there is no problem as Mela is coming to Kieferhof next week to investigate the home. I do have the feeling that as time passes I will be taking a more active part in the affairs of the homes. One of the men in the Central Office says that the opinions of a relative outsider are of particular value as he might see and hear things in an entirely different way than the regular members of the Central Office.

This morning, we left Kieferhof and began our departure with the mile walk to our truck. Eight boys with packs on their backs carried my equipment to the truck. I felt almost like an African explorer! As we started out in the truck, I discovered that there were no brakes at all. For some unknown reason the brake fluid had leaked out. There was nothing else to do than to drive very slowly the 10 kilometers down the mountain using the motor as a brake. Only once was it necessary for Herr Rohm to help with the handbrake, which worked, fortunately. In Lienz it was a simple matter to get more fluid and bleed out the air. Then back we went to Mittewald, only to spend the night.

April 2—VIP Visitor

Thursday morning, Herr Rohm and I picked up Lou Schneider at the train station in Villach. He is one of the commissioners from Paris and is visiting the Austrian program primarily, I suspect, to evaluate my program. We first took him to Cap Wörth on Wörther See to see the site of the new home that is now under construction. When it is finished in July it will take 200 boys. Then, we stopped in Mittewald for him to see the facilities for the girls and to meet the camp director. Then, we headed north over the Katschberg Alps. The road here is the steepest of any road in Austria; at one point the slope reaches a 29% grade. We found snow only on the upper part. Lower down the farmers were spreading manure and some were even getting on with the spring plowing. By suppertime we made it to Moosham where we stayed until yesterday and where I went on with my program for Lou to observe. I put on my music program, played Ping-Pong and volleyball with boys, and talked with the group leaders and the director at length. I hope Lou got a good impression. I think he did but as he is a rather quiet person, I didn't get much out of him. He understands German well but spoke practically none.

My musical presentation always includes a couple of Negro spirituals and I usually say something about their origin. One of the boys asked as to the status of the Negro in American life. I have had that question a number of times and I always say that phase of our culture is one about which I am not proud. And yes, it is true that to a large degree the Negro is a second-class citizen in America. However, I always point out that there are many people working to change this. This particular chap asked further, "Since you admit that in America there are second class citizens, how can you justify the fact that America entered the war against Germany on the grounds that Germany treated some of its citizens as second class, namely the Jews?" As my program develops and I find myself more at ease in it, I am being asked questions that are more penetrating, more questions that dig into fundamentals and not so many like that first one about how to join the US Army. Oh yes, one question came up about Unions. "If the Unions in the States want to really be of service to the workers why are the CIO and the AFL always fighting each other? Why don't they merge?" I wish I knew more about Unions. Actually, I am surprised that there is not more interest in unionism. This subject seems to arouse about the least interest of anything.

April 3—German Interlude

Saturday morning Lou and I left Tamsweg leaving Herr Rohm behind. We headed north over the Tauernpass and reached Salzburg by noon. We had a bit of trouble getting gas there as the Army has a new rule permitting no sale of gas until the vehicle is inspected. My truck was OK except for a broken stoplight, and there were no stoplights available—so no gas. The Captain finally relented and allowed me to get five gallons that would get me to the first station in Germany where they don't have this rule! At 2:00 p.m., according to prearrangement, we met Nuschi Plank, Ruth Dross, and Paul, all from the team in Vienna, and together we drove to the DP children's home in Bad Aibling near Rosenheim. There, I finally delivered the half truckload of kindergarten toys that I had carried all over Austria from Vienna for the AFSC team to distribute in Bad Aibling. The children here have hopes that a home can be found for them in some foreign land. At least by being here they are eligible. There is a tremendous amount of work here for the five AFSC workers.

Today Lou, Ruth, and Paul went on to Munich. Nuschi was busy with the children so Alice, who is now working here, and I went to Bad Reichenhall up on the Predigstuhl for another fling at skiing. I fear I had forgotten what I had previously learned from her. At any rate I learned it all over again.

April 8—Tour Completion

Monday morning, on my return to Austria I went a bit out of my way to deliver Nuschi to a social workers' conference in Saalbach near Zell-am-See. Then, alone I headed east past Marlis' castle that is occupied again by the US Army. I went back over the Tauernpass and reached Moosham by 6:30 p.m. The campers had not been sure I would make it that day so they all cheered as they saw me driving up. They knew my coming meant movies that night. I might mention here that I bring somewhat different movies each time I come. Some of the new ones on this trip included:

- *Geography from the Air*
- *Ski Sonntag in Cannonen* (A Swiss film on skiing)
- *Alte Sussex* (Travcloguc on Sussex)
- *Iceland on the Prairies* (Migrations from Iceland to Canada)
- *Erdölleitung* (Construction of the 'Big Inch')
- *Cowboy* (Dispels the 'romantic' cowboy idea)
- *Unsere Gross Glocknerstrasse* (Construction of Austria's most famous highway)
- *Ein Volk in den Alpen* (Life of the Swiss Alpine dweller)
- And then, my farm film continues to be a "best seller"

Tuesday, Herr Rohm and I spent most of the day driving to the home at Sigmundsberg. This time we were able to drive clear up to the house, but only after we had put on chains. Then yesterday, we came on to Spital. Finally, this evening after doing the evening program we drove on through the night back "home" to Vienna.

Now that I am well into the EDREC program, I can't help but wonder how well it is really doing. It is hard for me to judge, particularly, at this early stage of the program. There is as yet not much concrete evidence on which to make a judgment. It is a continuing process and the results will not be known until long after I have left Austria. The only standard by which I can judge it yet is by what the ÖGB says. So far, they seem quite happy about it. The really tangible result that may come is the more definite realization on their part of the need for an educational program in the homes. I hope that by the time I leave they will be able to have an Austrian, full time on the job, to do what no foreigner can do. If I can show the way and break the trail, so to speak, it will be enough.

I have been on this job long enough now to see three areas or programs that badly need help. First, I find that their libraries are woefully short. I hope I can remedy that lack a bit through the help of Mrs. Cook.

Secondly, some of the leaders have indicated that a handicraft program would really be good for some of the apprentices. I am at loss as to how to start something of this nature. Thirdly, is the lack of just plain recreational equipment. The boys play Ping-Pong only when they bring their own balls. They play soccer only when they bring their own soccer ball. The chess sets are all broken or have pieces missing. The group leaders feel that recreation is very important to the boys. A month's rest of sleep, food, and my programs are fine but recuperation means more than all that. They need to have the opportunity to play together. The Central Office is concerned about all this but just does not have the funds to do anything about it. One soccer ball, for example, costs $12. I will work on three possible sources for this equipment: the British Army, the US Army, and the AFSC. For your information, let me list what we could use: 4000 Ping-Pong balls, 30 soccer balls, 60 volleyballs, 30 chess sets, and 15 croquet sets. This would be a bare minimum, as it would be divided among 10 homes.

April 20—Vienna Interim

The minute I got back to Vienna, I got caught up again in the whirl of youth activities here, or so it seems. That first Saturday night I helped Louise handle the usual Saturday night folk dancing group. Several nights last week I showed some of my films to different youth groups at the Center. Monday after Easter is always a big Austrian holiday. A large group of the young people from Quaker House took a long hike through the Vienna Woods that day, and both Louise and I went along. There were nearly 50 Austrians and as we two were the only Americans, we practically lost our national identity for the day. It was a good feeling to feel so accepted by them.

I spent some time with Mrs. Cook with the US Army Information Service and through her good efforts was able to get over 200 books from them for distribution in the ÖGB homes. There are about 15 different books and about 12 copies of each so each home can have about two copies of each. Not much, but a whole lot better than none. I also spent some time showing Mela some of the films I use in the homes. She seems to think my programs are very well received and that the homes are always very glad to have me come. Again, I spent more time collecting films from various agencies in Vienna for my next trip. I even spent some time loading cereal into my truck for delivery to some of the homes.

I, of course, attended the two staff meetings held while I was in Vienna. One was particularly focused on what our purpose in Vienna had become. Our discussions are never as good as they were in the old group two years ago. People just don't speak freely as most of them fear to make a mistake for fear it will be held against them. I, purposely, don't worry about it and blurt out whatever I think. I do some how feel quite removed from the group as I feel I belong more to the ÖGB. Then, too, I miss most of the staff meetings by being out of Vienna. After one of the meetings I spent a whole evening calming a most irate Annalies. She had a tiff with George and was much upset about it all.

Last Sunday was Easter Sunday. I went to Mass in the biggest church in Vienna, St. Stephan's. It wasn't very inspiring. The priest was talking about the Mindzenty trial in Hungary. It seems it is usually the case here that politics is pulled into the church. The people weren't paying much attention and seemed rather restless. At the door were the usual beggars plus a few people selling pamphlets on Mindzenty. Then I spent the rest of Easter at the office writing reports!

April 26—On the Road Again

Thursday morning Herr Rohm and I left Vienna for the all day drive to Mittewald, the girls' home. About 2:30 p.m., I noticed that my oil gauge wasn't registering. It turned out that we had a broken oil line and that all the oil had been pumped out through this break. I finally got it plugged with a piece of wood and we went on, stopping every so often to see if we still had oil. At each stop I had to add oil so by the time we reached Mittewald, I had used up all the 10 quarts I had brought with me. Despite the delay we were in time for a program that night. Friday, all 110 girls and the leaders took an all day hike and, of course, that included Herr Rohm and me. We went with a few of the group and one of the leaders up to the top of a mountain. But it would have to begin to rain! We found a cabin which enabled us to stay inside until the rain ended an hour or so later. It certainly was a good way to get acquainted with the young people. Then Saturday, I went into Villach and spent all morning getting a new oil line made and assembled.

Yesterday we drove on to the little home at Kieferhof. I was pleased to find that a much more acceptable group leader has replaced the former one. I plan to stay here until Thursday when we go back to Mittewald to meet a new group of apprentices. Before we left Mittewald, George called from Vienna to announce that he and Virginia are coming to Kieferhof tomorrow to watch me in action. I am a bit fearful of the visit for I feel he won't like it. Lou Schneider, from Paris, was a great visitor but I am not so sure about George.

Unplanned Vacation

May to June, 1949

May 4—Scarlet Fever?

Wednesday morning I woke up with a severe chill so I stayed in bed all day. Before evening, George and Virginia arrived. Upon discovering that I had a fever of 103, they diagnosed me as having a case of strep throat. They left the next morning but I stayed in bed all day. By Friday I felt a little better as my fever was down to 101, but the Home Director felt that a doctor should see me. Herr Rohm walked the two miles to the nearest telephone, called a doctor in the nearby town of Winklern, and came back with him later. After examining me, the doctor said I had scarlet fever. He particularly pointed out the red spots on my body that I could not see. At that, the wheels were set in motion. The Director called the hospital in Lienz and Herr Rohm called Vienna. A couple of hours later an ambulance arrived within a mile of the home. As it could not come any closer, some of the boys carried me on a stretcher to the ambulance and within the hour, I was quietly reposing in the hospital in Lienz.

In the room with me were two other scarlet fever patients. One girl was a year and a half old and the other girl was three. The three-year-old was quite frightened that a man was going to share their room. The nurses took very good care of me. However, the food was horrible. I was given the same as the babies with one exception. When they got milk, I got coffee. Here is the menu: breakfast—one cup of coffee and black bread; lunch—coffee, black bread and a sort of cake. Naturally I did not have much of an appetite.

Sunday, back in Vienna, Mela went to work to get me transferred back to Vienna. She sent Herr Bartel to Kieferhof to get my truck and return it to Vienna, arranged with the hospital in Lienz to release me, had Mel arrange with the US Army 110th Hospital in Vienna for me to be admitted to an isolation ward, and arranged for an Austrian Red Cross ambulance in Lienz to transport me. She had gone to a top official of the ÖGB and had gotten agreement for them to pay for the ambulance. This morning at 2 :00 a.m. the Red Cross ambulance with a driver and a nurse picked me up and started the trip to Vienna, 400 kilometers away. Later on in the morning, a wheel bearing burned out and that delayed us three hours. I was fearful of our being able to go through the Russian control on the Semmering, as the Russians have been known to prohibit the passage of any ill people through their line. However, I guess they have no objections to sick Austrians as they passed me through without checking to see if I were an Austrian.

However, getting into the US Army 110th Hospital in Vienna where we arrived at four o'clock that afternoon was another matter. The MPs would not allow the ambulance to drive into the hospital's courtyard, as the ambulance was an Austrian one. It took quite a bit of persuasion and finally I had to talk to the MP myself before they would let us drive in. Then we could not find the entrance. Two more MPs on duty there did not know where the entrance was. So finally, the Austrian driver and the nurse carried me into the nearest door where we found ourselves in the middle of the dispensary where over 20 patients were waiting to be examined. Again, they were stopped and were required to place me on the floor and leave immediately. Their crime? They were Austrians. Presently a Captain came over and wanted to know what I was doing lying on the floor. I explained that I had scarlet fever and had arranged to come here. He asked if I could walk and I replied that I did not know, as I had not been allowed to try for five days. "Well, get up and walk," he said. I managed to wobble into his office where he examined me. He told me that since I had no fever, there was nothing wrong with me; I had simply had too much bed rest. I protested and tried to explain to him what had happened. He said get up and get out and not come back for a week. After that, if I still felt weak he would see me again. This was quite a shock to suddenly be well! So out I walked.

I tried to call the office for transportation but suddenly remembered that it was Monday afternoon and the team was having a staff meeting at George's home. I didn't know his phone number so I walked the half-mile to our garage, only to find they were on a new schedule and had gone home for the day. Therefore, there was nothing left to do but to take a streetcar. I got off at the Red Cross Center planning to take a shower, get a haircut, and generally get cleaned up. But, I had forgotten that the Red Cross is closed on Monday. So finally, I went to the Regina Hotel where we sometimes eat lunch and waited until I could contact someone from the staff who took me home. Am I tired!

May 19—Viral Pneumonia

I am writing this letter from my hospital bed. Until today, I did not have access to a pen and paper. Let me go back a bit. After being dumped from the hospital on Monday May 4, I made it home to my apartment for the night. The next day I didn't feel very well and moved into Arthur's apartment above the office. My fever kept rising and the Staff was getting concerned. On Thursday Mela took time off from her work at the ÖGB and took me to Dr. Baier, the ÖGB doctor. He said he couldn't say this late whether or not I had had scarlet fever but he suspected that I had not. He attributed my red spots, which had been diagnosed as scarlet fever, to have really been caused by the sulfa I had been given. After putting me under a fluoroscope he found a couple of dark spots on my lungs that indicated lung trouble.

On Friday, Mela took me to one of the top lung specialist in Austria, a Dr. Primarius Brausmüller. He also put me under a fluoroscope and determined that I did not have TB but had viral pneumonia. I was quite relieved by his diagnosis, but, he indicated I needed two or three weeks' treatment in a hospital. Back to the 110th I went, where, since I had some fever, I was admitted this time. The doctor said that at this stage of pneumonia penicillin would have no effect. All I needed was bed rest and good food. And I have had plenty of both.

After a week and another x-ray, the doctor said it was time to start the penicillin. So every three hours since then, I now get a shot. It must do some good for I feel much better now. I have had no visitors until this week when Mel, Sven, and George came yesterday. Normally, only immediate family is permitted in this isolation ward. Until yesterday I have been completely isolated from the team and the world. At last, today they were able to send in my mail, pen, and paper. I have spent most of the time reading detective stories as that is about all the hospital library has.

I was pleased to learn that George had sent a strong letter of protest to the hospital commanding officer regarding the way I was first treated when I came here on May 2. By the way, I found out today that my hospital stay costs 10 dollars a day. It will all be paid by the Blue Cross insurance that was taken out on me by the AFSC.

May 21—Someone Else's Trouble

I learned of this problem last week but am taking the time now to write it down. Arthur, one of the longest running and stable team members, has developed a problem. Last Monday he pestered George all morning about some new theory of his. Then, at the staff meeting that afternoon he seemed to completely blow his stack. He announced that Quakers weren't important anymore; everyone was going to join up with the Russians anyway. He announced that he is now world citizen #1. He has never liked some of the things George has done but has been discreet about it. However, at staff meeting, he broke out against him, often with the truth, but with things you just don't say. At any rate, they finally got him calmed down enough to agree to come out here to visit me.

George told him he had to have a shot to immunize him against my pneumonia. But the shot was really to keep him quiet. At the last minute he caught on and it took eight people to hold him in his anger. He really told off George for having tricked him. The next day he was flown to Germany to a psychiatric hospital. There seems to be a difference of opinion among the team about the wisdom of tricking him into taking that shot. It certainly is a sad situation. The trouble now is that everything he has said and written during the last few months will be completely discounted even though he has made some excellent contributions to the sanity of the team. He probably will be sent home to Kansas shortly.

May 25—Secret Revealed

Another item that was revealed last week probably affects me more. It turns out that Mela and her husband got a divorce last December. They had not gotten on well for a long time and she wanted to get a divorce after the war, but he had opposed it because her name gave him prestige. Since there wasn't any particular need for a divorce, she didn't push it. In the meantime she and Mel had fallen it love so she now wanted the divorce. Her husband had now agreed to it since he is well enough established in his profession to be willing to make it official. They got the divorce but have kept it secret on her account. She felt that with an election coming up this year the divorce might be bad for the ÖGB in the election.

At any rate, she and Mel are planning to get married in two or three weeks. In September, they plan to go to a farm in New York State. Because of politics, the Austrians will not learn of the divorce and the marriage until after the election. But they have to get married now if they want to go the US in September. In order for an Austrian wife to get a US entry permit, she must be married to an American for at least three months. At the ÖGB, the intimates know only that she is leaving the ÖGB for America in September. By the way, Mel and I know the ex-husband pretty well and he and Mel are the best of friends.

This development affects me somewhat. I will have to get used to working with her replacement at the ÖGB and I will be the sole AFSC-ÖGB liaison with Mel gone. That is not too bad, as by now I know most of the ÖGB personnel. Probably my role will be more or less one of closing out the AFSC-ÖGB relations before I leave in February.

June 2—Out At Last

On Wednesday, May 25, I was released from the hospital with the warning to take it easy for a time. And that is just what I have done. I found I was rather weak. I have been sleeping 10 hours a night, napping a couple of hours during the day, and eating very well. The doctor suggested that a week or so in a mountain resort might be the best way to recover. Some members of the team have urged me to do something like that. Then yesterday, George called me in and told me he had made reservations for me at the Predigstuhl mountain resort near Salzburg, but in Germany. Now it is a rest and rehabilitation (R&R) center of the US Army. He didn't ask me if

I would like to go. He just told me I was going. I am afraid this is typical of his way of handling every situation. At any rate I am going! I'll be taking the train Saturday night to Salzburg.

June 3—Arthur

The big discussion of the week has been Arthur. He called up once from Wiesbaden in Germany and sent a letter saying he was all right and we should let him come back to Vienna. Rumor has it that they are going to send him to the States next week and they will allow only one visitor before he goes. In the phone call, he asked me to be that one visitor. But I am told I am still too weak to make the trip. Therefore, George thinks he will go. He claims that since he worked in a mental hospital for three years in CPS he understands these things better than the rest of us. But he is the very person whom Arthur cannot stand. Arthur feels that George betrayed him with the shot at the hospital. When Arthur phoned, one of the Austrian secretaries took the call as no one from the team was in. We have the same Austrian staff that has been here for three years, so most of them feel they know Arthur better than George does. At any rate, the Austrian staff felt I should hear about the phone call before George did. Finding me took them some time but they felt better being able to tell me first. A number of them including two of the Americans feel that perhaps Arthur was not really sick at all. So you can see it is rather a mess.

I should mention here that Mel and Mela got married this morning. Their only attendants were George and Virginia. Mel apologized for not inviting me. When he had to record the witnesses some days ago he didn't know if I would be well enough to come.

June 9—R&R

As planned, I took the night train on Saturday and came up here to Predigstuhl on Sunday. This resort is high up in the mountains and can only be reached with a long cable car ride. The high altitude, the quiet, and the good food ought to make anyone healthy. During the week there are only two or three others staying here. You should see the style that the waiters use to serve the meals, and I am usually the only one in the dining room. Well, not quite. I did have company as Alice was spending a couple of days here. Tuesday, Alice and I went down the cable car from where she took me in her car to Chiem See, another Army resort nearby to meet with some of her Bad Aibling team. As further R&R, we even went sailing that afternoon, but with an experienced sailor to run the boat. Then we went on to Bad Aibling where I spent the night. Then Wednesday, she put me on a train that took me to Innsbruck. I found myself much at ease just getting back into Austria. One noticeable difference is that in Germany Americans are not allowed to eat in civilian restaurants, but that is not so in Austria. I went to Innsbruck at the behest of the team, if I felt able, to visit two families who had been helping the Innsbruck team before they left. They also wanted me to interview a prospective candidate as a possible member of the upcoming Salzburg work camp planned for July and August. She had been tentatively accepted but my interview clinched the deal.

I went to a hotel and slept until noon today. Then by train back here to Predigstuhl in time for a late supper. I had to change trains four times and go through several customs inspections, which are just part of the usual travel problems. One of the minor problems is the time difference. Austria has middle European time the year round, but Germany went on daylight saving for the summer. So that causes some confusion. They are having a horrible time getting the train timetables right.

You might be interested in the prices I paid to eat and sleep in Innsbruck. Food prices are about 20% higher for me than as advertised because I had no ration coupons. Here is what I paid at a regular restaurant, figured at the legal rate of exchange, which an Army person would tell you was foolish to do.

- Lunch—$0.55. With beef and plenty of potatoes, spinach, lettuce, and soup.

- Dinner—$0.77. The same as lunch except pork chops instead of beef.

- Hotel room—$1 .70. Very nice.

- Breakfast—$1.10. High because I got it in the hotel. But very substantial with two eggs, marmalade, rolls, butter and coffee.

Although I spent a good while just riding the train, it was very restful to be in Innsbruck. Something about the place always seems to perk me up!

June 10—Permission and Travel

This morning I received a phone call from George Mathues who is now working with CARE in Stuttgart. He had been to Wiesbaden the day before to see Arthur and he said that Arthur had been asking for and expecting me to visit him. I called George Little in Vienna and got his reluctant permission for me to visit Arthur if I felt my health was up to it. At 6:00 this evening, I again went down the mountain at Predigstuhl and got to Munich by train at 9:30. I tried to get a sleeper on the military train to Frankfurt, but to no avail. However, I took a chance and got on the coach anyway. Soon I got in touch with the sleeper porter and talked with him a bit. He seemed most impressed that I could speak German, as this was a US military train. At 11:30 p.m. he hunted me down in the coach and told me he had found a berth for me. So I am riding in style to Frankfurt after all.

June 11—Arthur Again

I stopped for a time in Frankfurt to get breakfast and get cleaned up. Then, an hour's train ride took me to Wiesbaden, which is the headquarters of the US Air Force in Europe and was the base for the Berlin Airlift. It seemed positively American as I think I saw more Americans than Germans. Then I went to the hospital and found Arthur where we had a good two-hour conversation. He seemed very calm and in pretty good spirits. He was entirely rational but his memory was very faulty. He just cannot understand what made him lose his rationality in Vienna. He gets electric shocks every second day and is hopeful he can return to Vienna in three or four weeks. The nurse told me that was doubtful. Ah, it is a sad case when you can't hold on to your senses, but he seems as good ever, probably due to the shock treatments. He was most happy I had come. I do feel that it was worth it. There are many people in Vienna who wanted someone other than George to talk with him and I have done that.

June 13—Back "Home" Again

After leaving Arthur on Saturday, I spent a couple of hours wandering around in Frankfurt. The shops seem to have many goods on display, restaurants are operating, and outwardly, things looked something like in Vienna. However, there was an intangible difference. People looked sullen. Here and there were groups of young fellows clustered together as if fomenting some mischief. Clothing was obviously much worse than in Vienna. I didn't feel as if I wished to get to know any of the people—quite different from my feelings in Vienna. In Frankfurt, you get the feeling that the war has just ended with conquerors and conquered everywhere together. In Vienna, a new life has pushed that all into the past. I got a night sleeper to Munich where I got the local to Predigstuhl and arrived in time for Sunday lunch. In the afternoon George Mathues called and invited me to go with him to supper in Salzburg. Back down the cable car I went for a delightful supper and chat with him. And so back up the cable car for my last night at Predigstuhl. Then this afternoon I went back to Salzburg where I had reserved a sleeper to take me back to Vienna. While this had not been the rest that George Little had envisioned for me, I thrived on the activity and it was good to have the Predigstuhl as a home base. Thanks George.

EDREC & Other Duties

July to October, 1949

June 26—Retooling in Vienna

Since getting back to Vienna on June 14, I have been busy getting reorganized for my EDREC work. I had some conferences at the ÖGB with Mela, Noverl, Herr Rohm, and Mel. One criticism of my work is that I have not been making enough noise about Quakerism. One of the boys had reported that he thought Quakers were a movie company. I don't understand how he got that idea. I have a couple of good films on war and peace as well as one on CPS. I think showing one or two of these will open up opportunities to talk about Quakerism. I spent time renewing contacts with Viennese film distributors, getting Russian gray passes in order, taking pictures of Nuschi's kindergarten, and showing films several nights at the Quaker Center to different youth groups. On Friday, the 17th, four girls from the German AFSC arrived for a weekend visit. Alice Roberts was one of them and I had known two of the others, Carolyn and Wendy, briefly. So as usual, I got elected to show them around. Saturday night I collected them with David, Paul, and Sven and we went up on the Kahlenberg, a high hill overlooking Vienna, for dinner. We really splurged spending $3.00 a piece for the dinner. I might add that the girls paid their own way. They spent a good bit of their time in Vienna visiting Nuschi's kindergarten.

On Monday, June 20, I drove down to Graz where I spent the afternoon at the office of the British Army Coordinator of Civilian Supply. My purpose was to solicit athletic equipment for the ÖGB recuperation homes. The British officer was very friendly and concerned and promised to do his best with the proper authorities. I was also able to buy British gas coupons for use in the British zone. There are no recuperation homes in the Graz area but we do drive through the British Zone quite often to reach the recuperation homes. Friday and Saturday I got my truck loaded for my next trip. This time I also included half a ton of cereal to take to a summer home in Vorarlberg. We had intended to ship it directly from Vienna, but the Russian permit to ship food takes at least a month and by then the need for it will be over. By taking the cereal in my truck, I can pass easily through the Russian control, as all they are interested in is the proper pass for the people, not the goods. I also loaded some kindergarten material to take to Klagenfurt for Nuschi. I guess I have to combine AFSC transportation needs with my EDREC trips! Tomorrow I start out again for the ÖGB.

July 11—One Recuperation Home after Another

After leaving Nuschi and her supplies in Klagenfurt where she will spend a week with kindergarten teachers, Herr Rohm and I then went over the Turracher Alps to Moosham, my first home since my illness. Since then we have been in Sigmundsberg, Mittewald twice, Kieferhof, and now back in Moosham. It has been good getting back on the job again. I feel that the program is going very well in the homes. I have learned how to better communicate with the apprentices and I am really getting to know some of the group leaders since the same ones are in the homes every time I visit. I just wish I could come up with more recreational equipment. At least in the absence of such the apprentices spend more time mountain hiking, and I do join them in some of their hikes.

After leaving Mittewald the first time, we went to Salzburg where I picked up Al Johnson who had been the CPS camp leader in Ames, Iowa. He is leaving the AFSC program in Poland and is passing through Austria on his way to Italy and then home. He spent the whole time with me when I was in Kieferhof. It was great to catch up on old times and sad to hear his tale of woe about the hard life of the people in Poland. In driving Al from his train in Salzburg to the home in Kieferhof we drove over Austria's most famous highway, the Gross Glocknerstrasse. The toll for the highway was $1.60, but it was hardly worth it for as soon as we started to climb we drove into dense fog. The fog, which lasted throughout the drive, was so thick I could only see far enough ahead of the truck to barely drive. It may be a beautiful trip but I wouldn't know. After putting Al on a train in Villach, I drove over to Wörther See to visit Arthur who had arrived there last week to recuperate. He is far from well yet. He can think of nothing but his illness.

July 13—A Real Mountain Climb

Monday we arrived here in Moosham in time to put on a program that evening. Then yesterday, two of the group leaders whom I have come to know well, persuaded me to go on a full day's climb with them. We drove west for about 20 kilometers up a valley to the little town of Zederhaus. There we left the truck about 8:00 in the morning and started to climb. After an hour, we rested a bit at an Almhütte. I was pretty well done in from the fast climb but it had not yet been very steep. Then on we went for another hour at an easier pace until we were above the timberline. There we rested for a time and picked Edelweiss, the famous alpine flower that is so rare and hard to find. We found lots of it and I picked a number of them. I have since found out it is forbidden, but we had seen several hundred! Then on we went, up and up, past the grasslands to the rocky slopes over loose rocks and finally over solid rocks to the peak.

I was just done in by then but after an hour's rest and a sandwich, we went on. We followed a ridge for another hour that was really on top of the world. You could look down at least 4000 feet on both sides of the ridge if you wanted to. I didn't while I was walking. The ridge was easy, in fact, all, so far, had been easy. We came to the high peak at about 10,000 feet. From there one had a wonderful view over many of the snow-covered ranges of Austria. At two, we started down another way. At one point we had to climb down a nearly vertical wall of rock with a good 500-foot drop. But the handholds were good, and the other two fellows were experts. They found the right handholds for me and were right with me the whole time. The dangerous part only lasted about 10 minutes, but I didn't look down any during that time. I faced the rock wall and held on. Finally, toward evening we were back at the Almhütte, milk, rest, and in half an hour were back at the truck. This was one of those long to be remembered days. We did make it back in time for another evening program for the boys.

The mountain climber!

July 14—A New Leader

Yesterday we stopped at Sigmundsberg to put on one program for the boys. We found the home all worked up about the impending announcement of the new director for the ÖGB Youth Program who will replace Mela when she leaves for the States in September. Just before supper last night, word arrived of the naming of the new director. The home director and the group leaders had been on edge about the naming of the new director since many felt their jobs might well depend on him. There was great relief when the new name was announced. It turned out to be Herr Seebauer, the former director of the home in Frankenmarkt, where I had first met him when I went there two years ago and got the load of apples. He is very well liked and should turn out to be an excellent choice.

July 19—Work Camp

Thursday I put Herr Rohm on a train for Vienna and I headed west to join a work camp near Gross Raming for a few days. I find that Philadelphia has expanded my EDREC job a bit to include visiting work camps, taking pictures, and showing some of my movies to many groups. This camp is not an AFSC project but is under the direction of the international Civil Work Camp Organization. There is little difference. The camp is made up of a dozen Austrians, one English girl, one Finnish girl, one Danish boy, and two other Americans. The only member I know well was Louise Powelson from our team in Vienna. The camp is supplying labor to help build a new road to a small town since the old road will be under water as soon as the dam is finished. Friday I worked all day with pick and shovel with time out for picture taking.

Sunday I showed movies at a nearby DP camp. Some of our campers went along and now there is the beginning of a good relationship between the groups. Sunday night a group of local youth came with a little band and played, sang, and danced until midnight. I even called a square dance for them. Last night, while the camp had a business meeting, I spent time in the kitchen popping corn and then later helped them eat it. I hated to leave the congenial group today but must get on with my work.

I headed east again to arrive back in Vienna this evening. Here I discover that Arthur has been in Vienna a couple of days on his way to Denmark to see a famous brain specialist. Sven leaves in a couple of days to get ready to attend Wilmington College this fall. Mel and Mela are out of town making a last visit to all the recuperation homes.

July 25—Brief Time in Vienna

This past week has been a rather quiet one for me. The weather here is so delightfully comfortable. Today was the first day this year in which I was slightly too warm with my suit coat. As usual, I have been getting ready for my next foray to the recuperation homes. It seems to be farewell time in Vienna: First, several parties were held for Sven; then Arthur had been here for a few days; Paul left last week at the end of his term; and of course when Mela leaves in a month, so does Mel. No replacements are at hand and if I stay too long in Vienna, I may get saddled with my old transport job again. Off I go tomorrow to Moosham.

August 5—Good Trips

Since leaving here on July 26 I have had three very good recuperation home visits, first to Moosham, next to Mittewald, and finally to Sigmundsberg. My companion on this trip was Herr Rohm. My good relationship with the group leaders continues to improve.

In Moosham after several good chats with group leader Pritzel, I selected him to go to Vienna this fall for a short course on handicraft work. He can later bring his new knowledge and skill to the homes. He is enthusiastic about this project.

Herr Rohm (second from right) with me and home personnel

Monday, in Sigmundsberg my clutch broke, so I spent several hours in Maria Zell getting it repaired in an Austrian garage. I arrived back in Vienna only yesterday and in a few minutes, I am leaving again. Only this time it is not to a recuperation home. I am going to an AFSC work camp in Salzburg for a week. Next Thursday I will start my recuperation home visits again.

August 11—Guggenthal

I have spent this week in a very good spirited work camp near the little town of Guggenthal, in the mountains above Salzburg. This camp's project is not one of physical labor but is focused on helping refugee parents in seven refugee camps around Salzburg handle and educate their children. The conditions in the camps are still very bad. Many of the residents have vague hopes of going to America some day. Quite a few of them are from Russia and speak no German.

Of course, most of the AFSC group is from Vienna. One of them, Edi Stopfer dressed up in his new suit one day for me to see him in his Sunday best. There are three or four new Americans, two from Denmark, two from England, two from Germany, and one from Ireland.

Edward Stopfer all dressed up

One of the Germans was sent by the AFSC team in Ludwigshafen. She is a most attractive young lady. I think I will have to visit this camp again later. I should mention one outing the group took last week to Berchtesgaden, across the border in Germany.

Guggenthal Work Camp group

We visited Hitler's mountain home of Berghof, where I had been two years ago. This time the group went inside the ruined villa and I snapped a picture of them looking out of his famous picture window.

Guggenthal Work Camp group at Hitler's
Berghof picture window, August 1949

August 21—Another Good Recuperation Home Trip

Again, I have done the same three homes, Moosham, Mittewald, and Sigmundberg and continue to have good feelings about the visits. This time Noverl was with me instead of Herr Rohm. He is every bit as good with the apprentices as Herr Rohm except that he doesn't give a sex lecture. Since the new home at Cap Wörth on Wörther See needed some last minute help to get ready to open and is not far from Mittewald, Noverl and I spent some hours each day working beside Mela, Mel, and others scrubbing floors, moving beds, etc. It opened on the 17th but I will not do a program there until my next trip. I think this was the last work that Mela will do for the ÖGB before she and Mel leave for America.

When Noverl and I got back to Vienna, I discovered that the long awaited visitors, Sam and Becky Marble had arrived. Sam is president of Wilmington College. I spent most of the weekend showing them around Vienna.

August 23—Mountain Hike Preparation

Yesterday, Monday August 22, I drove a regular 6x6 truck to Guggenthal. Sam and Becky went with me. I also had three other passengers, all Austrians. One was Herbert Linhardt from the present Community Center group. The second was Walter Knödel from the old Community Center group. And the third was none other than Noverl. We spent the night in Guggenthal. The next day I parked the truck that we had brought from Vienna, which we will use in a couple of weeks to return the Viennese campers to Vienna. Our trip on west now was by train. Sam and Becky were going on to Switzerland but we four got off the train at Bludenz to begin a week's mountain hike. This hike was the last of my allotted vacation time. Actually, we took a narrow gauge train southeastward to its end where we caught a bus to travel on another 10 kilometers. We easily found a Gasthaus in Partenen and put up there for the night. We were put in a bedroom for five and found the fifth bed occupied by a conductor on the Vienna streetcars. He proved to be a very jolly person as well as an experienced mountain climber and we invited him to join our group.

Street car conductor (left) posing with me, Herbert, and Walter

August 29—A Mountain Adventure

The next morning, Wednesday, we got up too late to catch the first car up the mountain and had to wait an hour. We made good use of the time by going through a power plant run by a huge turbine. The water came down the mountain in two huge tubes about six feet thick. At 9:00, we got on the cable car. Actually it was only a freight car pulled up by a cable. It was nearly two miles long and raised us some 3000 feet. Now the mountain tour really began. Our first obstacle was a mile long tunnel through which a very narrow gauge train could haul freight; we had to walk through. I had a tiny flashlight I had bought in Partenen. After an hour or so of easy walking, we came out to the dam where the huge tubes began. From there we could see the mountain peaks covered with ice and snow. Way off in the distance we could see the Saarbrückner Almhütte, where we planned to spend the night.

The day had clouded over so it was cool. Even so, after a couple of hours of steady climbing all our shirts were off. Stopping to eat some of the black bread we had brought along, I saw in the distance to our left another artificial lake. By looking at it and studying the map I figured out that it was the same lake to which Irwin and I had come two years before on a motorcycle. We were at least three miles from the place we had been so we never actually got to that point this time.

Up to the Almhütte we went, arriving there about 2:30. The hostess here was a jolly young lady who seemed to be a jack-of-all-trades, cooking, serving, washing, cleaning, cashiering, and even sewing up a tear in my pants. As there were no more Almhütten within reach, we spent the rest of the day in the Almhütte particularly since it began to rain. We played chess, wrote post cards, talked, and signed the log (I looked clear back to

January of this year and found that I was the only American who had been there—most of my fellow countrymen don't seem to like such strenuous vacations!).

Saarbrückner Hütte hostess

We found we were a very congenial group. In these Almhütten, everyone turns in early at 8:00 or 9:00 at the latest. The five of us got a six-bed room

Hostess mending my pants

this time. There are no sheets, just the mattress and two blankets. In the mountains, these bedrooms are called mattress storerooms. Luckily, I had brought along winter underwear that saved the day or rather the night as far as warmth was concerned.

Thursday we woke up at 6:30 to beautiful weather. After breakfast we started out to climb the Gross Litzner. We started out across a glacier that appeared to be the only way to the top. After an hour we were out of sight of the top and we felt we were lost. Only the streetcar man had been here before and that was 27 years ago. We had a book describing the way but it too was old and the face of these glaciers becomes unrecognizable after three or four years. We really were lost. Noverl and the streetcar man both had picks and they were able to help us by digging holes in the ice at the steepest places. About noon, we reached a ridge over which we thought we might go to reach the peak. Instead it was a dead end. We just didn't have enough time left before dark to retrace our steps and start over again. The ridge where we were was the Austrian-Swiss border. We could look many miles out into both countries and the beauty of it all was breathtaking. On our return to the Almhütte we passed a small abandoned shack, which had been a shelter for the German soldiers who had guarded the border during the war. It has been a beautiful and not too strenuous day.

Friday we were up at 4:00 by candlelight so that by 5:00, when gray dawn began to break, we were already on the trail. We started out from the Almhütte again over the glacier but this time it took us over an hour a half. It was so early in the morning that the glacier was hard and we couldn't get a good foothold. After Walter slipped and slid about 50 feet, we tied ourselves together with a 90-foot rope and had Noverl dig each step for us as needed. From 6:30 to 7:00, we rested where we had been the day before and watched the sunrise on the snow. We had heard that the hike we were doing generally takes about nine hours. Until 10:00, our way was fairly easy. We skirted the Swiss border and were on rocks, not ice. At 10:30 we started up a long glacier with the rope and soon were in Switzerland on the Silvretta Glacier.

About noon the weather began to go bad on us and by one, we were enveloped in fog. The glacier was covered with snow and was developing dangerous crevasses. Twice, Noverl was walking ahead and suddenly the snow under him gave way and he was in a crevasse. You just couldn't tell the difference between ice and a dangerous snow bridge. But each time he fell in we pulled him right out. I actually never fell for I always managed to jump at the right times, but then I never went first!

From time to time, the fog would lift and we could see what natural beauty was around us. At about 3:00, it began to rain and the joy of the day was gone. At 3:30, we hauled ourselves up out of the sixth valley we had gone through and there in the distance we could see the Wiesbadner Almhütte, our goal for the day. You can imagine what a lift it gave our soaked spirits to see it. It was only a mile or so away. We thought we were almost there. I was in the lead clambering down over rocks and then the trail led into snow again. I started out over it and suddenly found myself marooned, the next step was shear ice, and my last step back had slid away. I just stood and waited. Presently the streetcar man came to my rescue with his pick, but he passed me by and dug steps until he reached the end of the rope. Then each of us made the trip on his steps to him. Off again he went to the end of the rope digging more steps. We kept this up for an hour and a half in the rain until we came out on a less steep portion of the glacier where we could walk normally again. At that point, we met a mountain man from the Almhütte who, having seen our predicament through his binoculars had come to our rescue. It was indeed good to arrive at the Wiesbadner Almhütte at about 6:00 and change to dry clothes. These Almhütten were generally pretty well filled with other folks who were doing what we were, although most of them had guides. I am thankful we had the streetcar conductor with us.

On this day, Saturday, we had planned to climb the Piz Buin, the highest mountain in Vorarlberg. We did not; we were so done in from the day before and our clothes were so wet that we stayed in the Almhütte until noon. Again it was a wonderful day. After lunch, we started again to climb but this time only on a four-hour trip to Jamtaler Almhütte. On the glacier, we caught up with two other people, a Viennese man and wife. It turned out they were friends of a Viennese family to whom Fairview Friends in Ohio had sent clothes. This tour turned out to be the most treacherous as far as crevasses were concerned. We had to weave back and forth a lot to avoid them. About 5:00, we got off the glacier just as it began to rain again, with nearly an hour yet to the Almhütte. It was easy going on a dirt, or rather mud path. Suddenly, when we had spread out from each other because it was so easy, I came to a shear cliff with nothing to hold onto except the slanting dirt path under foot. It was still raining and as slick as could be; it was the only time I was really scared. Thanks to my nail bottomed shoes I made it. Again, we were in a mountain Almhütte to dry out, sit around and chat, eat the evening meal, which always tasted so good, and off to bed in a room for 20 people.

Today, Sunday, was the last day of our tour. We were again up at 4:00 so we could be off at the crack of dawn. A two-hour down hill hike brought us to Galtür in time to catch the only Sunday bus. We got out when we reached the main rail line before Landeck and walked a mile or so to Grins where I had visited two years ago and where there was a work camp last year. I spent an enjoyable two hours looking at the town and finding that the Quakers had not been forgotten. Then we took the train to Innsbruck where our hiking group broke up. Noverl and the streetcar man headed on to Vienna, Walter went to a mathematics convention while Herbert and I got a hotel room. It has been an unforgettable week in the mountains.

August 31—Another AFSC Work Camp

Herbert left Monday for Vienna but I took a narrow gauge train up the mountain from Innsbruck. It wound its way in and out of tunnels for two or three hours over one of the most beautiful railway lines I have ever been on. At the German border, the cars were all locked for the time we would be traveling through Germany. Shortly after going through Garmisch, we reentered Austria where the car doors were unlocked. At 4:00, I changed to a bus in Reutte and arrived in the little town of Grän by 6:00 where the campers at this new work camp met me. I had known many of them in Vienna. Their project here is to work on building a dam to control floods. I spent yesterday feeling like a real VIP as the campers showed me their project work. In the evening, the camp had a Ping-Pong tournament with the young folks of the town. I have never seen anything so serious in all my life as the way those town people took that tournament. They set up judges and acted as if each point was a life and death matter. After some practice, I was placed in the number one spot on the AFSC team. That put me up against the town's number one player who was the son of the mayor. I was badly beaten, as was most of our team. Still, it was great fun. I was particularly interested to see how vitally important it seemed to the local folk!

Today I was up at 6:00 to take a bus back to Innsbruck. Then I rode the train until 6:00 this evening to get to Salzburg. An hour's hike brought me back to Guggenthal to join the campers.

September 4—Guggenthal Work Camp Conclusion

I spent the last three days helping the camp conclude its work and make arrangements to depart. As usual, I had to do some truck maintenance before our return to Vienna. I also spent some time getting better acquainted with a German girl the AFSC group in Ludwigshafen had sent to the camp. I can relate two minor incidents about her. When I was here some weeks ago, the cooks told me they would love to have some cheese for the group but it was unavailable on the market. When I was in Villach I bought and shipped a 15-pound block of cheese to the camp. I thought it might have made an impression on this girl whose name, incidentally, is Helga Hoecker. When I asked her how she liked it, she told me she never ate cheese. On another day, I treated her by taking her to the Army ice cream parlor that was formerly the Tomaselli Café, a top one in Salzburg. In order to please her I bought her an ice cream soda, something unknown in wartime Germany.

She drank it and told me it was wonderful. Later I mentioned to one of the other campers what I had done and he told me that Helga would never drink milk. Guess she was just trying to be nice to me! At any rate, we got on famously. For two people from such different backgrounds we seem to share ideas so well.

This morning we broke camp, so to speak, with one jeep and two trucks. We left the two Germans at the Salzburg train station and took off for Vienna. We picked up some more campers at Enns from the Gross Raming camp and we all arrived back in Vienna about 7:00 this evening. En route, I was stopped by two MPs for having three in the front seat of the truck. We had to lose an hour to go into Linz to the Army Police Court. There they told me they had no jurisdiction over civilians and we should proceed on our way!

September 11—The Temporary Boss

George took his vacation this week so for the week I have been the "boss." I find that George has had 101 details to worry about as mission chief. One I had to handle was concerning the winter coal supply. First, I had to figure out how much we would need; then what kind of coal to order; then go to the proper Army office to fill out the order; and finally go to the coal yard to deliver the order. At the Army office they were out of order forms and wouldn't have any for a month; without a proper form, one doesn't get coal. The officer finally admitted that he had two forms left and after a lot of persuasion, I got him to issue one of them to me. Now we have coal at $15 per ton. And so it went all week. I find that George had been busy!

This week at the ÖGB we began the process of transferring the EDREC program to the Austrians so that it will continue operating after I leave in January. By this I mean that Herr Rohm and Noverl took the truck out and are visiting three homes without me. They have gone to the three homes that are in the Russian Zone so it is the first visit for the EDREC to these homes, as of course, I can't go into the Russian Zone.

We spent considerable time this week moving the AFSC office from its original location at 17 Rotenturmstrasse to the Quaker Center at 13 Jauresgasse. This is in the embassy section of Vienna. In fact, the office is just across the street from the German Embassy.

Then I spent more time in meetings and talking to people. Monday night I spent with Mel, Mela, and her parents. It was their last night in Vienna. Tuesday we took them to the train for Paris. I spent several hours later that day talking with Mela's successor, Herr Seebauer, about the future of the EDREC program. That night I drove a truck up the mountain above

Vienna to take a load of former work campers to meet others from work camps, all to have a farewell evening. Ed Wright, who had come for a few days from Paris, was delighted to meet old friends in that group. Wednesday night he and I were invited to Inga Peinlich's (an Austrian girl) home to meet some of his old friends. Thursday night I put him on the train for Paris. He is now head of all AFSC work camps in Europe. Friday night I spent the entire evening talking with fellow team member, Louise Powelson, who was just back that day from a work camp. Saturday night I attended the weekly folk dancing group at the Quaker Center. Then this morning I attended a session of the youth staff to plan for the coming year. It was held then, as Ruth Dross and David Winder leave tomorrow for a two-week vacation. In fact, Ruth leaves permanently for Germany in October. This is in line with a Philadelphia directive that our team must be down to four by spring. It has been quite a week. Welcome back, George.

September 12—Parental Questions

Let me try to respond to a few of your questions. No, I didn't get to any of the sessions of the Salzburg Festival. Tickets were sold out two months in advance except for scalpers whose beginning price was $10. You can see the same thing in Vienna in winter and I, at least, did see all the locations for the Festival.

You ask as to my mission in the work camps. In addition to what I have written I guess I could say it was to take pictures for Philadelphia and to be a general troubleshooter.

You ask how to spend the $42 Orville Hunt's church raised for sports equipment for the ÖGB homes. The most welcome items would be lots of Ping-Pong balls as well as paddles and nets. Also welcome would be chess and checker sets, volleyballs, soccer balls, and nets. Forget about the bats, baseballs, and softballs. They just don't go over here. I am glad to hear that the whole Yearly Meeting seems to be taking up my need for recreational equipment. However, let's not carry this too far. If the contributions get up in the hundreds of dollars maybe it ought to go to some other AFSC work.

You asked if we cooked in the mountain Almhütten. No, meals are prepared and served by the summer residents of the Almhütten. Food and lodging cost me $3.00 per day. We always carried bread and meat for lunch. I am sorry Steve Cary didn't get out to see you. Rumor here has it that he may soon take over from Clarence Pickett as AFSC General Secretary.

September 13—Long Overdue Report to Philadelphia

I will give some excerpts from my report to Philadelphia.

"Trips: My visits to the homes proved much more satisfactory after my initial trip. By getting to know the group leaders better on subsequent trips, I was able to relate better to the apprentices. Every month the group representatives write a report of the month. We noticed that from the July reports in every case the apprentice writing the report stated that he or she was most appreciative of the EDREC program. From this, we realize it would be better to spend more time in each home, but there just isn't enough time to expand the visits. As it is, I have been in Vienna a total of 10 days since June 27. However, don't forget that besides visiting the homes I have visited three work camps in Austria and have had a week's vacation climbing mountains in Vorarlberg.

Films: The major improvements in the film program have been four-fold. 1) Up-to-date news reels from the US information service. 2) A British film called *Man-One Family* which is very good on the race question. 3) *Boundary Lines*, a film showing the absurdity of the artificial boundary lines man his imposed upon himself. 4) A 20-minute film I brought with me about CPS camp at Big Flats, New York. It is an excellent medium for bringing a bit of Quaker ideology to the groups. I am still looking for a good film on Russia. I should add that I have put on several film programs at both the Salzburg and Gross Raming work camps. In both cases, the majority of attendees were DPs from adjacent DP camps.

Music: The interest in the music program is somewhat spotty. In the girls' home, there are always a number who are very much interested. Often the request is for more popular music rather than my program of American folk music and classical music. In one instance, American folk music was very enthusiastically received. This was in Kieferhof in July when Al Johnson was with me. We favored the boys with a bit of 'barbershop' and despite the fact we had never sung a note together it was an overwhelming success. This was just one more proof that canned music can't equal the live variety. I have stumbled onto another avenue of musical contact. I now take my clarinet along on all trips and often join in with the apprentices who are always playing an accordion, a guitar, and a piano together. I have even appeared in a couple of skits with them. There are indeed many ways of making contacts with people.

Sports: The search for sports equipment has been long and not altogether fruitless. In July I managed to get a few items from the Army Special Service warehouse, items that it later turned out we should not have been allowed to take. In the lot were six volleyballs, 80 Ping-Pong balls, a dozen packs of cards, eight Ping-Pong paddles, and a couple of chess sets. In August, Mr. Grossman from USACA Youth Activities let us have four soccer balls, 30 Ping-Pong balls, and a volley ball net (also four sets of boxing gloves, which are of no value in the recuperation homes). Then as you know, my local church group in Ohio became interested in the need for recreational equipment and raised $50 for equipment, which is now en route here. I hear that Wilmington Yearly Meeting is now involved in raising some money for this same project. Another possibility came through former team member Ned Weaver, who is now stationed in Wels. The Army Colonel in charge of Army Special Services in Austria knows Ned and knew that he had worked with the AFSC. It seems that this Colonel subscribes to the 'Friends Intelligencer.' Upon reading Elise's report in the July issue, he went to Ned to find how to get in touch with me. At Ned's suggestion I visited the Colonel in Wels and explained the program to him more fully. He said that although officially Special Service could not help us he would be glad to turn over a truckload of second hand equipment as soon as his Wels warehouse is in shape. He promised that it would be around the middle of September. It sounds like a good prospect but I'm not counting on anything until I see it. Finally, I visited a Mr. McKenna, Chief Civil Affairs, of the British Army in Graz. He promised to do what he could but nothing has yet come of that. All in all enough supplies or promises of supplies are trickling in to give us something of a sports program. The last two times I went around to the homes I spent a good bit of time introducing various games such as ring tennis and volleyball.

Handicraft: At last, the handicraft part of my program begins to look like more than just an idea. One of the group leaders, Herr Pritzel, whom I have gotten to know well, will be released from his present position about November 1 in order to devote full time to a handicraft program. He will first get some training through the Army Special Services and will then plan programs for the homes.

Recorder: We are still waiting for the arrival of the recorder. We have the installation instructions for the 50-cycle pulley conversion but that is all of the recorder that has arrived so far. A number of useful ideas about its use are running around in Herr Seebauer's head—not all of which have yet come out!

Mela-Seebauer: This summer certainly has been an interesting time to be in the homes. At first began the rumor, and then the announcement of Mela's leaving. This was followed by a 168-point questionnaire sent by Mela to all the homes for each director to study in preparation for the directors' meeting in July. Then slowly the realization came that from this meeting the announcement of Mela's successor would probably come.

Rumors really ran wild at this point. I imagine it was something like picking the replacement at the AFSC for Clarence Pickett. Perhaps it was even more serious to the individuals in the recuperation home program. Many of them felt that their jobs depended on the right person being chosen to lead the program. I was in the homes during this director's meeting and little else was discussed. I will remember for a long time the relief displayed that evening by the director of that particular home in which I was when it was announced Seebauer would take over. I feel that there was more unity of feeling about his appointment than would have been with any other appointment.

Fall Plans: Herr Seebauer is now planning a conference for all directors and group leaders for sometime in January. He also is planning to have a reunion celebration for all past recuperation home attendees for December, although it may not be possible to rent a large enough hall to accommodate all of them. The blow of AFSC withdrawing all food contributions to the ÖGB has been eased by a contribution from the Swedish Save the Children. Food has been delivered this week in enough quantity to supply 1000 apprentices for four months at a comparable rate to what the AFSC has been supplying.

Future EDREC Plans: As my contract runs out January 31 and as the homes won't reopen until about that time, my effective operating time in the homes will end in December. The question then arises what happens after I leave. Herr Seebauer is planning to continue the EDREC after AFSC withdrawal. The personnel probably will be a combination of Herr Rohm, Noverl, and Herr Pritzel. Naturally, the international flavor of the program will be reduced when I leave. The main job for me now seems to be to get the program well established so that it will operate without me. In planning for a continuation of EDREC next year, I am operating on the assumption that the AFSC is willing to turn over my equipment to the ÖGB. This seems to be agreeable to the team. The ÖGB has agreed to make the equipment available whenever possible to Quaker House. The one exception will be the truck. The ÖGB is not interested in having the truck either as a purchase or as a gift because it consumes so much gasoline. By Christmas they hope to have a small car ready for the program. The EDREC truck will then be turned back to the general AFSC truck pool in Germany for further disposition."

September 14—Downsizing

In my last letter, I forgot to mention a bit more about future personnel plans. Since Philadelphia wants us to cut down to four people by next spring, they stated that someone already here should be designated as mission chief. George and Virginia were told to leave in December, partly because they are expecting another baby in November. Since I will not be doing any EDREC work next year, the group asked me to stay on as chief until next June. I didn't agree, only promising to stay through March.

The hope is that a replacement will be here by then, although there won't be much of a team to coordinate by then. David and Louise will be the youth staff, Annelies Becker will continue in clothing, and Joan Freeth will still be in DP work. It seems that this cut is to all AFSC projects because not enough money is coming in. My first year in Austria we had a budget of $600,000. This past year it was down to $125,000. Philadelphia then cut us down to $50,000 for next year (beginning always in October) and now the figure is down to $24,000. Italy, Spain, and Finland are being closed completely.

The timing is tough on George because he is a professor and it is hard to get a job in December or January. He went to Paris yesterday to see if there wasn't some way out for him. If no way can be found he will be leaving in December and I'll have his job. The rest of the group has been urging me to agree to stay until June but I have not done so. April is a much better time to arrive on the farm. There is one other variable factor in the picture but I'll come to that another day.

September 18—Quick Trip to Germany

Last Wednesday night I took the Mozart night train to Munich. Thursday morning after a two-hour layover, I took a train to Mannheim from where I walked across the Rhine to the Quaker Center in Ludwigshafen. I had known Jean Merlin, the Frenchman who joined the AFSC team three years ago in Paris, but the other team members were new to me. Friday I began getting a jeep ready to take back to Vienna. AFSC has a surplus of jeeps at last and is beginning to sell them. However, the market in Austria is better than in Germany. The only catch so far is that the Army won't let us sell any of them for marks or schillings. It is indeed a queer arrangement whereby the Army can control what we do with our private property. We hope to get the rule changed.

At any rate, I was to take a jeep to Vienna. Later that morning Earl Fowler, the present head of AFSC work camps in Germany and a former classmate of mine at Earlham, took me to the AFSC Central Office for Germany in Darmstadt. There I met some of the AFSC big shots for Germany. After I got back to Ludwigshafen, I went to visit Helga, from the AFSC work camp in Salzburg. Her father met me at the door and almost turned me away because I didn't make my identity clear. She heard me from the kitchen where she was washing her hair and saved the day. Saturday afternoon we went over to Heidelberg. Since she had gone to school there she was able to show me around. It is a very picturesque German town. I had always wanted to see it and I did find it to be most quaint. That evening I had dinner with her family. It was a genuine German experience, made even better by the way that Helga and I get along with each other.

At midnight, another chap from the Salzburg work camp and I started to Vienna in the jeep. About 5:00 in the morning, a connecting rod bearing went out and we were stranded on the autobahn. He thumbed a ride to Munich and I just waited in the jeep. By 10:00 a.m., my patience was exhausted so I caught a ride for the 40 kilometers to Augsburg. There I was able to get a jeep to come out and tow me into Augsburg where I left the jeep at a garage and took a train into Munich. It turned out a jeep had left Munich to come for me at noon and I had missed it. I was able to arrange for the Munich team to get the jeep from Augsburg the next day and have it repaired. From Munich I took a train to Bad Aibling where I had supper with Alice at Chiem See. Then a night train took me back to Vienna. Now, here I was back from a long trip to Germany without the jeep I had gone to get.

September 21—Iowa Farmers

In addition to getting ready for my next recuperation home visits I was busy Monday and Tuesday entertaining four Iowa farmers. They were official AFSC visitors for some reason or other. I had never met any of them before but we got on famously. Yesterday I was up at 5:00 in order to leave Vienna at 6:00. We left with my truck, a station wagon, a half load of food for a DP camp in Salzburg, Herr Rohm, George, and the four Iowa farmers. George went on to Salzburg to unload the food while Herr Rohm and I took the farmers through an artificial insemination station in Wels. The station was a part of the program of the Brethren Service Committee so a couple of Brethren showed us around. We also visited a farm, a large one for Austria, a farm of 80 acres. In Salzburg we turned the farmers over to one of their German team who took them on to Germany. Herr Rohm and I then drove on to Moosham to start another round of visits to recuperation homes.

September 22—Question

In writing you about my future plans, I mentioned one "variable factor" but did not explain it. I am not quite ready to go into detail about it yet but I do have a question. When I get home in February, March, April or whenever what chance is there of finding some place else to live besides with you at home? In other words, it begins to look as if I will be wanting a house. You know how you always said you wouldn't want two families living in the same house. Now don't go advertising this because it is not all settled. They say there is many a slip between the cup and the lip. But you might at least be looking around.

October 1—Another Recuperation Home Circuit

Since beginning another recuperation home tour on September 21, Herr Rohm and I have been to Moosham, Mittewald, Sigmundsberg, and the new home at Cap Wörth before returning to Vienna this evening. It was a very successful trip with one minor exception. Some weeks ago Mela asked me for my reactions to the group leaders. I was glowing in my appraisal of most of them, with one exception. I told her of my feeling about one leader at the girls' home at Mittewald. I felt this leader who was excellent in many ways still seemed to retain some of the Nazi racial ideas. Then I forgot about the conversation. When we arrived in Mittewald this leader would not even speak to me. Later, she finally broke down and told me she had been fired, effective November 15, because, according to Mela, I had said she was a Nazi. So you see what a hole that left me in particularly as the director of the home feels that this girl is the best one of her group leaders. My statement to Mela had been exaggerated, but I shouldn't have said anything. Further, Mela was most indiscrete in passing on this whole affair. I won't be on such intimate terms again with some of the group leaders in Mittewald. Now that Mela is gone, there is not much I can do to rectify the situation. I will, however, relate this to Herr Seebauer. We did have a most successful visit to Cap Wörth with its 200 boys. I am going to miss these visits when I leave Austria.

October 4—Fall Opening of the Quaker Center

The Community Center, now called Quaker House, was set to open for the fall youth programs last Sunday. Ruth and David were to preside at the opening but as of noon that day, they had not returned from Denmark. Louise and I hurriedly improvised a program and speeches for the opening. At the last minute, Ruth and David showed up so we didn't have to speak after all. I shouldn't have had to anyway, as it was not my project. The plans for the year were explained, new people were introduced, and the year with youth work was off to a new start. Now again every night finds a group of young people coming to the Center. Every night this week I have been involved there, partly in showing movies. I was also able to assemble and try out the new recorder, which just arrived from Philadelphia.

October 6—Leadership Problems

George had just come back from Paris where he and the Commissioners had worked out a new financial plan, which would enable him to remain here until June. The team didn't exactly accept that with open arms and Staff meeting was a most difficult session, particularly for him. There was nothing for the team to do but accept the proposal, but some of the team who will be here next year remained silent about his staying and George was just not given any support. Finally bowing to that lack of support, he stated that it would be best if he went home in December. That would mean that I would become the temporary chief.

I guess the next step is for me to say whether or not I will stay past January. I think it is hardly fair to take over only until April and I don't want to stay past March. Then too, I don't like the idea of taking over a job that is made vacant by the team sort of pushing him out.

Also, there is the other factor that I hinted about last week. This is an involvement that determines whether I accept this job for a little time or for a longer period. I would prefer to resign as of February 1 from the AFSC, then stay on here for a period of a few weeks and work out this other matter. Then I wouldn't be all tied up in Army red tape. I'm sorry I am leaving you so much in the dark about this "other matter." However, I have hesitated to commit anything to paper as yet. All I can say is that great progress is being made, at least to the point where I asked you that question last time "Where could a house be found?" I will be, hopefully, in a better position to write more next week. I leave in a couple of hours again for Germany.

Officially I am going back to get another jeep, probably the one that broke down before. It has been towed back to Ludwigshafen for its repair. Please don't jump to any conclusions. As I said, I hope to be more explicit when I write you next week

October 16—That Other Matter

I'm sorry I have been so vague about this "other matter." I did hint at it a month ago when I wrote asking about the possibility of finding a house. Now I am in the position to clarify my reticent writing. I am now planning to bring someone home with me. The last obstacle to my getting married is where we can go in the States or in the New Vienna area where I can farm. If you can put up with me on the farm, I'll be glad to stay around New Vienna for some time.

I suppose you are concerned with my not having come through with more details sooner and I probably should have. I guess I'd rather have this sort of thing all definite before I go alarming you at home. My point now is that it's as definite as can be from this end.

Now for some of the missing factors. I would much prefer to bring her home entirely unknown. I don't know why, but I guess you wouldn't put up with me if I didn't tell you some of the details. Don't go alarming all the community and the relatives just yet. No, it is not Alice, although she is a fine girl. Why do I know that it is the right thing? Well, of course, I don't for sure. But is seems nearer the right thing than anything else I have ever done. Her name is Helga. I think I mentioned her before. Her name sounds Norwegian but she happens to be a German from Ludwigshafen. She speaks nearly perfect English but we haven't decided whether or not to admit that at first. It might be fun for her to speak only German for a few days.

We met in July at Salzburg where she was a member of the Guggenthal AFSC workcamp. She has worked with the AFSC team in Ludwigshafen for nearly two years.

There are, I suppose two drawbacks if one looks at it objectively, which I am not in a position to do. One is her age. She is nine years younger than I. However, as far as I know all the books say that is not too much. The second objection could be that we have not known each other long enough. That could be a very valid objection. It could also be said that I have remained single so long because I got to know the other prospective wives too long and thus too well. However, getting to know someone is not necessarily a matter of the passage of time. I am sure we understand each other much better than I do any of the Viennese whom I have known for three years. I could go into a long description of Helga but then I suppose it would be little different from the description most people make when contemplating marriage.

We found each other to be kindred spirits in the beginning and that has developed to where we now are. You can be absolutely sure that I am not being taken in by a European girl who just wants to go to the States. Our greatest differences seem to be that she does not like milk, cheese, or tomatoes! She has never been a Catholic but belongs to a sect known as Free Religion. But during the past two years, she has practically become a Quaker.

I have now been in her home twice. Her father is 48 and is a foreman in the IG Farben Chemical Works. His division is engaged in extracting nitrogen from the air for fertilizer. Her mother is 45. I don't know when I have seen such a close mother-daughter relationship. The separation will be tough for both of them. She has one brother who is 23 or 24. I get along very well with him.

She and I have been together a total of five times: the first when I visited the work camp in July; the second when I passed through Salzburg on the way to that mountain tour; the third at the end of my mountain tour; the fourth when I went to Germany to get that jeep; and then again last week when I went for the second jeep. I was in Ludwigshafen from the seventh to the twelfth of this month. That sounds short, I know, but if my memory serves me correctly I think you told me you two got married the 12th or 13th time you met!

There have been innumerable technical problems involved in all of this. I come under the US Army rules, or at least I thought so and so did the Army. The mass of red tape this involves is horrible. You must ask the Army for permission six months before the marriage if she is a German, only three if she is Austrian. We had to get a US Army Chaplain's permission, which we did last week. We both had to have physical exams in an Army hospital, which we also did last week. I could not apply for permission from the Army to marry until I had a statement from a German official that she had applied for a military exit permit from Germany. However, they would not accept her application for that until she had a statement that a US visa was in hand. She cannot even apply for that until after she is married, a typical Army technique. On Thursday, I found an old ruling which classes AFSC the same as Cocoa-Cola or Pan-American, etc. That means, I come under the State Department rather than the Army and that makes it so much simpler.

By State Department rules, we could get married tomorrow and would not have needed the Army physical. Of course tomorrow is too soon. Under Army rules we had thought of having the wedding in January, but now that we are under the State Department, we are thinking of Christmas. The sooner we can get married, the sooner the visa application can be made, and that takes three months.

You might wonder why I don't come home and let her come later, but that is now impossible. She cannot apply for a visa until after she is married!

Now I need your help. In order to get married in Germany I need three copies each of the following:

- A certified copy of the marriage certificate of my parents
- A copy of my birth certificate
- A statement from the office where my birth certificate is that I am an American citizen (This sounds unnecessary since I already have a passport, but I must have it.)

When she applies for a US visa I will also need the following:

- Certified copies of my financial condition including:
  - Bank statement of deposits
  - Statements of other securities
  - Statement of property held—in my case none
  - Copy of last year's income tax receipt
- Certified statement of job opportunity
- Certified statement that a home is available
- Copy of birth certificate (included in original request)

How will we get married? In Germany, you must have a civil wedding and you may also have a church one, which usually means a Catholic one. In our case, after the civil one, we plan to have a Quaker one at the AFSC Center in Ludwigshafen. I have talked over our plans with Lou and he promises I can officially stay in Vienna until April. Despite the money cuts, they can carry me as a third youth worker during that period or as chief of mission if Philadelphia hasn't found one yet.

The most pressing thing for you to do now is first to get that paperwork done I mentioned before and secondly to find a house. It would not be wise to put Helga in with complete strangers at first even though they are you. Most any house will do for the time being. Helga has lived all her life with her family in two rooms and a kitchen. I do hate to be in the position of begging for a house but I don't know what else to do from here. If it is impossible, or you feel that it is, then let me know so we can change our plans. If I apply soon enough I could probably stay on here another year, or at least get a job with some other organization that pays some sort of salary. I would rather be at home on the farm. As I mentioned earlier, don't go around spreading the good word right off. Let it simmer awhile. And do not let Aunt Elsie put a notice in the paper. In fact, you had better not tell her anything of this yet for she surely would have it in the paper the next day. Time enough for that later.

October 28—Tour to All ÖGB Homes

I have probably finished my last complete tour of the homes as Cap Wörth closes for the winter next week and Moosham closed today in order to start building a permanent structure so the boys will no longer have to live in those old, windy barracks. I started this tour a week ago Tuesday, beginning at Moosham, going on to Kieferhof, back to Mittewald, on to Cap Wörth, and finally to Sigmundsberg before coming back to Vienna this evening. I am glad to report that since this was the last full tour I will do, it also turned out to be one of the most successful. I feel I have in general provided the apprentices a real alternative to just eating and sleeping in the homes. Herr Rohm and Noverl are well prepared to carry on the program next year. Noverl accompanied me on this trip. It has been great getting to know the home directors and the group leaders. I would almost like to stay on with this program another year. Although the homes will be closed in December, the ÖGB has other plans afoot for then. A two-week training program is being planned for all the personnel. Before we went on this trip, Herr Seebauer made a brief speech on my new recorder and I was able to use it in each home. Then the directors, some of the group leaders and few apprentices told of their camp experiences, again on the recorder. Next week, here at the ÖGB headquarters, I will play some or all of those recordings to various ÖGB officials. The recorder is certainly proving to be of real value.

Marriage or Not?

$$\rightarrow\!\!\!\!-\!\diamond\!-\!\!\!\!\leftarrow$$

November to December, 1949

November 4—Problems with Parents

You think we should live with you for a few months? I realize from a practical standpoint that might be wise, but I am surprised. You have always stated that young married folks should not live in the same house with in-laws. Now that the case has become concrete, you back down from that view! I know it may be difficult to find a place but even so, I don't want to live at home. I haven't gone into detail with Helga on this point but implied that we would be living alone. A letter from her this week comes right to this point without her realizing how timely it is. She says, "Since I don't know the country and the people, I think it will be wonderful for us to live alone. If we don't have anybody around us to give us advice we can build our future ourselves!" You stated that you lived with grandfather and grandmother McCoy for four months. That was different, as you were Americans. The culture and thought patterns are a bit different in this case. You talk about her sharing in the cooking and the yard trimming; maybe she doesn't want to trim yard. Then I would have to do it to please you. That is only a small example but I hope you get the idea. Please don't start taking her in as a daughter. You don't even know her yet and there is always the possibility that you wouldn't particularly fit each other at all. The relationship should have a chance to develop on a basis of friends who go to see each other as often as they like but not be thrust in to live with each other.

I am not clear on another point. I have been under the impression that the farm was not up to full capacity with me gone. With me there should we add chickens, add custom work, etc.? Maybe we should rent some land. You have been getting along with the present operation without me. Maybe it would be better for me to start thinking in terms of some other work for a while. There is always the AFSC on a maintenance basis that is not so good. There is CARE with relatively good money. You even mentioned the Farm Bureau in Columbus as a possible employer. Any of these options would be better than coming home, living with you, and feeling superfluous on the farm. I suppose I am foolish to be planning all this before I have $20,000 in the bank and a home. If we put this off, well, the world is pretty unsettled and I think you had better take things as they come, and not put them off until tomorrow, which may never come.

November 8—More Red Tape

Every paper these days needs to be stamped with a rubber stamp. The papers I need quickly may be copies but they must be stamped. I told you before that I need copies of my birth certificate, your wedding license, and a statement from the clerk of courts that I am a US citizen. The stamp should be official looking from the appropriate office. It doesn't really matter as long as it is official looking. You could probably use a Farm Bureau stamp for all of them and we would get away with it. I do need them by November 25 if at all possible. After I get them, they must be translated into German with an official stamp of the translator. Then they need a stamp of the German license bureau. Finally, they must be stamped by the French Army officials who are 30 miles away from Helga's hometown. This last is necessary as she lives in the French occupied zone of Germany. With all of these properly stamped papers, we can then apply to the marriage bureau and pay them a fee of 500 marks. Then after all the papers are approved, our application is posted on a bulletin board for a minimum of 16 days. This must be done so that during that time anyone who wants to object can do so. Then we get the license. The 500-mark fee is the fee required whenever a German marries a foreigner. I guess that is to catch Army money! However, they did tell me that if I submit a statement that I am working with the AFSC and don't get paid we might get off with a fee of only 10 marks.

Another problem we seem to be facing is getting her into Vienna. Even though she will be married to an American, the Russians still consider her a German citizen. As such, she will not be permitted to go through the Russian Zone of occupation into Vienna. Our only recourse seems to be to fly her over the Russian control directly from the American Zone of Germany to the British airport in Vienna. The American airport is so far out of Vienna that one must go through a Russian control post to get to Vienna.

This comment is not exactly in the category of red tape. It is just a quirk in the German language. I am at last on a "Du" basis with the rest of the family rather than a "Sie" basis. "Sie" is the more formal way of saying "you." "Du" is used only to children, friends, and family. I guess I have arrived as a family member. This detail means an awful lot in German and to be at all accepted you had better get it right.

The Quaker staff in Ludwigshafen has graciously agreed that we could have our wedding ceremony in the Quaker barracks (really the Quaker Center). This will not be official, as the official wedding must be at the Standesamt (marriage bureau) earlier in the day. At the Quaker ceremony, each of us will have to say a few words as in usual Quaker weddings.

This last item also does not quite qualify as a red tape one. However, it is a plan that does not seem to be working out. You wrote earlier that Fairview Meeting would like to host a young Austrian for a year. You even said that there was some thought of him living with the Donald Bernard's. I told you I had just the right candidate in a young man named Egon Winkler, but Fairview is taking too long to make up its mind.

Moreover, they would have to arrange some housing change whereby he could live for two or three weeks at a time with different families. In the meantime, he tells me that although he has no other immediate plans, if something good here turns up he would take it in preference to waiting for the Meeting to act. Furthermore, a few days ago he called the office to tell us he had just broken his leg. He would have been a good candidate for this cross-cultural experience.

November 13—Is It Still a Secret?

The news concerning Helga and me has been seeping through to most of the Quaker House folks this week. Lou Schneider has asked that I inform Philadelphia so that he will have a freer hand in explaining the administrative job here to them in the light of my wanting to stay until April 1. So within a few weeks the news will probably begin to filter through. Sometimes I sort of worry that as a married man I will no longer be able to come and go in independence. But I guess it is not so bad if you voluntarily give up part of your independence.

November 17—Helga's First Letter to My Parents

"I read your letter over and over again, and I know that you will be my parents when I am with you in America. Though Bob assured me that nobody among his family and friends would mind that I am a German and that I would be heartily welcomed in the States, I sometimes was a little afraid. But your letter convinced me of all that Bob had told me before.

I find it very hard to leave my family and my home, and yet I don't need as much courage as you think, for it is Bob for whom I leave all this. Our love will overcome that very easily I hope, and I know Bob will share my troubles and concerns as well as I will his.

My mother loves Bob very much, which makes it a little easier for her to give me away. I translated your wonderful letter for her and she is very happy that you will accept me into your family and help me as much as you can.

Bob and I are planning to get married before Christmas if he gets all the papers in time. After the legal wedding, we will have a Quaker ceremony in the barracks of the AFSC, where I am work-ing. You will hear from me again when everything is definite. Then I also will send you a picture of me if it is ready.

Many greetings and love to you both.
Your Helga"

November 21—A Final Quick EDREC Trip

The week of November 6 to 13, I spent most of my time in the office. George and Lou spent the week visiting DP camps all over Austria so I sort of took George's place in the office. This past Monday after staff meeting, Herr Rohm and I took off, arriving at Sigmundsberg in time to put on an evening program. The next morning the ground was covered with about eight inches of snow so we had to put on chains in order to get over the mountains. After we thought we were out of the snow, I took the chains off but shortly after we hit an icy stretch and skidded worse than I had ever done before. Somehow the truck pulled out of it and we had no more trouble. We made it to Mittewald that afternoon and stayed there until Friday. This was one of the best visits I have yet had to any of the homes. I spent some time in each home making recordings to be used by the ÖGB office in Vienna. Thursday evening Herr Seebauer (Mela's successor) arrived. Friday morning we drove over to Cap Wörth. Even though the boys were no longer there, 18 group leaders and the camp director were still there. We spent the day and evening talking with them, mostly about the future of the EDREC program. On Saturday, we (Herr Rohm, Seebauer, and I) went on to Moosham where again the camp had closed for the season. Seebauer needed to go there to negotiate about buying the land before the ÖGB can start building a new home to replace the old barracks. Then yesterday, we were back again at Sigmundsberg to make more recordings and to put on our last program for the boys. This morning, the three of us headed back to Vienna, arriving here about one this afternoon.

It seemed a bit odd after a week in snow country to be back in Vienna where there has been no snow yet. It was particularly interesting on this trip to have Seebauer along. It gave me more of an opportunity to get some insight into the workings of the organization. He is extremely well liked. One reason is that he is trying to institute a new policy in the homes, one that is making the people feel more secure in their jobs than before. Under Mela if someone made a mistake, he or she often went out on his or her ear. Seebauer operates on the theory that if a person is basically the right one for the job, he or she should be entitled to the privilege of a few mistakes. It will help the whole spirit of the work if the workers feel a certain security in their positions.

I think I should mention a couple of things here that have nothing to do with the ÖGB. Last Sunday evening I attended a lecture at Quaker House on Unitarianism. The interesting part is that none other than Arthur gave the speech. Yes, he came back to Vienna some days ago. The second item is that since Virginia's baby is due about now she went to the hospital today. The doctor has a new method of inducing births, but he was too busy today to do it. Despite the fact that she is not yet in labor, tomorrow he will give her a special hormone shot that is supposed to do the trick.

November 24—Marriage Requirements

Just before I left on my last EDREC trip, I got a letter from Helga telling me that in Germany you can only get married on Saturday. The Saturday before Christmas is a holiday and the Saturday before New Year's is also a holiday. Therefore, our only open Saturdays would be January 7 or December 17. But January 7 is bad for us because I should be in Vienna with the beginning of the New Year with George just gone. Can we work it out for December 17 with all the problems? She tells me that you have to apply at the German marriage bureau for permission at least 16 days before the permission is issued, and one must make an appointment to go in person two days before that. Since I am a foreigner, the papers must then be sent to the French for their stamp of approval, which usually takes eight more days. When you add eight and 16 to make 24 you find that we had to make our application in person by November 23, which we did yesterday, to make it possible to get married on December 17.

In your last letter you said you would get those papers off soon. I was beginning to worry that your soon might not be soon enough. Hence, on November 15 I sent you that cable from Spittal. I tried to make it as short as possible because they charge by the word including your name and address. I tried to sign it just Bob but they insisted I must use and pay for my last name! At any rate, I was counting on the papers arriving in Vienna by last Monday when we got back from the EDREC trip. I planned to take the night train to Ludwigshafen, arrive there on Tuesday evening and be able to go to the marriage bureau on Wednesday, the last workable day for us. I had written Helga to make that appointment for Wednesday and I told her I would call her on Tuesday to cancel the appointment if the papers didn't come. Not only did I hope I would not have to call to cancel the appointment but I hated to call anyway because her parents have no telephone. In order to get Helga on the phone I would have to call the nearest neighbor with a phone, the local bakery, and have them run up to Helga's home and get her back to the bakery!

As soon as I got back from that EDREC trip, I checked the mail and found that the papers had not come. I resigned myself to calling Helga Tuesday and calling off the wedding until next year. No mail ever comes in the afternoon but in desperation at 5:00 p.m., I went to the post office and found your letter with all the papers. By 7:00, I was home where I first unpacked and then repacked. Then I got the nine o'clock train to Munich but had to sit up all the way as no sleepers were available. At least I saved two dollars! Then another train ride put me into Ludwigshafen by 9:00 Tuesday night.

Wednesday morning, Helga translated the papers you sent. Then we took them to some office to have the translation officially approved and stamped. In the afternoon Helga, her parents, and I went to the marriage office where it took an hour and a half to get all the papers filled out and all of our signatures on it. Her parents' signatures were required to give their approval of the marriage. It took two men all that time to get all the papers filled out and signed.

They were so concerned by the McCoy name. The greatest trouble was with the "H" in my father's name, Arthur H. McCoy. "What does the "H" stand for?" they asked. I told them it stood for nothing, it was just a letter. "But that is impossible," they said. Then my mother's name bothered them too. One paper had it as Eva M. Thorp McCoy and another had it Eva Marie Thorp McCoy. Why weren't the names in agreement? It was of great concern that my middle name, Thorp, was also my mother's maiden name. In addition, why was my middle name on a paper, Thorp, when in my passport it was Thorpe?

Finally, why did my birth certificate name my birthplace as Green Township when another paper said I was born in New Vienna? We finally came to an understanding with them and paid the fee of $4.00. We just hope the French don't charge the customary $125 to approve my application. Now all we can do is wait. But we made the deadlines.

November 25—Ohio Home Search

In my last note to you, I forgot to comment on your good efforts to find a home for us. The 60-acre place next to Jordan's doesn't sound like a bad idea. As I remember it, the land does lie better than the land in the Snow Hill direction. $200 an acre does seem high if the land is poor. But then the Snell place sold for $600 an acre. Probably the 60 acres would not be self-sustaining but if worked in conjunction with the home place, it might work out. You say there is a good, fairly new barn and chicken house there and though the house is small, it is in good shape. Of course, the ideal setup would have been the Ridgeway place, but it is now sold. The Gall place might also work out. You will have to decide as you are on the spot and know best how to integrate the farming. As I think I wrote before, I am not against the idea of a trailer for a time. Just keep looking. It sounds like you are doing a good job for us.

November 26—Helga's Problems Getting to Vienna

On November 10, I was able to get permission from the American Border Control Office in Vienna for Helga to come to Vienna by air. They immediately cabled this permission to the French Border Control Office in Baden Baden. On November 14, she went to Baden Baden to gets the permit stamped in her passport. They said that they had never received any such cable. They further stated that even if they had received such an American permit they could not grant their permission until she had a permit from the mayor's office in Ludwigshafen. She could not bring that permit to Baden Baden, but would have to let it go through channels to Baden Baden, after which Baden Baden would send their permit to Ludwigshafen, but only through channels. And all this would take up to eight weeks. She then went to the mayor's office but was told they would not grant a permit until she had proof that the French would grant her permission. They also require that she have an Austrian visa. But the American Office in Vienna told me that no such visa is necessary, in fact, it is not possible for any German.

Tuesday, on the way to Ludwigshafen, I stopped in Stuttgart at the American branch of the border control and met one of the French officials from Baden Baden. He seemed nice enough and told us to go to Baden Baden on November 26, today, and he would see what he could do for us. I managed to borrow a jeep from the AFSC and off we went to Baden Baden, but no one had ever heard of this French official. They further told us that even if that cable had come they would not have honored it, as they are the French and would take no orders from Americans. The cable giving Helga permission to enter Vienna must come from the Allied Commission (impossible because that includes Russians) or from the French in Vienna. On Monday, when I get back to Vienna, I must pay a visit to the French there. Then, after Baden Baden receives this cable, Helga must go to Mainz to apply for the permit as she lives in the northern half of the French Zone, which is administered from Mainz. But she won't yet actually get it. They must send it to Baden Baden where she can pick it up. Wow! Helga is pretty discouraged about all this paper work and so am I. I can't admit that to her.

Farewell, ÖGB

December 1949

December 4—Routine Vienna

I arrived back in Vienna on Monday and immediately got the French to send the permit to Baden Baden. Hurrah! The rest of the week I have been picking George's brain as to details of his job. Philadelphia has sent no hint of a replacement for him so I had better learn quickly. I spent considerable time hunting a place in Vienna for Helga and me to live. I finally found a two-room apartment in the 18th district. It is close to where I lived three years ago, but it is very expensive. It costs us $30 a month, whereas the one-room apartment where I am now costs only $15. I have also been busy getting our vehicles relicensed and helping out at Quaker House. Last night, we had about the biggest crowd ever at the Quaker House Youth night. It also included five of the ÖGB home group leaders. Then tonight, most of us went to the Staatstheatre to see *Pygmalion*. I have also been busy helping the ÖGB youth officials (including Seebauer) get ready for the planning school he has scheduled for the next two weeks.

December 11—Final ÖGB Contact

Monday morning, all the ÖGB camp directors and group leaders met at the end of the subway line on the west end of Vienna where two buses took us an hour and a half west to the nearest ÖGB home at Innermanzing. Yes, that was way inside the Russian Zone, but since I was the only illegal, the group covered for me nicely. The group is having a two-week training school in preparation for next year's programs. It had been originally planned for January but was rescheduled to December. I could only attend the first week as I do have something else planned for next week. Each day, lectures were held from 8:00–11:30 and 2:00–5:30 by all sorts of experts. I found that I got nearly everything in the lectures. Maybe I could go to college in German after all. An outstanding educator on the handling of delinquent children gave one of the lectures. Then the next day he spoke about the philosophy of Quakerism. It turned out he is a Viennese Quaker and he did an excellent job of explaining Quakerism. I was continually amazed at the things that came out in these lectures. As a result, I feel that we Americans have little or nothing to contribute to these people in the realm of new ideas. All we can do is establish a bond of friendship with them. I really had a great week between lectures. I already knew most of the people there from my work of the past year. In fact, I probably had been to more homes than any one person there. The week there made me feel that my year in getting the EDREC program established had certainly been valuable. It was a most fitting occasion for my farewell to the ÖGB.

Our Wedding

———⟨⬦⟩———

December 1949

December 16—Ready?

Tomorrow is our wedding day. My goodness, the way you keep writing about the great news, the great day, etc. It is not going to be so world shaking. Please don't go making such a big fuss over it. It all seems very natural to me. You take life as it comes more or less. This happens to come now, so...

I am glad Elmore was able to work out a telephone call from the McCoy clan tomorrow at 4:00. It is nice to have someone in the family associated with Ohio Bell. I forgot to mention that I did get away from Vienna Wednesday night. When I arrived in Ludwigshafen Thursday night, I found Helga's mother and her aunt, Rosel, busily baking. They had been working at it all day Thursday, and continued with it today. We are really going to eat tomorrow. This afternoon, Ellie Myers of the Quaker staff here and Helga's brother, Otto, took us shopping. However, Ellie and Helga did it all, while Otto and I trudged along bored stiff. Then the AFSC staff invited us for supper. Tonight comes the traditional German pre-wedding Polterabend (Bachelor Party) night out for the groom. He is supposed to celebrate his last night of freedom with his drinking buddies. Since I don't have any such buddies here, I relegated my role to Helga's brother, who was quite happy to oblige. He was supposed to pick up her wedding dress, but he went so late to get it that he must have taken it to the Polterabend party. It is midnight and he has not yet returned. It seems we always have some problem or other! Helga had not planned to get a special dress, but her parents wanted it and the Quakers gave her the material. The dressmaker promised to have it finished today. It will be white with large buttons all down the back. She will also have a thin veil.

December 17—The Great Day

Otto showed up early this morning with the wedding dress. The Polterabend had gone on until 6:00 this morning! I'm glad I didn't have to go. Later, Helga's Uncle Karl and Aunt Rosel came from Mannheim. He, Helga's father, and the two of us went to the Standesamt, the bureau that handles marriages as well as many other legal matters, for our 9:15 wedding appointment. Another uncle, Willy, and his bride to be met us there, for they were to be married today too. We planned to use the same two witnesses, Helga's father and Uncle Karl. We were the 13th and 14th couples of the day. The official reluctantly agreed to have a double wedding although he feared he might marry the wrong couple. The four of us sat facing the "judge" with the two witnesses on either side. The judge then read for a couple of minutes about how we are to take care of each other, how serious it all is, etc. Then we stood and he asked the usual question, "Do you take this woman?" etc. I don't remember the exact words. At any rate, we got our Jas (yes-es) said properly after the uncle and his new wife said theirs. We all four signed papers, the witnesses signed, and we were married. The judge also waved the usual 500-mark wedding fee for us and charged us only 10, since I was working without pay for the Quakers. I think I forgot to tell you earlier that the French also waved their $125 fee and charged us only $12.50, all for the same reason.

In Germany, a couple is always expected to ride in a car to their official wedding. Otto had promised to borrow a car from his boss but at the last minute that failed. He then tried, in vain, to get a taxi, so we just took a 15-minute streetcar ride and walked the rest of the way in the rain. No, Helga was not wearing the wedding dress for this ceremony.

When we got home, Helga's mother and aunt had rearranged the room with a long table loaded with food, and the day of feasting began. Someone had to answer the door all the time, as I don't know how many pots of flowers arrived from friends and neighbors. We also got a telegram from Wilmington from the Marbles and Sven. I even got a congratulatory letter from one of the directors in the ÖGB.

At 1:15 p.m., Ellie came in a station wagon and took most of the relatives to the Quaker Barracks. Then she returned for the two of us. As we got out of the car, what seemed like a battery of friends and well-wishers turned cameras on us. All the rest of the day picture after picture was taken. I hope we can get some of them. We then went into the back room to wait until every one was seated. Yesterday, someone had prepared the room and had even waxed the floor! The audience faced one way and there were five chairs in front facing the audience, the five chairs serving as the facing bench. The ceremony began with the playing of a record, Bach or something. The clerk, Trudy (I forget her last name), went in first to the far right from the viewpoint of the audience. Helga's mother went to the other end. Then came Helga's father, then Helga, and I sat between Helga and Trudy. Trudy is a genuine German Quaker from Heidelberg. Helga says she is a very nice person who is about 55.

We sat there quietly for five minutes or so. Helga and I stood up and I started with the usual words to Helga. "In the presence of God and these our friends, I, Robert, take thee, Helga, to be my wife, promising with Divine Assistance to be unto thee a loving and faithful husband as long as we both shall live." Then she said the same thing to me in German. We put on the rings I had had engraved in Vienna and we sat down. About 10 minutes later, Ruth Dross from the Vienna team stood and said a few appropriate words. Then in about five minutes, Trudy spoke too. A few moments later Trudy shook our hands and that concluded the ceremony. We then went into the next room where everyone filed in to shake our hands, kiss the bride, meet the parents, and sign the wedding certificate. We found a table with a number of nice presents including a delightful cuckoo clock from the Vienna team and all employees. Of course, coffee and cake were served to all. In the middle of that, your telephone call came through just at the right time. Thank cousin Elmore and Ohio Bell.

Those people who had to go left at this time. The rest of us indulged ourselves with a bountiful repast all prepared by Helga's mother. We stepped outside for a few pictures and then back in the barracks for a bit of dancing. It was so good to have so many friends of both Helga and me come to the wedding. From Vienna came George and Virginia, Ruth, Annalies, Louise, and Herbert and Ellie Foster. Marlis, formerly from the Vienna team, came. My old friend, Alice, made it as well. George Mathues had wanted to come but he was best man today for some friend in Munich. From the AFSC German headquarters near Darmstadt came Lou Schneider, Ruth Dross (formerly with the Vienna team), Lucretia Wood (a Westtown classmate of mine), and Earl Fowler (an Earlham classmate of mine). Quite a few of Helga's friends, both AFSC members and German friends, stayed as well. After the dinner, the Vienna group left to drive to Vienna and George and Virginia left to fly to Boston.

Our wedding day

By now I thought we had had enough food for the day. We went back to Helga's home to, at last, change our clothes for traveling and found a family party had begun with more food. All the family was present including Uncle Willy and his bride. They had not come to our Quaker wedding but had stayed home all day after the civil ceremony. At 10:00, Connie Hunter (an AFSC team member in Ludwigshafen) and Otto took us to the train station in Mannheim where we found the mainline train that we had to catch in Heidelberg was an hour late. They took us on to Heidelberg where we got a direct sleeper to Garmisch where we will spend our honeymoon. That family party at Helga's home probably will go on until morning, but without us!

December 23—Honeymoon

Sunday we arrived at this officer's hotel at Riessersee just outside of Garmisch. It is a beautiful spot just north of Germany's highest mountain, the Zugspitze. Riessersee is a small lake about five acres in size and is available to guests for fishing and swimming. However, at this time of year it is only to look at with the Zugspitze looming in the background. Surprisingly, we have the hotel pretty much to ourselves. Yesterday, we took the cog railway through a long tunnel to the top of the Zugspitze. It was raining here at Riessersee but on top, the sun was bright on the deep snow covering the beautiful mountains. It certainly seemed more beautiful this time than it had when I was first there some time ago. I wonder why?

Helga at the Zugspitze

Me at the Zugspitze

Travel Problems and Christmas

December 1949

December 20—How Get To Vienna

Tuesday, we went up to Munich to try to get Helga cleared by the US Army for her to travel by train to Vienna next week. However, our attempt was in vain. A WAC to whom we applied said, "What, a German? They don't have any rights. Here in Germany we never give permission of any kind to Germans, including the right to ride on military trains." This was hard on Helga making her feel like a second-class citizen. It seemed to me to be as a Negro must feel in our South. Having anticipated this problem some time ago, we had decided that in this case she would fly to Vienna and I would take the train. The flight costs $18 and the train only $4. Arthur thought that was so horribly unromantic that for a Christmas present he would give us the difference so that I could fly with her. Trusting that the French permit for Helga will come next week we decided to make flight reservations now. We first tried Pan Am. They would not let her fly with them because she didn't have an Austrian visa. They said that once she is in Vienna she will become a US Dependant and could then fly with them. Does that make sense? We finally got a reservation with KLM, the Dutch Airline, for Wednesday, December 28. They simply didn't bother to ask whether or not she had an Austrian visa. This evening, we are eating wurst and rolls here in our room. Helga was fed up with hotel fare!

December 26—Christmas

Saturday morning, we took the train to Ludwigshafen, arriving at her home about 5:00 in the evening. Christmas is always on Christmas Eve in Germany. After supper, as soon as Otto and his girl friend, Gerti, had arrived, we went into the other room where her folks had set up a three-foot high tree covered with real candles. With the candles lit and Christmas music coming from the radio, we had a few moments of a real Quaker Meeting. Then, of course, came the opening of the presents. We had gotten something for each family member. Helga had knitted a sweater for me and I gave her a watch. Her parents gave me a brief case. We also had a number of small items for each person. Afterwards, we went visiting and saw some of her friends. Then yesterday and today, we spent most of the time visiting more of her friends. She has become right famous in the neighborhood because of her anticipated move to America.

December 27—The French

All this time Helga was getting more and more discouraged about the fact that her exit permit from the French had not arrived. She had gone to Baden Baden on December 6 and found that the French had received the telegram from their office in Vienna granting her permission on the strength of the US Army's permission for her to come to Vienna. But, of course, the French had to put the permit through channels, which would take a week. However, by Christmas, the permit had not arrived. Since Christmas and December 26, Monday, are holidays there was nothing we could do about it until today. This morning I managed to borrow a jeep from the Quakers and we went to the French office in Ludwigshafen to see if the permit had arrived. And the answer—no. Off we went on the 100-kilometer drive south to Baden Baden. There we were told that the permit had been mailed according to protocol on December 12 to Mainz, but it had never come back to Baden Baden. Off we went back the 100 kilometers to Ludwigshafen and further on north 80 kilometers to Mainz. Yes, they had received the permit, but on December 23 had mailed it to Neustadt since Neustadt is the local office in charge of Ludwigshafen. Neustadt is 40 kilometers south of Ludwigshafen. Back to Neustadt we drove. This time we hit pay dirt. Helga had her permission.

December 28—To Vienna at Last

Despite our busy day yesterday, including packing, we were up at 3:00 this morning to take a taxi to the train station. Late morning found us in Munich. Then to KLM where we boarded the "Flying Dutchman" for our flight to Vienna. This was the first beautiful day in weeks and we could see the view all the way to Vienna. To the north was Czechoslovakia and to the south were the snow-covered Alps. It was a magical trip. It was Helga's first flight and my second. It almost looks like our legal troubles are over. Of course, we have to get her trip to the US worked out. The trip took just over an hour. Once in Vienna, after supper we went back to my old apartment for a good night's sleep.

Last Days in Vienna

January to March, 1950

January 5—Getting Settled

Last Thursday, we managed to get our luggage from the station and move into the new apartment. It is not too satisfactory. It costs more than twice as much as the old one and has no services. Supposedly, we can use the kitchen but that doesn't seem to work out. We cook on the heating stove. We had no dishes but now we have the few that George left. I guess I was spoiled by my former landlady. She was so much nicer than the present one. Helga has been seeing a number of her old friends from the Salzburg work camp. Several of them came to a New Year's Eve party hosted by Mausi (a Quaker Center Austrian member), where the biggest hit of the evening was telling our fortunes using liquid zinc on water.

Since George and family left for the states after our wedding, his work now falls on me. I find that his responsibilities were considerable. In addition, the ÖGB has been calling on me to clean up odds and ends with them. In addition, I should be applying for Helga's visa but must wait for the paper work you are sending. The most needed is the financial report proving I am able to support a wife. That requires a bank statement about my $135 bank account, a copy of the bit of Farm Bureau stock that I own, as well as a copy of the income tax report from last year. Can you think of any other assets? Then, as I think I wrote, I need a statement from my employer, you, that I will have a job when I return. I thought I was finished with paper work!

Then there is the matter of the house. I am glad to see that you finally bought the Birmingham place. The only problem is that it has no running water. Helga was a bit dismayed at that disclosure. Though she lived in a small place, she cannot imagine having no running water. However, I was able to placate her with your statement that you would try to have running water installed before we get home. And, as you said, it would be nice to install a bathtub. You should know that I don't care where you put the bathtub as long as its placement doesn't make it too inconvenient. At least I am glad that you finally got a house.

January 6—Helga's Second Letter to My Parents

"Dear Parents,

First of all, I wish you a Happy New Year! I hope that you can celebrate many more with us in the States and that we can contribute some happiness to your future life. I want to thank you very much for that nice Christmas present. I was so happy that you had not forgotten me and that you gave something to me that will last forever, always reminding me of you. I guess the presents I

*made for you arrived after the Holidays. It was not much what I
sent, but I made it with love.*

*I have been in Vienna for two weeks now and I like this big
town very much. When I went through the illuminated streets for
the first time, I behaved like a little child. For it is wonderful to
see these big shop windows with all those wonderful articles displayed. A picture like this I had seen very often in my hometown
before it was destroyed. But this was almost 10 years ago.*

*Bob's friends and mine welcomed me very heartily here. We
have had many invitations already and I liked it everywhere. Bob
and I would very much like to have guests also. That seems almost
impossible right now, because we really do only have the dishes
we need for both of us. Since two days we have our breakfasts at
home, which saves us a lot of money. I think Bob wrote you all
about our present home and thus I need not do that again. I feel
that these two rooms can never be that home we love and I am
looking foreword to our household in Ohio.*

*Enclosed I send you the pictures of our wedding with some
explanations. These are the first pictures you see of Bob together
with me. I hope you like them.*

Much love and best wishes, your daughter,
Helga"

January 15—Another German Trip

Wednesday I went alone to Helga's home in Germany to get
some of her things sent to the States and to bring other items to Vienna.
Of course, she had to stay behind in Vienna. We don't need any more paper
work now. Sometime in the next two or three weeks you should be getting
four parcels sent with Army mail from Mannheim. I only insured the largest
one. It contained most of the wedding presents. The second contains a tea,
coffee, and cream pitcher that Helga bought. The other two are some more
presents and odds and ends. We had the family buy china for us. This consisted of a set for twelve made up of 88 pieces. We packed it all for shipment
but the Army post office said it was way too heavy for them to handle. Otto
is repackaging it in three parcels and will give it to the Quakers to ship for
us. The china cost 260 marks, about $65.

Speaking of money, I'm wondering if you could add maybe $200
to my bank account at home. Incidentally, I don't understand your statement
that I have over $200 in the account. In the fall, you wrote that I had around
$130. What makes it grow that fast? Since January I have written one check
for $100 on that account. I don't need any more yet, but I will when it comes

time to go home. It took some time to get these items taken care of so I did not get back to Vienna until this evening.

January 18—More Red Tape

Thanks so much. All the papers we need arrived in Monday's mail. The next day we got them all signed and certified copies made. Off to Washington they went. We were told that if we mailed them to the Washington office directly it would take at least six weeks for them to be processed. However, if we knew someone in Washington who could present them in person it would take only about one week. Since there are so many details to be handled after the approval comes back, time is of the essence. So, I sent them to Herbert and Ruthanna Hadley and asked them to hand deliver the papers. I am sure they will be happy to help. Then to add to our woes, our landlady tells us that she was visited by the CIC (Army Counter Intelligence Corps) yesterday, to ask if Helga was a Nazi or a Communist. The landlady had never even seen Helga until three weeks ago!

January 20—Another Letter from Helga to My Parents

"Dear Parents,

We just received a letter from you, for which I thank you very much. Bob is not in the office right now, and thus he did not have any chance to read it yet.

You write so many wonderful things, which I, as a German girl, can hardly believe. You tell me how everybody is eager to meet me! I always thought it would be very hard for me to come to the United States as a German. I do not know if you understand me right, but here we sometimes have to feel that we are "those bad Germans." Up to now, I always was a bit afraid of coming to the "New World," but now I can hardly wait to meet you and all my friends-to-be.

I am happy that you are interested about all the details of our wedding. Right now, I am not going to write about it, because the letter I sent you last week might be enough description. You are right; the Quaker Ceremony was the real wedding for us. Bob and I, in fact all my family and our friends, liked it very much. It was good, that we could have it in the Quaker barracks. Thus, we were able to invite all our friends. I am so sorry that you were not there! I am sure you would have liked it, too.

I wish so much that you could meet my folks. I know they would like it very much. Bob showed them the film he took of your

*home in Ohio and thus they have at least an idea of where I am
going to live and where Bob comes from. They also saw you in these
movies.*

*Sunday, Bob came back from Ludwigshafen. He had been
with my folks for four days! They had a wonderful time there, my
mother wrote. They were sorry to see him leave so soon. Nobody
realized that I was alone in Vienna and missed Bob most.*

*I like it very much here in Vienna. Everybody is so friendly
with me. In fact, I have a lot of friends already. Our home is quite
nice, too. We have two rooms, a bathroom, and the toilet. The
apartment is in a small house in a very quiet district of Vienna.
It is a bit far from the office, but as long as we can go by car, it is
all right. We sleep in the smaller room, and the one with the nice
comfortable furniture we use as our living room.*

*We have had some guests for tea already and they all like this
room with a desk and chair, two easy chairs, one davenport and
some little tables, very much. The only problem is that we don't
have a kitchen here. This means that I cannot cook anything but
coffee, tea, or cocoa. This is all right as far as eating is concerned
because we have a big dinner at noon downtown every day. I would
so much like to cook! I had to prepare meals for my folks during
those bad times after the war when my mother was in the hospital
(she is a diabetic). Now I think it must be wonderful to cook with
all those good thing you can buy again.*

*I am looking foreword to our home in America. I thank you
very much for everything you are doing for us. Please don't start
with the rebuilding of the house before we come there. I would like
to see it grow. Then nothing can be strange to me and I am sure
to love it. There is only one thing I would like you to do. That is
to arrange that we have running water in the house when we start
with the rest of the building. I guess Bob told you about it already,
didn't he? I think having water in the house makes it easier for me
to keep it clean from the beginning on.*

*My Mutti—that is how I call my mother—wrote me how
much she loved your letter. A friend of mine translated it for her.
She says, "I am so happy that I can get in contact with Bob's
folks." She is going to write you soon. She is so happy that you are
going to replace her and want to be my mother.*

*I know this English is not very good and I am a bit ashamed
that I am not able to a write better. But I am sure you can
understand all I want to say. After being in America, I am sure I*

will learn your language very quickly. Bob said I might go to some
courses at Wilmington College. Do you think that is possible? I
would like it very much. I am also going to have driving lessons
with Bob, which I like very much too. Isn't it exciting to drive?

I hope you'll soon let us know how you liked the pictures of
our wedding. Do you like your new daughter—on the picture, I
mean? Please, let us soon hear from you again.

Love and best wishes from your daughter,
Helga"

January 30—My Letter to Uncle Leo and Aunt Elizabeth

My goodness, it still scares me to write 1950. Why, I'll be an old
man before I know it. At least that is what my wife says! How do you like that
—my wife? I'm just not used to my use of the term yet. I imagine you heard
from my folks that we did get married. We had a bit of trouble getting all the
papers in order for Helga to come to Vienna, but now we are here. The latest
problem is again from the US Army telling me I have to get out of Austria by
March 17 since I am married to a German! Hope we get that solved in order
to stay here until our sailing date sometime in April.

Well, you folks have made quite a hit with Helga. She loves the
popcorn you sent. Did I ever thank you last fall for sending those 10 cases
of popcorn for the apprentices? They certainly appreciated it too! Helga
pops it for guests, sent some to her parents, and generally enjoys it in many
ways. We have even had our eggs cooked in the coconut oil you sent. Her
mother baked a really good cake with it too. The only trouble was that the
usually white cake turned out yellow! Maybe we ought to just buy that pop-
per you advertise and stay over here. I believe a person could really make
some money here if he went into the popcorn business. But I guess we'll be
coming home anyway. At any rate, thanks so much for this second install-
ment of popcorn.

I'm getting my taste of office work these days. I don't have a
chance to run around all over Austria like I did last year; I have to stay in the
office and push the pencil. There is only one indication that I am a big shot.
I have three phones in my office, but I never have been able to get a call in
on all three at once yet!

I keep feeling that there ought to be something I could do about
all this Russian business while I am still here in the middle of all the fuss. I
just don't know what it might be. Everyone seems pretty calm here. I guess
when you are in the middle of it you aren't as scared as when you are way off
in the States. You get much more frightened reading US publications than

you do reading European ones! Time to call a halt. Thanks again for that popcorn. Hope to see you both one of these days.

February 18—Ski Week

Louise and others from the Quaker House organized a ski week for Quaker House participants. They managed, with my help, to get the use of the ÖGB recuperation home in Moosham. Last Sunday we drove 54 youth in two trucks to the home for a week of fun and skiing. Since there was no one left from our team to drive the second truck, I managed to borrow my old sidekick, Noverl, from the ÖGB to drive it. Of course, Helga could not go, as we always must cross the Russian occupation border coming here. We had no great difficulties and the ski week is turning out to be a huge success. Tomorrow, Sunday, we will return to Vienna.

February 19—Helga Again to My Parents

"Dear Parents,

I was so happy about your letter that I am going to answer it immediately. I am glad you like our wedding pictures, which a friend of my brother's took for us. We also had some moving pictures taken, but they are not developed yet.

Last week, Mr. and Mrs. Roberts from New Jersey, and their daughter, Alice, who is working with AFSC in Bad Aibling, Germany, paid a visit to Vienna. We tried to show them as much as possible of this wonderful town. I think Bob did a marvelous job. The Roberts' seemed to like it very much. They also had tea with us in our home, and I think they are going to write you about it.

Right now, I am a grass widow, which I don't like at all. Bob and all the others left Vienna last Sunday as scheduled. Unfortunately, I could not get a permit for the Russian border control, which forced me to stay here. All I could do was replace a secretary who has gone with them. I do look forward to their arrival in Vienna tonight.

Last week, we were informed that Washington granted my visa. All I need now is the permission from the CIC—an Army division—here in Vienna. This should be granted if they are convinced that I am no Communist, have not been a Nazi, and have not committed any crimes. Besides that, I have to have a valid passport, of course, which is not so very easy to get, as I am a German. Despite all that red tape we hope to be able to leave

Vienna by the 1st of April, go to Germany for a few days, go on
to Paris and London and sail on the 26th of April.

My mother is very happy about the correspondence with you,
and I think she is looking forward to your next letter. When I am
with you the writing won't be so complicated any more because I
can do the translation.

Did Bob write you from Moosham? I don't know if he will
be able to write you next week because we are going to have a
visit of Julia Branson, head of the Foreign Section of the AFSC
in Philadelphia. She will spend all next week here in Vienna. I
think everybody will be busy in talking to the "big chief."

Hope to hear from you again.
Greetings and Love,
Helga"

March 4—VIP Visit

Helga was right. The "big chief," Julia Branson, arrived on
schedule on February 23. She was here to spend the week getting acquainted
with all of us, and learning of our programs. The first few days she spent
in Vienna interviewing many government and nongovernment officials, as
well as all of us. In her conversation with me, she said she would like very
much for Helga and me to stay on here for another year. However, I told
her we were not interested. For one thing, it is not good for Helga. She can't
cook in our little apartment and thus comes to the office where there isn't
much for her to do. She can't leave Vienna when I do. Altogether, it just
isn't satisfactory. We want to get to New Vienna, Ohio. She is a bit fearful
of going to America, but wants to face the challenge up front. I think she
fears that she may be treated as a second-class citizen, since that is what she
gets here all the time from Army Americans. Your writing that Negroes still
cannot go to school with whites in Wilmington alarmed her. She wonders
are Americans like the US Army here or are they more like the AFSC workers here?

March 5—Other Matters

Monday night, Julie went with us to a party held by the Austrian
government for all foreign relief workers. Then Tuesday morning, Frau von
Katherine, an Austrian team member with us, Joan, Julia and I left at 6:00 to
drive to Klagenfurt. Here, Julia talked for some time with Dr. Keller about
a possible resettlement project. Yes, that is the same man whom I had failed
to contact two years ago. The next morning she interviewed a number of

officials about the possible project. We then drove on to the ÖGB home at Cap Wörth where she met the director and some of the group leaders and learned more about my EDREC program. This gave me a chance to say farewell to the leaders I had grown to know in the past year. She had more official talks in Villach. Then, I put Joan and Frau von Katherine on a train back to Klagenfurt and put Julia on a train for Germany.

I drove up to Mittewald to say farewell to the leaders there and they pushed me into spending the night with them. It was certainly good to be once more in the recuperation homes. What a different relationship from the way it was a year ago when I was just beginning.

March 5—Relieved

After spending the night at Mittewald, I drove north. In order to go north without a great detour, I drove the jeep onto a train that took me through the Alps from where I drove on to Salzburg. There, I met Dave from our team. He and I went to the appropriate US Army office and after a long delay, I was ushered in to a very friendly and sympathetic officer. After hearing my tale of woe in negotiating with many Army branches, he issued the proper authority for me to stay in Austria past the March 17 deadline. Despite having a German wife, I now have permission to remain until April 10. For the night, we then went to the Army rest center at Predigstuhl where I had spent several days in recuperation.

Friday morning, we went to Kitzbühl to check on the house that the AFSC had inherited. We were not able to clear up the title to the property due to the intransigence of the French occupation authorities. We were tempted to take a beautiful 12 by 12 carpet woven with a huge swastika, but our good sense returned before we could make off with it. And so back to Vienna we drove.

Last night, we took in a chilling movie called *The Third Man*. It certainly captures the mood of Vienna as I experienced it in 1946.

As usual, it is very difficult to get passage to the US. However, as Helga told you, Paris has us booked on the *Ile de France* from Southampton on April 26. We hope to leave here about April 1 and spend some time in Germany, Paris, and London. Maybe we will have time to hunt the McCoy ancestral home. Was it in Ireland or Scotland?

You wrote, "Do you hear lots of war talk in Vienna? It begins to sound ominous to us." I have asked many people since you wrote and the reaction is always the same whether they are Americans or Austrians. "What war talk?" It seems to me that tensions have eased considerably. I thought that maybe it was just that I had not been reading the papers enough. But everyone else backed up my feeling that there was nothing particularly new on the subject right now. Maybe it is this Vogeler case that you have been reading about in the papers that scares you. At any rate, here in Vienna, which would get it first if war came, there is no war scare. It is the general feeling that people in the States are always much more alarmed than people here. To what recent incidents are you referring? We just don't know here.

I think I asked a few weeks ago if you could put $200 in my account at the bank. As you haven't mentioned it, I don't dare write any more checks until I hear from you. The AFSC is not supporting Helga and we will need a little more money before leaving here and for traveling home.

March 6—Helga's Note to My Parents

"As you know, today is Bob's birthday. He was quite pleased with the presents you sent, and they arrived in time. He will be writing you about them later.

Right now, I am sending this note to include a picture of Bob, as the representative of the AFSC, receiving an award from Dr. Theodore Körner, the mayor of Vienna.

This was done at the celebration the city put on a couple of weeks ago for the work of reconstruction by foreign relief agencies."

Much love,
Helga"

Receiving an award for AFSC work in Vienna from
Dr. Theodore Körner, mayor of Vienna

March 14—Another Note from Helga

"Thank you very much for that nice letter and the plan of the house. I'm afraid I don't understand it all. Bob promised to answer all your questions concerning this. I want to thank you very much for all those good things you have done for us already. I'm looking forward to our coming to the USA and I'm very excited to see the place that is to be my new home. So far, everything has gone all right with my papers, and if all goes well we'll leave Vienna by 1 April. I hope that we can go to Italy before we come to Germany. I really would like to see that part of Europe, which is said to be so lovely, and it is a place to which I have never been.

Just think, it is only seven weeks until we sail on April 26. I can hardly believe that I really will leave this continent where I've been living for more than 20 years. I'm glad the Roberts' liked the time they spent with us in Vienna. I'm looking forward to seeing you.

Much love,
Helga"

March 16—Letter from Helga's Mother to My Mother

"I thank you heartily for your lovely letter. It pleases me very much that we are to be good friends. I am glad, also, that you find me, with my 46 years, still so young. You will see more of us than just the picture when that young couple comes home. Soon it is Easter. Helga and Bob will come to us on April 12, stay here a few days and then come to you.

Many times it is hard for me, when I think about it, that I must be separated from Helga for such a long time. It is a comfort to know what loving provision will fall to Helga's lot. I thank you for the great care you have taken that Bob and Helga may have so good a beginning. It is beautiful that the two of them will be able to have a house of their own and a piece of land which they, themselves, can build up to call their own.

I know that Helga, busy in the first few weeks of household arranging, will not have much time remaining. She is a trained little housemother. She will also be happy on your farm. Ludwigshafen is an industrial city, so it has always seemed good to Helga, when we, in our vacation, could drive over the country. As she was also in the country during the war, on that account she will *not feel entirely strange in her new surroundings, especially as she has your Bob. So they will both be happy. I am proud of Bob and Helga and you and your husband will have a great joy from them. Still more than these words can tell you, you will soon be convinced when you know them personally. I hope that you can translate this letter. In the hope that all goes well with you, I greet you and your husband with all my heart...*

Your friend,
Ella

PS Many greetings from my husband and Otto."

March 18—Newspaper Write-up

In today's mail, I received a clipping from the Wilmington, Ohio News Journal, which included not only the picture of the mayor of Vienna handing me the award, but also a write up about my work in Austria. It is not too accurate and sounds like it might have been written by Aunt Elsie. It goes as follows: "The picture shows Bob McCoy of New Vienna, Ohio in the Vienna, Austria City Hall receiving for the AFSC Unit in Austria a medal and scroll in appreciation of the achievements of the Quakers who have been working in that country. The presentation was made by a Dr. Körner, the Mayor for Vienna, since so much of the AFSC work has been in that city.

Bob spent 1946–47 in Vienna as head of Relief Transport and 1949 in charge of recreational and educational work in recuperation homes for undernourished, teenage apprentices. Each month he traveled through Austria stopping at several recuperation homes where up to 1000 apprentices were kept for a month in order that they might have additional food to build up resistance to disease. In each home he talked to the group as a whole, to smaller groups, showed constructive movies, played records of fine music, loaned good books, went on hikes with the boys, supervised games and talked over individual problems. After training two Austrian men to take over the work at the beginning of 1950, Bob was appointed leader of the Austrian AFSC Unit until the expiration of his term of service, April 1. This work is largely administrative and involves the coordination of the various activities of the Unit."

March 30—Last Days in Vienna (Really)

These last few days have been terribly busy. First, there is all the last minute administrative work to clear up in the office. Philadelphia has not yet appointed anyone to replace me, so David Winder will fill the role until someone else comes. Secondly, we have been busy packing our stuff and sending most of it through the Army post office because of all the traveling we will be doing en route home. Thirdly, we have been inundated with invitations galore. Then last Sunday, we had a party at our little place for all those who had been at the Salzburg work camp last summer.

Yes, it will be sad to leave Austria again, but this time I think I can make it. After all, part of Europe is coming with me. I will also miss the ÖGB people. After all, I spent most of my time with them.

April 2—Start of Our Italian Trip

Yesterday, we tearfully left Vienna and flew to Venice. Helga still has to fly over the Russian Border Control. Then today, we met up with David Winder from our staff, Gerti Feifar and three other Austrians. Tomorrow, the seven of us will head south in the AFSC jeep station wagon to visit Rome. Since this is my second trip to Italy, the others think I should know my way around!

April 12—Italian Trip

We turned out to be a very congenial traveling group. It was just as well, as we were a bit crowded in the station wagon. At any rate, we made Rome sometime Tuesday afternoon and after spending considerable time found proper housing. I did feel a bit like a tour guide to those who had never been to Rome before. Then a couple of days later we headed south, parked the car in a garage and took a vegetable boat to Capri. Again, since I had been there before, I became the tour guide. Capri seems like a wonderful place to go to get away from all the problems of the outside world

Easter Sunday, instead of going to Mass somewhere, we took a ferryboat back to our jeep and headed north. We made it to Rome at midnight and realized we couldn't change any money then. We discovered that among us we only had enough Italian money to buy gasoline to get us back to Austria but not enough for any food. So, after filling our tank and three jerry cans we again headed north, eating the last of our sandwiches and oranges.

The next day it was a relief to get to Villach in Austria. There we were able to get a good meal at the British Army Hotel Post. Then out to the ÖGB home at Mittewald where we said farewell again to the Austrian leaders and to each other.

My old EDREC truck was waiting there for Helga and me to drive through Salzburg to Ludwigshafen where I will turn it over to the

AFSC European travel pool. The rest of our Italian trip group then headed back to Vienna.

Helga and I picking up the EDREC truck.

On to Ohio

---◆---

Spring 1950

April 25—Last Days in Europe

We arrived at Helga's home in Ludwigshafen on April 12. Helga spent a joyful and tearful time getting ready to leave Germany for who knows how long. However, I think her mother is bearing up well at the prospect of a long-time separation. Then on to Paris by train where we stayed only two days, mostly at the AFSC office there. Then we had a long day on the 21st when we first took a train to Calais, then the boat to Dover and finally a train into London. Again, I had interesting conversations with various Quakers at the London Quaker Center. We visited the Helen Harris family. Daughter Margaret took a good bit of time showing us around London.

April 26—The Last Letter

We have boarded the *Ile de France* and are more or less settled in our tiny stateroom. It was good to get on the ship and out of the steady drizzle in England. We just met up with Merlin and Eloise Mather. He was a member of the AFSC team in Ludwigshafen and of course knew Helga. They are also going home, which means Iowa. It is good to have someone on board whom Helga knows.

They tell us we will land in New York next Tuesday, May 2. Then we are expected to stay in Philadelphia until May 10 for "debriefing." So on that day you will pick us up and drive us to Ohio? That should be just in time to start corn planting.

Love,
Bob

Epilogue

Once in Ohio, we turned our attention to becoming a typical Midwestern Quaker farm family. Despite our relative isolation from the world, my life of "planting the good seed" on our farm offered its own bit of Europe, with my German wife, Helga, by my side. My first major project was to acclimate her not only to life in another country but also to life in rural America. She soon made friends with my contemporaries and in 1953 became a doting mother to our daughter, Pamela. We became active in local farm organizations, in our local Friends Meeting, and in the Wilmington Yearly Meeting.

In 1960 and 1964, we organized and directed two Young Friends tours to Washington, D.C. and New York to introduce our local Meeting Young Friends to the Friends Committee on National Legislation (FCNL) and to the United Nations.

Helga in Ohio in 1951

We kept in touch with a wider Quaker circle by attending the third Friends World Committee for Consultation (FWCC) Conference in Oxford, England in 1952, the ninth FWCC triennial meeting in Waterford, Ireland in 1964, and the fourth FWCC Conference in Greensboro, North Carolina in 1967.

Despite these diversions, I still found life on the farm a less than satisfactory profession. I missed both interacting with a broader social circle and contributing to the larger community.

Helga and I in 1996

In 1963, James Read, Wilmington College president, offered me a position at the college as Director of Admissions. With the understanding that I would combine this role with my farm management duties, I gladly accepted this new challenge. It fit me well and I remained there in several administrative roles until my retirement in 1989. In 1966 Helga joined me at the college, teaching German until her retirement, also in 1989.

During our work at the college, Europe remained ever in our sights. From 1969 through 1989 we organized and directed twelve different college student semester study abroad programs in Vienna, Austria. In 1973, 1978, 1983, and 1989 we led alumni tours to Germany, Austria, Czechoslovakia, Hungary, and Italy. Through all this activity I continued managing the operation of our home farm. I had at last found my professional niche in life—a dual role of planting seeds on the farm and planting seeds of intellectual inquiry at the college. Since retiring from the college, I have kept my hand in farm management and maintained close contact with family and friends in Europe.

Over fifty years have passed since Helga and I came home on the ship mentioned in my last letter. I look back on those years in Europe with fondness, knowing I did my best to carry out the AFSC mission and make some difference in the lives of people caught in that troubled place and time. While not visible on a grand scale, I know my efforts helped many on a personal level, including French families that I moved to livable homes, our Austrian team that I equipped with road-worthy vehicles, and the hundreds of boys and girls educated and entertained at my EDREC programs. As to the many people I met who were suffering the consequences of war and occupation, I can only hope that my efforts helped to renew some faith in the power of love and in a life beyond the material vein.

I am grateful for the experiences I had in Europe and for the gifts I brought home with me: an ability to work with all types of people; a knack for navigating through layers of bureaucracy, courtesy of the Army; a renewed appreciation for our modern farming methods; and the many friendships that I enjoy to this day. I had a world of fun there, especially in the Tyrolean Alps, and best of all, I discovered my life's companion.

When we first met in Salzburg in 1949, Helga and I knew almost immediately that we belonged together. The intervening years certainly proved this to be true. After over fifty years together, Helga died of cancer on January 29, 2003. Going on without her has proven to be most difficult. However one particular item, found amongst her papers after she died, has helped to sustain me. This poem, penned by my Helga, gives a glimpse to her inner self and it seems a fitting note on which to end this account of *Planting the Good Seed.*

What Is Love?

A closeness of mind and body
Two persons needing and wanting each other
caring and sharing
Two individuals growing to new heights together
but not in each other's shadow

Love is honesty, trusting, feeling alive
It is giving of oneself unstintingly
It is understanding, supporting, encouraging
It is tenderness, happiness and pain

Love makes us whole, complete
It gives our lives meaning and our actions purpose
It is worth fighting for and preserving

Love is the most precious thing we can give
And the greatest gift we receive

Glossary and Abbreviations

ALMHÜTTE

A building located in the mountains intended to provide food and shelter to mountaineers and climbers (According to Wikipedia Encyclopedia at http://en.wikipedia.org/wiki/Alpine_hut)

AES

US Army Exchange Service (Civilian use only)

AFSC

American Friends Service Committee (Quaker organization for social justice, peace, and humanitarian service) with Headquarters in Philadelphia. In conversation instead of saying "AFSC Headquarters" we just said "Philadelphia"

CARE

International Consortium dedicated to reduction of world hunger

CO

Conscientious Objector

CPS

Civilian Public Service Camps (CO camps in World War II)

DEMENAGEMENT

French word loosely meaning the process of moving of persons and their goods

DP

Displaced Persons (homeless ex-Germans from Eastern Europe)

EDREC

Education and Recreation Program of the youth department of the Austrian Trade Union (ÖGB) presented by the AFSC (author's program)

ETU

European Transport Unit (Branch of the AFSC European relief work)

FISCHHORN

Marlis' family castle in Bruck an der Glocknerstrasse near Zell am See

FOR

Fellowship of Reconciliation (International Peace Organization)

G-4

US Army Logistics Division

HQ

US Army Headquarters

IRO

International Refugee Organization of the UN (Succeeded UNRRA)

ISB

US Army Information Service Bureau

JDC

Jewish Joint Distribution Committee

KER BERNY

ETU home in le Pouliguen near St. Nazaire, France

K rations

US Army emergency field rations

MAISON ROSE

ETU home in la Jonchere near Bougeval, just west of Paris

MCC

Mennonite Central Committee

MP

US Army Military Police

NAAFI

British Army restaurant and supply outlet

ÖGB

Österreichischer Gewerkscschaftsbund (Austrian Federation of Trade Unions)

PENDLE HILL

A Quaker study center near Philadelphia. It was home to all relief workers during orientation for overseas work

PW

Prisoner of War

PX

US Army Post Exchange retail store

RAF

British Royal Air Force

QM

US Army Quartermaster Corps provides field services

QM DUMP

QM used vehicles and parts supply

UNRRA

United Nations Relief and Rehabilitation Administration—the umbrella organization for private relief groups

USACA

US Allied Commission for Austria

USFA

United States Forces Austria

USAT

US Army Transport

WACS

Women's Army Corps